HOW TO

ARGUE
AND
WIN

EVERY TIME

OTHER BOOKS BY GERRY SPENCE

From Freedom to Slavery

Gunning for Justice

Of Murder and Madness

Trial by Fire

With Justice for None

HOW TO
ARGUE
AND
WIN

EVERY TIME

AT HOME, AT WORK,

IN COURT,

EVERYWHERE, EVERY DAY

GERRY SPENCE

ST. MARTIN'S PRESS   NEW YORK

Production Editor: David Stanford Burr

Design: Sara Stemen

Library of Congress Cataloging-in-Publication Data

Spence, Gerry.
How to argue and win every time / Gerry Spence.
p. cm.
ISBN 0-312-11827-9
1. Persuasion (Psychology)   2. Interpersonal communication.
3. Persuasion (Rhetoric)   I. Title.
BF637.P4S66 1995   94-43552
153.8'52—dc20   CIP

To my darling Imaging who taught me that love,

at last, is always the winning argument.

Contents

HOW TO

ARGUE
AND
WIN

EVERY TIME

My Argument for This Book

The art of arguing is the art of living. We argue because we must, because life demands it, because, at last, life itself is but an argument.

I have written this book because I must. Argument is my profession. Arguments are the hammers and nails by which I have, for over forty years, constructed winning cases for my clients. I believe, as Native Americans believe, that the greatest gift is the gift of learning, and that that gift is not complete until it is passed on. My dream, therefore, is to share with you what I have learned about argument. Otherwise I fear that all the pain, the self-doubt, the fear, the failures I have experienced in learning how to make the winning argument will be wasted.

Argument is, indeed, an art. There is a technique to it, a mindset, but anybody can deliver the winning argument. We can make the winning argument in the kitchen, the bedroom, the courtroom, the boardroom, at work—anywhere. I argue that the powerful argument comes not from disavowing our divine uniqueness in favor of someone else's style or values, but from tapping into the wondrous well of our own personhood. But how? That is where the magic of argument lies, and we shall learn that magic in the pages that follow.

We have traveled to the moon and back, but when we launch ourselves into outer space, we send forth a severely retarded species. In essence we remain the brute, for when confronted the brute attacks, and when faced with need or desire it takes by force from the weaker members of the hierarchy. It is an anomaly that we can split the atom, but we are nearly powerless to persuade each other to embrace justice. We can recombine our genes, but we cannot, in simple ways, ask each other for love. The ultimate danger, of course, is placing the power of technology in the hands of the savage whose ability to argue has advanced little over the grunt and growl of his ancient ancestors. In short, we have learned how to dominate people as *things*, but when relating to people as people we still tread wearily in the Dark Ages.

I do not expect to save the human race by this effort. I believe, however, that we must and can make small beginnings. In the same way that man began his technological journey by first chipping away at stones, we must learn simple and effective ways of speaking with each other. We must learn to speak to and to hear our mates and our children. We must learn how to effectively forward our interests at work. We could advance the human race enormously if we but learned to communicate honestly with our neighbors. We could experience a staggering breakthrough for the species if we but learned to achieve our needs and realize our dreams through argument, rather than by splattering human bodies all across the landscape.

I have arguments to make of my own, arguments that define who I am and that support my life's purpose as I envision it. I can think of no better place to deliver my own homilies than in a book on how to argue. You will encounter me herein. I have thrown open my doors. I have not only made my arguments on how to argue but, in doing so, I have ardently, with premeditation and unabashed forethought, argued for causes and ideas that are critical to me. I hope I will be successful in my arguments, that they will engender change and bring about evolution. But I make room for your disagreement, for your arguments. For without the power to argue back, you would have no power to hear or understand me in the first place, is that not so? Without your power, I would be alone.

I dream of a book that will help you achieve what you want in your life. Life is brief. It needs to be lived with every advantage. I dream of a book that will help you emerge from this experience with new wings that will enable you to break free of the cocoons of convention. I see you flying. I see you arguing for what you want without fear of banishment. I see you communicating your needs without injuring yourselves or your relationships. I see you creating, playing, winning. This dream brings me much joy, for out of these psychic chippings I hope—yes, I predict—that one day we shall have evolved into the species that we, as our own creators, have envisioned for ourselves from the beginning.

March 1995
Jackson, Wyoming

Getting Started

Everyone wants to argue. Everyone does. Everyone needs to. Sometimes the argument is screamed through tears. Sometimes it becomes only a paroxysm of impotent rage. Sometimes it is a tiny mumble in the corner of the room. Sometimes it is engaging, charismatic, moving. Sometimes, in the dark of night, in a lonely bed, the argument we wanted to make is shouted silently, safely, into the mind's desolate ear.

While birds can fly, only humans can argue. Argument is the affirmation of our being. It is the principal instrument of human intercourse. Without argument the species would perish. As a subtle suggestion, it is the means by which we aid another. As a warning, it steers us from danger. As exposition, it teaches. As an expression of creativity, it is the gift of ourselves. As a protest, it struggles for justice. As a reasoned dialogue, it resolves disputes. As an assertion of self, it engenders respect. As an entreaty of love, it expresses our devotion. As a plea, it generates mercy. As a charismatic oration, it moves multitudes and changes history. We must argue—to help, to warn, to lead, to love, to create, to learn, to enjoy justice—to be.

Everyone, every breathing person can make the winning argument. Many are forced into the mire and mud of the stagnant, immutable past. Locked in their psychic closets, many do not argue. And many who dare fail in their arguments and are frustrated or silenced. Many more argue almost blindly—like those who have never held a bat in their hands who strike at the ball, strike and strike until finally, and by sheer chance, the ball collides with the bat.

The enemy is not the *Other* against whom our failing arguments are made. The fault is not God's, or fate's, or the bad luck of the draw that has left us with wee voices or unimposing presences. We do not fail to make a brilliant riposte or persuasive argument because we lack electric genius, or lightning wit. We do not fail because we possess but a sparse fund of words. We fail to make the successful argument because we affix certain *locks* to ourselves, locks that imprison our arguments, or, having made the argument, locks that bar us from assuming a successful stance or from adopting a winning method.

The method of this book is to identify the locks from time to time and to offer the key with which to unlock them. The lock is, of course, your lock. But you also possess the key. I have fashioned this book itself as an argument—an argument that identifies the disabling LOCK and provides the enabling KEY. The structure I have devised here reflects my method of communicating with people, in the courtroom and out, at work and at home. It has been developed and refined over a lifetime in which I have been a worker, a prosecutor, a trial lawyer, a husband, and a father.

I have divided the book into three parts. Part I offers that which many writers of how-to books ignore, a matter best explained by a Wyoming cowboy I once knew. When he saw a rich dude come loping up on a typical dude plug clinging to an expensive silver-inlaid saddle he exclaimed, "Why look at ya! Ya put a thousand-dollar saddle on a ten-dollar horse! Ya can't get no place on a ten-dollar horse no matter how fancy a saddle ya put on him." So it is also true that no matter how clever the orator, no matter how many slick tricks of argument he has mastered, no matter how eloquent the rhetoric, technique, in the end, is nothing more than the thousand-dollar saddle. If we have mastered the skills, the procedures, the methodologies, yes, even the art of argument, but are still locked behind our psychic doors, we cannot win. If we have no concept as to when to argue and when to remain mute, if we do not understand how to use power and how to avoid its devastation in our own hands or the hands of others, we cannot win. If we do not grasp the incredible power of credibility or the magical power of listening we can argue with all the skill and artistry of the greatest orators ever spawned by history, but we will never win. To win, we need a saddle, all right, but we need to mount it on a powerful horse.

I make room for the criticism that this book contains too much philosophizing and exhortation, too much psychology and storytelling and not enough of the black-letter rules written in easy-to-follow outline, as one reads in a book on how to construct a sailboat or plunk a guitar. But I argue that we can sail and plunk without much evolution of our selves. Such is not the case of successful argument. The magic of the winning argument is born of the person, not of words; of the soul, not of rhetoric. Those who become impatient to learn about saddle-making rather than the fashioning of the powerful horse that will run beneath the saddle may turn directly to the second part of the book, where I detail the structure, preparation, technique, and art of the winning argument. Yet even there, I embrace the magic of the person, for technique is useless without the artist's hand. We all have it, this magic, our own unique power that cannot be duplicated, not in the history of the world. It is the quest for this magic that most intrigues me and, I hope, that will engage you as well.

The third part of the book helps us understand how to argue with loved ones, with the kids, with the corporate and governmental Cyclops—with our employers. To argue successfully with loved ones, we must redefine what winning is, and what we wish to gain from our arguments. We cannot argue at home in the same way I argue to a jury in a murder trial. We cannot argue with our children as one might whip into line one's opponent in the courtroom. We cannot argue against the power of the boss without understanding his power. The last chapter deals with the notion that, having acquired the stuff of successful argument, it becomes our duty, as it is the duty of those who possess any powerful weapon, to put it to use for good and just purposes.

So, let us venture forth, hand in hand, like two entering the dark woods together. Once there I promise that the woods are not so dark, so deep, so fearsome. Once there we shall see that the woods are indeed lovely, and made up of splendid trees that shelter, that provide secret medicines and magical potions. Once there we will discover enchanted places where the sun comes bursting through. That is my promise. Let us therefore go play together in the woods. Let us learn both to argue and not to argue, to combat the power of others and to empower ourselves, to recognize our fear and to overcome it, to create, to sing, and to let our souls run free. Let us proceed with unrestrained passion in our play. Together, let us learn how to argue—and how to win every time.

PART I

Readying Ourselves to Win

1

Why Argue?

OPENING THE DOORS, FREEING THE PSYCHE

THE LOCK: I don't like to argue and I don't like people who do. So why not try to get along? Besides, when I argue I lose.

We *were born to make the winning argument* just as we were born to walk. We don't need the silvery hair and the booming voice of the great orator. We can speak quietly in our kitchens—and win. We don't need speech lessons. We don't need the vocabulary of a Harvard professor. We can speak with our employers or our children in ordinary English—and win. We can win our arguments in the courtroom and the bedroom. But locked in our psychic closets we can never make a winning argument.

Sometimes we've been locked in our closets by parents and teachers. Sometimes we've locked ourselves in—it makes no difference, the doors are locked just the same. Some like their closets very much. Some know no other world. Some know no spiritual space. Still others pound at their doors and beg to be freed.

How did we get so bound up, so hunkered down, so mute? From the moment we were born we have been conditioned to avoid confrontation. If we opened our tiny mouth to cry, a bottle was hastily used to muffle our cries. We've been taught, as puppies are taught: Don't bark! Thoroughly domesticated, we have been conditioned to comply, to remain silent, to plod on. We deem it barbaric that some Chinese, less than a century ago, should have bound the feet of their baby girls to conform to the Chinese idea of physical beauty. Can't you see the horror of it, a child with her little feet bound so that as she grew, her feet became ugly stubs? Can you see the child wanting to run and play and dance but holding back, shying back, because her feet were shrunken and crippled? What a greater sin to bind the souls of our children.

We've been taught not to let our emotions show. We cherish logic and disparage passion. Real men do not cry. Doctors do not suffer with their patients. Lawyers must not care for their clients, not really. Businesspeople are cold and calculating—impersonal, as if the world were populated by robots. By the time young lawyers face their first jury they have doubtless had the winning argument crushed out of them by professors who have never tried a case. In the same way, one day we awaken into adulthood only to discover that the sole source of our winning arguments has been smothered by parents and peers—those who hold power over us.

By the time we become adults the word *argue* calls up dark, negative feelings. Parents and teachers and preachers and priests have unleashed immense pressures upon us. They have forced us to accept their ways, their religion, their philosophy, their values, their conventions, their politics, their wisdom. The power of community norms creates boundaries of mind and spirit that stand intolerant of challenge. Early on we have been molded into walking, lumbering, laboring, mostly trouble-free machinery. We have been assembled and fabricated into well-behaved students, predictable consumers, and obedient citizens. Most of what is feral has been domesticated. We suffocate in an amorphous glob of sameness. We have learned it is better to conform than *to be*. Argue?

Masses of men and women, their eyes long ago dulled by disillusionment and disappointment, live their miserable, diminutive lives in quiet Thoreauvian desperation. Many feel so petty, so paltry, so picayune as not to warrant the wasting of a whit of reverence for their own perfect uniqueness. How dare we argue?

But the human spirit is like the dandelion growing in the garden. Chopped off at the ground, it will spring back up from a single hair root. True, what peeps up may be weak and tender. But it is alive. By God, it is alive and it will grow! The trick is to discover our own hair root, to cherish it, that blessed succulent amputated little root that's searching for the sun. That's me, that's you, that's us!

And how? The key to our freedom is embarrassingly obvious.

THE KEY: We need only give ourselves permission. We need only unlock our doors.

It is a curious sight, these people—we ourselves—locked in our closets with the key to our freedom clasped tightly in our fists. The key, of course, is *permission, our* permission to peer out of our closets, to step out—one step—to look around, to ask questions, to demand respect, to share our creativity, our ideas, to speak out, to search for love, to seek justice—*to be.*

THE LOCK: I'm afraid to argue. It just causes trouble.

How do we argue with people we love? Our arguments turn sour, the words ugly, the passages to the heart close, and the feelings of love are replaced by hurt, then anger. How do we fight the bullies on the block who have always won and who now, as our employers, have the power to throw us and thousands like us out of our jobs—usually at Christmastime? How can we argue with anyone? How can we alienate our families, aggravate our friends, antagonize our fellow workers, anger our employers, and isolate ourselves from the community? "You only lose when you argue." Our experience affirms that. Haven't we learned by now that silence, that bowed heads, that dead tongues are safe? Do we not hear ourselves echoing the words of In-mut-too-yah-lat-lat, the great leader of the Nez Percé, better known to us as Chief Joseph, who, on surrender, proclaimed through his tears, "I will fight no more forever"?

This fear that so disables us—how do we deal with it? I feel it squalling in my belly whenever I stand up in the courtroom to begin an argument. I feel it whenever I begin the cross-examination of an important expert witness who is armed with a much greater knowledge of the subject than I. Will I fail? Will I be seen as incompetent? How do I dare argue with him? Will I find myself slinking out of the courtroom, the jury watching, witnessing my shame, my opponents leering, mocking my misery?

THE KEY: Fear is our ally. Fear confirms us. Fear is energy that is convertible to power—our power.

Fear is friend and foe alike, adversary and ally. Fear is painful. I hate its frequent companionship. Yet it challenges me. It energizes my senses. Like the sparrow, watching, watching, in the presence of fear I become alert. In the forest, the great buck with the majestic presence runs at the first snap of a twig. Fear has caused him to bolt. How else did he grow so grand? It is the two-point buck, who was not afraid, who now adorns the fender of the hunter's car, the young buck who only stared with large, blinking eyes at the hunter, and did not run.

I have learned not to be ashamed of my fear, but to embrace it. One cannot be brave without it, for is not our bravery merely the facing of our fear? How brave is the soldier who does not understand the danger as he charges? How brave is the madman? The fool? And who is the more brave—the small boy standing on the stage singing his first solo before his Sunday school class, or the great opera diva singing at the Metropolitan Opera?

Fear confirms that, at my heart-core, life, not death, is the authority. The dead are not afraid. Fear is the painful affirmation of my being. To affirm myself is to experience the courage to make the argument—for all argument begins with me. To affirm myself is, as Paul Tillich once argued, "the courage to be." Once we have embraced fear, once we have felt it, accepted it, we have also proclaimed the imperative *I am!*, and the argument may now begin.

In the courtroom I sometimes carry on a silent conversation with myself about my fear, while the jurors look on wondering, as they must, what occupies this strange man who stands silently before them looking down at his feet. My conversation with myself most often sounds like this:

"How are you feeling, Gerry?" I ask.

"The jury is watching, waiting for me to begin my argument," I reply. "I can't just stand here saying nothing."

"I asked you, how are you feeling?"

"You know how I feel.

"What is the feeling?"

"You know what the feeling is."

"Are you afraid to say it?"

"All right. I'm afraid."

"Well, you should be. Big stakes. The prosecutor wants to destroy your client. He wants to destroy you."

"I don't want to think about it. Not now. Not standing here."

"It's all right to be afraid. You should be afraid. Go ahead. Feel it."

"But the jury's watching."

"They can wait a few seconds more. Fear is energy. If you feel your fear, you can also feel its power, and you can change its power to *your* power."

Suddenly I look up at the waiting jury. I hear myself address them in a clear, quiet voice, "Ladies and gentlemen of the jury." Suddenly I am vaguely aware that something is happening to my fear. I have looked it in the eye. I have stared it down. It retreats like a whimpering cur that is now afraid to face me! The pain of it recedes. I feel a new power well up. And my argument begins.

To argue in the face of our fear brings on the *magical* "*yes,*" the simple affirmation of our being. *Argument* springs out of our authority. It escapes from us as our thought and feeling, as our sounds, our music, our rhythms. When we give ourselves *permission*, the argument bursts out of our lungs, out of our throats, out of words formed and caressed by our lips, out of words born of our hearts. When we give ourselves *permission*, we rediscover our will to win—may I say it?—we become born-again gladiators.

THE LOCK: Even so, why argue? Why experience the pain? Why take the risk of losing?

THE KEY: The art of arguing is the art of living. We argue because we must, because life demands it, because, in the end, life itself is but an argument.

In important ways argument is a gift—a gift of ourselves to the *Other*. Without the gift of ourselves, we can never succeed as persons or parents. Without the gift of ourselves to the *Other* we can never achieve acclaim as artists or respect as employees. We can never win the cases of our clients or the love of our mates. In short, our victory in this life depends upon our ability to give of ourselves, and by such gift, to awaken in others their own knowledge. When I am convinced by someone else's argument the experience is often the awakening of what I once knew and accepted and have since forgotten. Such are these so-called earth-shaking epiphanies, which cause one to slap one's head at the sudden insight. As I see it, we engage in an intrapersonal archeological dig. The magic comes when, by argument, we unearth a bit of ourselves, and, thereby, we likely discover something about all others who inhabit the universe.

I argue because I must. Sometimes I argue to discover the efficacy of a thought or the validity of a plan. Sometimes I argue to tap the knowledge of others. We constantly affirm ourselves. A single corn plant growing in the basement cannot pollinate. It requires other stalks, the sun, the wind. Life—the search for truth, the pursuit of justice, the explosion of creativity—cannot bloom in isolation. Without loving argument, children can never experience the crucial gift of parenting or bring to fruition the parent-child relationship that produces the mature and functional adult.

Without argument the nation becomes a wasteland where nothing grows, nothing blooms, nothing is created, nothing lives. Thousands of rusting factories across the land, millions of unemployed, the wholesale abdication of our nation's industry to foreign lands, the mindless destruction of our natural resources, the decline of our education system, the slums, the crowded concrete cages we call penitentiaries, the disintegration of our justice system, the moral decay we so fervently protest—all affirm the critical need of our leaders, our employers, our educators, and our people to make and to hear our arguments, and to receive from each other the gifts we have withheld.

The art of argument is the art of living. If we are successful in our arguments we will bloom and grow. We can accomplish massive good and experience endless joy. We can prevent war and save the earth. Our success in life, our cultural immortality depends upon our ability to argue. I suspect that if we become experts at argument, we might even find ourselves arguing our way into the proverbial pearly gates. I daresay St. Peter rarely meets a candidate who has fully mastered the art.

THE LOCK: If only I could be like the great orators, at least like the preachers, at least like the guy next door who can talk his way into or out of anything—but I have no talent for argument.

THE KEY: You have a power of your own that no one else can ever match.

We have become focused not on how to identify our own uniqueness, but on how to mimic the mark and style of others. We have been told that if we can look like others, act like others, indeed, argue as others argue, perhaps then we can be successful. Be like John Wayne or the village priest. Be like Elvis or Lincoln or Jesus or Michael Jordan. At least wear the same brand of shoes. At least eat his cereal. We are taught to strive for sameness and work hard at imitation. But do we not admit that the value of a diamond is derived from the fact that each gem is distinguishable from all others? Why then do we strive to rid ourselves of our uniqueness? Why do we imitate *their* way of thinking, adopt *their* belief systems, and accept *their* values as our own? Why do we dress like them, speak like them, and, having purchased their bottled scent, even smell like them? Why do we strive for *their* goals and *their* power? Why do we embrace *their* authority and abdicate our own? By seeking to become like them, do we not cast aside that which makes us valuable beyond all comprehension?

The perpetual quest for acceptance as parts of the social machinery is a form of psychic self-destruction. I am repulsed at the thought of our need to conform—to give up that which distinguishes us from all others so that we may become mere impersonations! How can one argue at all if one argues not from one's own authority but from the inimitable imitation of another? When we imitate another we murder ourselves and, thus dead, are as powerless as the dead. As imitators we are, by definition, fakes, and the counterfeit is valueless. What a crime to commit against one's self!

So, too, do we commit homicide against the self when we deliver our authority to others—to the church, to a political party, to a creed, to employers, to McDonald's, who tells us what we deserve today, to Budweiser and Toyota, who advise us what our experience of joy and the meaning of our lives should be. Having abdicated our authority to the conventional, to stylish wisdom, to political correctness—having, indeed, succumbed to anyone or any entity that proclaims its own authority—what is left of us? How dare we argue out of nothing? If we raise our voices, whatever escapes is likely no more than a limp mumble, or worse, an explosion of impotent rage. Unheard, we plod on.

I argue that when my argument begins with me, when it emanates from my authority, it will be unique among all arguments. Do we not each possess fingerprints that can be easily distinguished from all fingerprints that ever existed? I speak of the fingerprint of personhood. That print, as well, is distinguishable from all others in the history of the world. The key to the winning argument is to understand that, and to believe it. The great quest is to find the individual "soul-print," the singular stamp that belongs only to us.

I have heard many a pretty argument by many a fancy lawyer. But when the fluff and feathers fall, there is nothing left. Nothing at all. There is nothing left because the argument, at last, is recognized by all who hear it as the pettifoggery of another technically proficient parrot. The argument may cause an audience to applaud. It may reward the person who delivered it with many a slap on the back. But it will never become a winning argument.

On the other hand, I have seen a young, frightened woman wearing a plain dress stand before a jury, her hair pulled back, mostly to be out of the way. I have watched her painful search for the right words. I have witnessed her faltering, her face burning red. I have seen the tears well up in her eyes. I have felt her caring. I have observed her stumbling, and courageously fighting back. And her argument, the faithful reflection of her uniqueness, out of her soul, became a winning argument. She had not graduated from a great university. She was not at the top of her class. When she walked down the street, no one looked at her. When she took her seat in the courtroom she blended in with the spectators. But her argument had *her* mark on it. There will never be another like it. It was hers, and because it was hers it became a winning argument.

THE LOCK: Why should anyone listen to me?

THE KEY: You are your own authority. That is enough.

How can I insist that others listen to me when I possess no special education, no expert knowledge? In this country we repose a certain faith in the wisdom of the "common man," for the "common man" is familiar with life in ways of which many are ignorant.

A certain hotel maid sits on a jury. Every day she labors long hours for a few dollars, and at night, after many hours cleaning the human refuse we leave behind, after scrubbing our toilets and changing our dirty linen, she trudges home to a small, nearly empty walk-up apartment in the other part of town. She is old. Her bones ache. When she climbs into bed exhausted, she automatically reaches over to where her husband once lay beside her. He has died. His side of the bed is empty and cold. And after she has wept silently in her lonely room, no psychiatrist listens at a hundred dollars an hour to aid her through her misery.

Now she is on the jury, this hotel maid. She is embarrassed about her looks. She wears her best dress—the one she wore to her husband's funeral—but her shoes are old, and she does not have the money to have her hair fixed like the banker's wife who sits next to her. When she is asked questions by the lawyers about her qualifications to sit as a juror, she is shy, because she knows she does not always use the English language correctly. The lawyers speak to the other jurors. They speak to the banker's wife. They speak to the schoolteacher in the back row. They speak to the manager of a local chain store. They speak to the lineman for the electric company. But they do not speak much to her. Yet who knows more about the human condition than she? Who knows more about sorrow and poverty, and hard work and loneliness? Who is more courageous? She harbors a deep knowledge. When she speaks the other jurors will have to listen carefully, for her voice is soft and it is difficult for her to find the words. But the words she finds will come from her heart because she knows no other way to argue. And indeed, for this is my experience, at last the others will listen, and respect her because they know she speaks out of an authority they do not possess.

Wisdom usually does not fall from high places. The mighty and the splendid have taught me little. I have learned more from my dogs than from all the great books I have read. I have learned more from my children than from all the professors who have importuned themselves upon me in the exercise of their tenure. The wisdom of children is the product of their unsullied ability to tap their innate fund of knowledge and innocently to disclose it. The wisdom of my dog is the product of his inability to conceal his wants. When he yearns to be loved, there is no pouting in the corner. There are no games entitled "Guess what is the matter with me." He puts his head on my lap, wags his tail and looks up at me with kind eyes, waiting to be petted. No professor or sage ever told me I might live a more successful life if I simply asked for love when I needed it.

The world is overburdened with those who claim to know life's secrets and who are eager to impart their knowledge—for a price. It is as if I stand on a busy corner where the great minds of the world and their imitators pass by, where sages and impostors, geniuses and fools all claim to know the way to Disneyland. Some cannot speak my language. Some are so blinded by their own brilliance they cannot see. Most have never been to Disneyland. The directions some give are incomprehensible. When I ask, "How do I get to Disneyland?" some respond by asking me for spare change. Some point in one direction. Some in another. How do I know who on this street knows the way? Only when I have traveled to Disneyland myself can I evaluate the directions given me. In the end, I am for me, as you are for you, the only authority.

My life has been devoted to poking around in the outer reaches of myself. In the same way that the universe unfolds as it is explored, so does my own. No sooner do I arrive at some new, inner galaxy than I can see heretofore unimagined worlds that invite further exploring. But the acceptance of external authority as my overriding authority blocks all discovery of the self. Such acceptance inhibits all growth and mimics death, for no act is more suicidal than casting aside one's personhood and replacing it with the alien authority of another.

THE LOCK: But if I am my authority, then aren't they also theirs? How can I win?

THE KEY: A winning argument is possible only when, speaking out of our authority, we address the authority of the *Others*.

Our authority, and theirs: When we are moved to tears by a scene in a movie, it is because the actor cried before we cried, cried out of his heart. The script did not have tears. The tears came out of the actor's authority. He does not weep out of the sorrow of others, but out of his sorrow. Had he never known his own sorrow, he could not have cried.

The actor's presentation that gives rise to our tears can be understood as his argument. He is arguing for our empathy, our caring. When he argues out of his own sorrow, that is, when he argues out of the authority of his experience, he does so acknowledging that we have experienced sorrow as well. If we had never experienced sorrow, if we had no authority of our own, the scene he presents—his own argument—would have utterly failed.

We begin to understand: *Successful argument is a communication between the acknowledged authority of both parties to the argument.* Moreover, that I argue concedes to the *Other* the right to argue back. That I speak and wish to be heard admits the *Other's* right to also be heard. But nothing in the bargain suggests that either should surrender his or her authority. I retain the authority, as does the

Other, to accept or reject those arguments that are true or not for me. We cannot argue to those who have no authority of their own. Our arguments to those without authority are like beseechments to fence posts, like preachments to stones. Unless the *Other* retains authority we are arguing to the dead. There should be a sign taped to the refrigerator of every home and on the boss's door in every place of employment. The sign should read, PLEASE ARGUE WITH ME. In the end, argument is not always combat conducted with words. Argument is often more like intercourse—an activity that is most satisfying and valuable when both parties join in.

AND SO: We have been locked in our closets by those who have sought not our love but our compliance, who have sought not our growth but our subservience. But the keys to our freedom are in our hands. We need only give ourselves *permission* to unlock our doors.

We are afraid. But fear confirms life and identifies the source of every successful argument—ourselves. We shrink from its pain. But we can experience its energy and convert its power to our power.

Many protest that they have no talent for argument. They cry, "If only I could be like them." But such lamentations are a wish for death, for in order to be like another we must relinquish our own perfect uniqueness. Still some protest they have no authority. But I say we are the only authority—for ourselves.

If, therefore, in the exercise of *your* authority, and out of *your* experience, you have accepted—as true for you—some of my arguments, you may wish to join me in discovering what other buried treasures lie ahead. And, having given each other permission to argue, let us continue in this dialogue, in this lovely adventure of arguing together.

2

When to Argue

WINNING WITHOUT ARGUING

THE LOCK: If I argue I want to win.

THE KEY: But first, "What is winning?"

What is winning? Is winning when we force the *Other* to lay down his emotional and intellectual arms and surrender? Do we triumph when the *Other* cries out, "You win! I was wrong! I am a foul, faithless, filthy knave not worthy of my space on this earth!"? Notwithstanding the overstatement, do we envision winning as when the *Other* hoists the white flag of capitulation? To win must we always knead the enemy's soul with salt, as Rome did the soil of Carthage? If so, I have never won an argument in my career.

I once believed, as most do, that if arguments are to be won, the opponent must be pummeled into submission and silenced. You can imagine how that idea played at home. If, in accordance with such a definition, I won an argument, I began to lose the relationship. Winning an argument merely meant that I had won the right to live in silence with the woman and children I loved. It meant that their ideas, their contributions to the relationship were diminished or demeaned or discarded. It meant that to win I disavowed their personhood, their uniqueness. It meant that to win I was left alone, preaching to myself, yapping, haranguing, demanding at an empty room.

The old saw, "Sticks and stones can break your bones but words will never harm you," is patently false. *Words kill and words maim.* The death sentence handed down by a judge is composed merely of words. Words of rejection, words of betrayal, words of hatred, words of denial can destroy as surely as a dagger. Words cause war.

Today, in this age of alleged enlightenment, words are the weapons of choice for combat between husband and wife. Words are wielded in affrays between business adversaries, in contests between employer and worker, in any struggles where issues, both critical and petty, are at stake. Although words vanish from the airwaves as quickly as they are spoken, the damage they do is often permanent. We can leave scars on the psyche with words as disabling as the wound from any bullet. War is war, whether it is conducted with artillery or words.

Using argument as a weapon of injury has given argument its bad name. I think of my neighbor, an explosive type who resembled a loaded pistol with multiple hair triggers.

One of the triggers—let us call it the "Go to Church Trigger"—was set off by his mother—continually and maliciously. Like a good son, he brought his aged mother to his house every Sunday for dinner. And before she asked him if he was feeling well or how her grandchildren were, she asked, "Did you go to church today, Henry?" More than once I witnessed his rejoinder, one as predictable as a recorded message from the telephone company.

He screamed, "Mother, you know I don't go to church!" Whereupon his mother let fly an equally predictable question that never failed to pull yet another trigger:

"Why don't you go to church? You know you should go to church, Henry!" After the verbal brawl produced many more virulent volleys, the mother suddenly stopped, seemingly quite happy indeed, and, after some further abuse of his mother, the son also stopped, seemingly quite contented as well. The exchange was not an argument but a means by which the parties engaged in their familial sport of mutual flagellation.

One day the same man's wife bought him a new lawnmower for his birthday. He couldn't get the damn thing to run. He pulled at the starting rope, and pulled and pulled until he was red in the face and sweating and cursing.

"This goddamned lawnmower!" he hollered.

Hearing his outburst—everybody on the block did—his wife appeared at the back door.

"What's the matter, Henry?" she asked. She could see well enough what the matter was.

"This goddamned lawnmower won't start," he bellowed. By this time he had fetched his tool chest from the garage and was trying to adjust the carburetor.

"That's a perfectly good lawnmower," she shouted back at her husband. "I paid good money for that lawnmower. It's brand new. There's nothing wrong with it." And with that, another of his triggers was pulled.

"What do you mean there's nothing wrong with this hunk of junk? Can't you see! It won't start." He was beginning to pull some of her triggers.

"You are calling that lawnmower that I paid good money for a hunk of junk?" she screamed back.

"You're damned right, I'm calling this hunk of junk a hunk of junk!" She began to cry.

"That's all the thanks I get for the present I got you for your birthday—you standing there calling it names!" She was hysterical.

"The son of a bitch won't start." He was ready to cry himself.

"That's probably because you haven't read the instruction book that came with it. You never do. You think you know it all."

"You don't have to be a goddamned genius to start a fucking lawnmower," he shouted.

"The problem is that that hunk of junk is smarter than you!" She said it as if she were protecting her only child.

Suddenly, wanting to kill her, he grabbed a hammer out of the tool box and attacked the lawnmower instead. He beat the poor thing in rhythm with her screaming and sobbing until the lawnmower was, as he had announced in the first place, a hunk of junk.

The wife could have avoided this brawl by simply "getting on the right side of the lawnmower," that is, for her to have said when the husband complained that the lawnmower wouldn't start, "I wonder why? It's brand new. I don't blame you for being upset." By getting on the husband's side of the argument, she would have pulled none of his triggers and the lawnmower would have lived to mow another day. In a similar manner the husband could have gotten on the wife's side of the lawnmower as easily. The minute she began to defend the lawnmower, all he had to say was, "I know how disappointed this must make you. Maybe I'd better read the instruction book."

In households, at our places of work, wherever men and women make decisions, the resolution of issues does not usually grow out of logic or reason or justice. The final accord, frequently the aftermath of exhaustive wrangling, is more often the result of attrition, so that the final position of the parties is an unhappy appeasement or a coerced compromise or a helpless surrender.

Moreover, many resolutions bear with them the seeds of wars yet to be fought. Woodrow Wilson believed the Versailles Treaty would end all wars, but its punitive terms were the progeny of wars to come.

Argument is not the process by which we seek to destroy the *Other*. Argument is a tool with which we can achieve an end, satisfy a want, fulfill a desire. Argument is the mechanism by which we reveal the truth—the truth for us. It is the incomparable art by which we connect and interact successfully with the *Other*.

Winning is getting what we want, which often includes assisting others in getting what they want. Winning may forward a just cause. It may help strangers. It may discover the truth. Winning may help a loved one to succeed, a child to bloom, an enemy *to see us* in a new light. But, whether winning is winning for ourselves or for others, winning is still *getting what we want*.

If arguing is the means by which we obtain from the *Other* what we want, then we must make room for the notion that argument may take multiple forms. Argument may, indeed, take the form of contest. It may be hostile and aggressive. It may attack and subdue. It may be contentious. It may engage in debate. Most arguments before a jury or a city council or a school board take this form. But the winning argument may also take the form of a love offering, of providing help, of understanding, of cooperating with the *Other*. The winning argument may be silent as when Imaging, my wife, sometimes listens patiently to my outbursts, says nothing and merely waits for the storm to clear so that the storm's author can see for himself another side. Sometimes the best argument is to permit the *Other* to talk himself or herself out of the argument. Sometimes the best argument is endurance coupled with the perfect power of silence. The trick, of course, is to know when to argue.

Argument—confirming that "I am": For some, argument is a means by which they attempt to confirm their being when, for them, their being is frail and in question. We see them every day—those who must prove that they *are*.

These people hassle and wrangle and bicker and balk because they are structurally weak. They interpret concurrence on their part as proof of the weakness they seek to disprove. If you could hear their splenetic little inner voices jabbering and whining they would sound like this:

The Other: Johnny, don't you think it would be fun to go to a movie tonight?

Johnny's inner voice: Don't agree. She'll think you're a first-class pushover.

Johnny: God, you know how I hate movies! Why do you always want to go to a movie?

The Other: Well, how about the basketball game? The Dips are playing the Dunks tonight.

Johnny's inner voice: She's trying to control you again. If you agree you'll be nothing but a sniveling, inconsequential, demented little piece of lint.

Johnny: Why can't we stay home just once? You're always trying to get me to do something or go somewhere.

The Other: Okay. Have it your way. (Whereupon she curls up on the couch with a good book, which is what she wanted to do in the first place.)

People like Johnny do not argue. *They disagree.* They never win arguments for they do not argue. They never win, for they never achieve what they want. But they prove but one thing—that they are *disagreeable.*

Argument and dissent: What about the great dissenters? The great dissenters argue in accordance with a life's principle that consistently governs and shapes their individual purpose. The great men of history were great dissenters. Christ was a dissenter who kicked the money changers out of the temple and dissented from the ideology of "an eye for an eye and a tooth for a tooth." Galileo was a dissenter who believed the earth orbited the sun. Marx was a dissenter who decried the exploitation of the masses. Jefferson, Lincoln, Martin Luther King Jr.—all were great dissenters. They all argued eloquently, and some won the great arguments of history. But they argued out of strength, not weakness, out of conviction, not insecurity. They argued toward the fulfillment of a purpose and in service to mankind.

Arguing to hear one's own wonderful voice: I know people who use argument merely to hear their own voices. They are noise-makers. These people seem perfectly secure, but they are enchanted with their words, enthralled with their own wisdom, and they are, to be sure, as boring as popcorn without salt. They have, during the course of their lives, made so much noise and filled the air with so much authoritative banality that they have had no time to form an original thought, nor have they given themselves the opportunity to hear and learn anything from listening to anyone else.

Argument and neurosis: I know people who argue because of neurotic traps into which they continually fall. To some, any authority figure becomes their oppressive father or their nagging mother with whom they have not yet settled their psychic accounts. I once knew a young lawyer who argued with the judge, even when the judge was attempting to assist him. He did not argue with his wife or his children. He was never contentious with his friends. But when the judge took the bench and began to give orders and make rulings, this young lawyer transmogrified from a pleasant human being into a screeching jerk. But he also spewed out rancor at his past employers, his sergeant in the army, and all other persons who chanced to occupy a position of authority.

In court, the more this young lawyer reacted to his authority demon, the more he displayed his totally unrestrained hostility, the more the judge came down on him. Finally his relationship with the judge deteriorated so badly that he was held in contempt, and in the end had to move to another community where this bizarre drama was likely played out all over again. Strange that a lawyer who must learn to argue effectively in the same way that a surgeon must learn to use the scalpel skillfully ultimately converted argument into a weapon of self-destruction.

I have known others who argue out of panic or paranoia. They hear every comment, every word that is directed toward them as criticism or censure. At a little country grocery store the other day I heard a conversation that fit neatly into this category. I was waiting in line to pay for my purchases when the checker, who happened to be the owner of the store, said to the woman in front of me, "Nice day."

"My bill isn't due. I paid it two days ago," she replied in a huff. "Haven't you gotten my check?"

"Yes, thank you very much," the grocer said.

"You don't need to thank me. I pay my bills, and I pay them on time."

"You certainly do," the grocer said, giving the lady a big smile.

"How would you know? Have you just run a credit report on me? There's no call for that whatever."

The grocer looked at the lady in utter shock. When he finally composed himself he said, "Why don't you take these groceries with my compliments?"

"You can't buy me off like that," she said. "Who do you think I am?" Fortunately for the grocer, he didn't answer her question. Argument and mental illness are rarely compatible.

I have known those who, in response to some traumatic childhood memory, become immediately fearful whenever someone launches any argument in their direction. Verbal abuse of some sort has brought them pain: pain from a parent who was so insecure the parent would not tolerate the slightest questioning from the child; pain from a parent who did not love the child sufficiently to permit the child to inquire, to explore, to question, to bloom and grow; pain from a parent who was so untrustworthy himself that he did not trust the child. One cannot argue with those who are afraid of a verbal interchange any more than one can do the jig with someone who is afraid to dance.

Winning without arguing: Early on my own Imaging taught me how to win an argument without really arguing. We had just returned from our honeymoon and had settled into our new home. The following morning was my first day back at the office. That evening I was about to go home for dinner, one that I knew Imaging had prepared especially for the occasion, when I decided, no, by God, I was not going home! I had been in chronic trouble in a previous relationship for having failed to come home on time. Without realizing it, I was still engaged in a struggle in a relationship that was over. Instead of going home, I went to a restaurant where I met a friend. We sat down to talk over a cup of coffee. The time dragged by, but I was not going to be home for supper on time. I thought, "I'm just entering into this marriage, and I am going to establish some ground rules the first night home.

Well, I drank coffee and chatted with my friend until I was over an hour late for supper. When I came in the door, what I faced astounded me. Instead of being met with scolding, or with the worst-of-all punishment, silence, I was greeted with a big kiss and a smile.

"Hi, sweetheart. Your supper's in the oven. I've kept it warm," Imaging said. She set a beautiful dinner before me and sat down to keep me company.

"I ate an hour ago," she said. "I hope your dinner is all right." And that was all the comment there was—no subtle questioning, no mild complaints, no hidden hostility, nothing but smiles and gentleness.

I couldn't believe it. Surely this was all just an act. I vowed to give it another test. The next night I again met my friend for coffee. Again I was an hour late and again I got the same loving treatment when I came home. As I sat down to supper I decided to discover what was really going on with this new wife of mine.

"Aren't you even a little mad at me for being late for supper?" I asked.

"Of course not," she said. She seemed surprised.

"Well, you had supper waiting and I was late and I haven't even said I was sorry."

"I figured you were busy at the office with important matters. Otherwise, you would have come home."

"Oh," I said.

"Besides," she said, "you're a full-grown man. Full-grown men don't need someone telling them when to come home to supper," and that's all there was to it. She won our first argument without arguing, and I have never since intentionally been late for supper in all of the years we've been married. She understood long before I did that arguments can be won without arguing. The power of the mirror, which we shall encounter again and again in these pages, did its work. Trust begets trust, and I became trustworthy. I learned again that night what I had learned so many times before and forgotten as often—that demonstrations of love, whether in the kitchen, the bedroom, or the courtroom, are the most powerful of all arguments.

Recently I met a very old and close friend for lunch. We were in trouble. He was formerly a heavyweight fighter, a champion, and for many years a successful courtroom lawyer and later a judge. He had retired from the bench and taken up the practice again. Over the years we had never been in a case against each other, having consciously chosen not to be adversaries. But as old chieftains, we were unable to know where our warriors, our young associates, might be warring. One day we discovered that our firms were against each other in an important case.

During lunch we skirted the issue like a couple of seasoned boxers in the first round. Finally we began to argue the respective merits of our clients' cases at Nora's in the little town of Wilson, Wyoming. Nora's Fish Creek Inn was a rustic log-cabin café with a barn-red ceiling and a double-sided counter running through the middle of the room with a comfortable jumble of amateur art and old photographs and mismatched tables and chairs on both sides. I listened to his argument. He spoke quietly, and his words reflected a deep caring for the seemingly irresolvable plight of his client. He spoke of the many years he had known my client as well. "Good people," he said. "The best." I was feeling distressed and impotent that these folks, all decent citizens, should be caught in this trap from which neither side could escape without irreparable injury. But my frustration and pain went deeper than that: I was caught in this same trap with my old friend.

We were about to leave the café when a man wearing workman's clothes happened by the table. The man nodded at both of us as if he knew us.

"Sit down here," my friend said to the man. Then my friend turned to me. "I want you to meet my client." I realized this was one of those serendipitous occurrences, my friend's client just happening to enter the café while we were discussing his case.

"Tell Mr. Spence your story," my friend said to his client.

"Is it all right?" I asked. I felt uneasy about that. Most lawyers would advise their client not to give any information to the opponent's lawyer, who might use the information against the client.

"Sure it's all right. The facts are the facts," my friend replied. In effect he was saying, "I trust you as a reasonable man to listen to my client, who will tell you the truth." I listened. And when, an hour later, I left the café, something had happened to me. The raw zeal I had first felt for my own client's case had now become tempered. I had gained a new understanding of the other side of the case as well. I saw his client in pain. I heard the small catch in his client's voice when he spoke of his dilemma. I saw the strain on his face, the hurt in his eyes. I understood the justice of his case from his perspective. I heard the sound of my friend's voice, a gentleness for an old warrior such as he. He made no demand, no suggestion that I submit, or compromise, or indeed, that I do anything. His argument was really no argument at all. He said, without saying it, "I trust you. You are a just man and I therefore trust you to do the just thing." The power of his argument came from vesting his opponent, me, with trust and reasonableness.

Without attempting any manipulation, my friend had placed a portion of the responsibility for justice on my shoulders. I felt it. I feel it now. We have not yet determined how to resolve the dilemma, for my client's case is a just case as well. But the conflict will be resolved, correctly, justly, by two old friends who know the power of making the winning argument, one that is in the best interests of their clients, without having ever argued in the first place.

AND SO: Learning *when* to argue is as important to winning as learning *how* to argue.

3

Understanding Power

THE PISTOL THAT FIRES IN BOTH DIRECTIONS

THE LOCK: I am not a powerful person. Those I face are always more powerful than I. How can I win against them?

THE KEY: All power, yours *and theirs,* is yours.

The secret source of power: When I argue, I face power, the power of the *Other.* It is the *Other's* power that I wish to overcome and that I fear. I am therefore fascinated by power and I wish to trace its source. If I understand power, if I understand its nature and where it abides, if I understand how to get it and how to resist it, I will have attained great power of my own. I want power. I need power to win.

What is power? The power peculiar to each of us is that force that distinguishes each of us from all other beings. Our power permits us to grow and to fulfill our potential. It is the surf, the swell, the wave, the storm we feel in our veins that propels us into action. It is our creativity. It is our joy, our sorrow, our anger, our pain. This energy is our personhood—the extraordinary mix of traits and talents and experience that makes up the fingerprint of our souls. This power belongs to us, and only us. Although there is a bountiful supply of power for each of us, it is, nonetheless, a precious thing. It ought not be wasted. It must never be abused, else it will come back to destroy us. It can never be abdicated or denied, else we will have lost our very selves in the process.

Understanding how power works: Power is first an idea, first a perception. *The power I face is always the power I perceive.* Let me say it differently. Their power is my perception of their power. Their power is *my* thought. The source of their power is, therefore, in *my* mind.

The power others possess is the power I give them. Their power is *my gift.* I give them all the power in the universe, as, indeed, the faithful give to God, or I give them no power at all, as, indeed, is the quantum of power we too frequently allot to our children. If I have endowed the *Other* with power that the *Other* does not possess, then I face my own power, do I not? My own power has become my opponent, my enemy. On the other hand, if the *Other* possesses power, but I do not perceive the *Other's* power as effective against me, he has none—none for me.

My perception of my neighbor, Mr. Suderman, is that of a nice man who tends his roses daily, and always has a wave and a smile. He has little power over me, for I have given him none.

If, however, I ask Mr. Suderman how to grow roses, I will have endowed him with the power to explain to me the loves and lives of roses. If I ask him to sign a petition to recall the mayor, I provide him with more power. I perceive him as one who can grant or reject my request and thereby affect the political career of another. If I have a heart attack as I am visiting him in his rose garden, as I lie on the ground among his roses I perceive him as one who has the power to save my life. But his power came from me, my perception of him as a man who can teach me to grow roses, who can help recall the mayor, or who can save my life.

To Mr. Suderman's ten-year-old son, Mr. Suderman has great power, that is to say, the boy perceives his father as the source of his food, his shelter, his sustenance, and his safety. His very survival depends upon the will of his father. Yet other children of the same age take for granted their right to the essentials of life, and more. Even as to the child, therefore, the father's power depends on the child's perception of the father's power.

Mr. Suderman still enjoys a position of power with his twenty-year-old son. This son lives at home and feels as if he lives under a monarchy, for Mr. Suderman demands that the son study hard, that he work when he wishes to play, that he attend church when he would rather go sailing, and that he join the family in its activities when he would rather be with his friends. But such domination of the father is likewise dependent on the son's perception of his father, for if the son chooses, he may give no power to his father at all and go happily, freely on his way, as many do at twenty.

And so we see that Mr. Suderman is powerless or all-powerful, depending upon who perceives him and under what circumstances he is perceived. Yet Mr. Suderman is the same Mr. Suderman in every case. Is it not clear then that his power is the product of our perception, that his power is merely the power that we give him— that his power is *our* power?

It is true that Mr. Suderman has power of his own. Yet he may see himself as a poor gardener of roses, and he may feel he has no power whatever when he signs the petition for recalling the mayor, even though his signature is one of those required to effect the recall. As to his children, he may feel they are incurably pigheaded, that he is incapable of controlling them or earning their respect. He may, at last, see himself as nothing but a living cipher whose sole solace comes from his roses. But his power, as ours, is the product of his perception.

As a young lawyer I stared at the ceiling numberless nights fretting about how to meet the power of an opposing lawyer in a case for a terribly injured client. My client had been brain-damaged by a defectively designed crane and was left without a sense of who or where he was. He deserved justice. But the insurance company refused to pay a penny. As they often do, they brought in their famous lawyer to defend the manufacturer. To get justice for my client, I had to win against this man.

I perceived my opponent's power as a superior presence, a more skillful talent, a more pleasing personality. I believed that the jurors would like the opposing attorney better than me because they would find him a more appealing person. Insurance companies have a proclivity for hiring lawyers with beguiling smiles and attractive personalities. Walk into any courtroom and you can immediately pick out the insurance company lawyer. He is stately in his appearance, always immaculate with a proper haircut. He usually wears a white shirt and his tie complements his navy blue pin-striped suit perfectly. And he seems quite unimposing, quite humble, quite kind, quite gentle, quite to-the-toenails right. People inevitably look to him and listen to him, and because they tend to believe nice people, he usually wins.

An iniquitous dynamic occurs here. This paradoxical character with the proficiency of the most pernicious pettifogger leads the jurors to believe that he is decent and kind, when in fact his only goal is to deprive a desperately injured person of his chance at justice. He reminded me of the Judas goat in the slaughterhouse. The goat is a smarter animal than the sheep. In fealty to his master, the Judas goat leads the sheep to the killing house. The sheep innocently follow, having put their full faith and trust in the goat. Once in the killing house, the goat is released to lead yet another flock of sheep to slaughter. How could I reveal the insurance company lawyer's treachery to the jury? How could I win?

I found myself completely obsessed with my fear of this handsome charmer, who was the epitome of wrong to me. I talked to every lawyer who would talk to me about him. The more I listened, the more I discovered that he had no apparent Achilles' heel. Moreover, everyone seemed to like him, even those whom he had beaten. I lay awake at night devising scores of arguments to the jury. At last I came up with this one.

"Ladies and gentlemen,

"Mr. Randolph Hightower is a mighty nice man. But when this case is over he will suffer neither loss nor gain from anything you do. His fee from his client will be the same, win or lose. No matter what your verdict, when this case is over he will simply pull out another file and try another case for the same client he represents here today. [We are not permitted by law to tell the jury that the client is really the insurance company.]* And when Mr. Hightower walks into court tomorrow, despite what the facts may be in that case, he will have the same nimble smile for the next jury, the same perfect demeanor, the same kindly exterior. It frightens me. No matter what the facts, no matter where justice lies, no matter how evil his client or his cause, he will always remain the same— kindly appearing, marvelously poised, unpretentiously compelling—in short, wonderful.

"I am afraid you will like him more than you like me, for, in truth, he is more likable than I. I am afraid you will feel closer to him than you do to me, for indeed, he seems like the kind of man you would like to have as a friend, while I am sometimes abrasive and difficult to approach.

---

*Most judges who care more for corporate profit than the right of people to justice believe juries will award a greater sum to the injured if the jurors know that an insurance company, not the defendant, will pay the bill.

"I am afraid that you will therefore decide the case in his favor, because you like him, when justice demands that you decide for my client. That is my fear. I have thought about it a lot."

Later I actually made this argument to the jury. To my bitter shock, the jurors found against my client. Afterward, one of the jurors was kind enough to speak to me about my argument.

"Mr. Spence, didn't you trust us?"

"Why, of course," I quickly replied. "Why do you ask?"

"Because, you took great pains in telling us that you were afraid we would approach this case as a personality contest. This case was not a personality contest, Mr. Spence. We decided this case on the facts, not on who the nicest lawyer was."

Suddenly I realized I had proven beyond doubt that *I* was not nice. Too late, I realized I had spent my time defending against the lawyer, rather than presenting the justice of my case to the jurors. I had given my opponent so much power that his case proved to be more just than my own. I realized I didn't have the first idea who my opponent was. As the years have passed, I now know him as a genuinely nice man who saw himself as merely representing his client's interests to the best of his ability. But back then I was facing the unconquerable giant I had created. Mine had been a self-defeating investiture. I had furnished this giant—in fact *my* giant—with all the power he had needed to defeat me.

In those days I had not learned what I want to teach here. It is a hard lesson to learn and to remember. We often encounter opponents who excel where we do not. Often our opponent will be wiser, brighter, quicker, better-looking. We can squander our time, our energy, indeed, all of our power in worrying about our opponent's power, and thus give our power to him. No argument, no matter how skillfully delivered, will change our opponent. The only people we have the power to change are ourselves.

I have long since refused to relinquish any of my power to my opponent. I keep my power. I use it to prepare my case, to care about my case, to care for my client. I have learned to listen to the wee voice that speaks to me: "You are all right. You are adequate. If you will spend your power in discovering and thereafter being who you are, if you will present yourself as genuinely as you can, if you will speak out of your core, out of the innocent center, out of the place where the last remnant of the child abides, from which, indeed, all true power is born, it will be enough." Then I say one more thing: "I hereby give you the power to win."

Power over death and taxes: If all power originates with me, why then do I not have power over, let us say, death and taxes? I have no power to destroy death. But I have power over me as I face death. I can face it in a variety of ways—in panic, bravely, even with joy in anticipation of the experience. How I face death is solely my power. I have no power to rescind the tax laws. It is the government's power to assess taxes against me. But only I have the power to determine whether I will pay the tax, fight the payment of taxes, avoid taxes, even evade the tax. The power of such a decision is mine—only mine.

When I find myself on a lonely street at night surrounded by a mob of thugs, I may have no power to escape. But I have the exclusive power to determine how I will react to their threat. I may be afraid, but I have the power to determine how I will deal with my fear. I can run. I can turn and face the mob. I can argue or fight or play dead. In the end, no matter what the situation, I am the source of all power—for me.

Understanding the power of those in power: When one among us is suddenly elevated to high office, something quite magical occurs. This person who may have been of average intelligence and mediocre talent suddenly becomes a quite different person. Think of the small haberdasher who wore thick glasses and who, by quirk of fate, became president of the United States. His power became immense. The buck stopped with him—in the kitchen where he took the heat. He decreed the death and mutilation of hundreds of thousands of Japanese during the Second World War. We gave him such power. And thereafter, we gave him the respect due a great president although he was but a haberdasher, and a rather ordinary one at that.

When Harry Truman took the presidency he did not become magically wiser, suddenly more intelligent. His elevation to the presidency did not cause an inexplicable burst of brain-cell growth. His transformation from a haberdasher to a great president came about in the man's altered perception of himself. But he was always the same man with the same education, the same experience, the same genetic bank, the same number of brain cells. The chief difference between the haberdasher and the president was the power he gave to himself, and, from our viewpoint, the power we gave him.

When one of my fellow lawyers was elevated to a judgeship,

strange transformations also occurred. This person was once a lawyer with pedestrian skills and a quite ordinary understanding of the
law. We called him Bill—just plain Bill. But once he donned the
black robe, we saw him as the judge. We called him "Your Honor,"
and while before we would argue with him, now we respected his
opinions and often found ourselves accepting his vacuous judgments without question. Where once his humor was flat and wanting, on the bench he became very funny. We laughed loudly and
too long at his jokes. When he was a mere lawyer he couldn't play
golf very well, but as a judge, he seemed never to lose.

But Bill saw himself differently as well. He believed the feedback he got from those who were once his colleagues. He loved to
be called "Your Honor." He liked it when people stood up when
he entered the room. He felt a sort of headiness, a sense of self-
love, a lightness of heart. He loved his power. He began to believe
in his infallibility. Both he and we began to endow Bill with certain
powers reserved for God. He could deprive our clients of their lives,
their fortunes, their children, their homes. He could withhold small
favors that, in a trial, could spell winning or losing. Indeed, he
occupied an airy place.

The perceived power of others is often understood on our feeling
level. We felt the judge was omnipotent. We therefore felt intimidated. Such feelings cause the strong to shrink and the brave to
slink away. On the bench, Bill became a tyrant. His demands for
respect were insatiable, his rulings harsh. While once he was one
of the boys, now he treated the humans below him as if their minds
had mysteriously dissolved. Within a short time this judge was thoroughly despised by all. His brutal, empty, often mindless use of
power revealed the nature of the man. Nothing intrinsic in Bill had
changed. The change was in our perception of the man. The
change was in his perception of himself.

Understanding the power of parents and teachers: We are trained
from birth to bestow power on others. As children we saw our parents and our teachers as quasigods. They possessed power we did
not have and could not understand. To you, my mother would
likely have been a pleasing and polite woman, perhaps a little
pretty, with penetrating but kind eyes. To me she was ineffable,
unfathomable, mysterious, a woman whose powers were beyond
understanding—and so she is to me even now, though she has been
dead these many years.

I understood intellectually that my father was a human being. But to me he was braver and stronger than others, wiser but more innocent than other human beings. He was my father. I had my problems with him, my arguments, but they were arguments with *my* father. *Father*—it is a word that for me is loaded with power. *Mother*—it is a word that for me is laden with mystery.

Take away the litigants and the lawyers and the judge is merely plain old Bill. Take away their children and our parents are only people, friends to their friends, employees to their bosses, numbers, mere numbers, on government records. Without *us*, who bestow power on them, those with power are powerless.

Understanding the power of God: In the same manner that we bestow power on our parents, we also bestow power on God. God's power is our power as well. If this were not so, we would not be continually and urgently implored to give our power to God. Having followed the admonition to deliver our power to God, we then beseech Him to answer our prayers and to return to us the power we vested in Him in the first place.

I say that we must deal with power from a *reality stance*. One cannot expect more from God than we have given God. If we have given Him no power, He has none to return. Therefore, if we recognize that all power is born of us ought we not keep our power in the first place?

Besides, no true God would want our power. He has plenty of the stuff, the power of the universe—all of the universes. No merciful God worth our worship would covet our puny power and at the same time admonish *us* not to be covetous ourselves. No merciful God worth our worship would deny us the kingdom of heaven for retaining our power, for our power was given to us—not to return to God, but to return to man, is that not so? By exercising our own power justly, wisely, lovingly, are we not acting in a way to please God, any God? Is not true respect for God the exercising of our power in such a way that we are respected?

The power to judge: All power entities attempt to judge us. We are told that God judges us. Our parents judge us and the judge judges us. But they have the power to judge us only so long as we have given them such power. Otherwise they judge us only for themselves, which was their right in the first place.

Several years ago I was defending Imelda Marcos in New York.

She was, contrary to her portrayal in the press, the truly little person. She had been kidnapped by the United States, widowed, and prosecuted in federal court by international politicians who had agreed to trade the hide of the former first lady of the Philippines for certain favors from the new Philippine regime. The press wanted her hide as well and had, by the worst sorts of infamy, brainwashed an entire nation against her. She was this evil, avaricious woman who stole poor people's money and squandered it on jewels and fancy clothes and who owned three thousand pairs of shoes. She was in a foreign land prosecuted by a foreign prosecutor for the alleged violation of foreign laws before a foreign jury, represented by a foreigner in whom she must place her trust.

One day on our way to court, Mrs. Marcos and I were driving along a crowded street when we came to a stoplight where the newsboys came running out to the cars holding up the latest papers. I saw one of them approaching our car holding up the *Daily News* with a full-page, grotesque photograph of Mrs. Marcos on the front page, below which was a four-inch headline. It contained one word: "OINK."

I tried to distract Mrs. Marcos, but she saw the paper right away. I reached over and touched her hand. "That must make you feel very bad," I said.

"No," she said. She had soft, kind eyes and her voice was gentle and without anger or hurt.

"No?" I asked.

"No," she said again. "That was not me."

She was right. It was not her. I heard much oinking during the trial, but none came from her. She was, as a jury later decreed by its verdict, an innocent woman who had been wrongfully charged by a government engaged in its international political games. But most of all, she was saying to me that she gave no power to the *Daily News*—nor to the host of Americans who despised her without knowing her—to judge her, for her. She was, in the end, the only judge of herself.

The power we deliver to a power entity is like depositing our week's pay in the bank. Before we opened the account, the bank had no power over us or over our money. The bank got its power only when we deposited our money. Thereafter we found that our money was subject to the bank's rules. The bank could use our money as it chose. It could commingle our money with the money of others, lend our money and earn interest on our money. We could take our money back only if we followed certain procedures established by the bank. We could enter the bank only at its bidding—when it chose, where it chose. We must stand in line with others who had also given their money to the bank. If we attempted to withdraw more than we deposited we could go to jail. After we put our money in the bank we became merely a number attached to other numbers. In fine, once we gave the power of our money to the bank, we were required to petition the bank according to its rules to retrieve that which was solely ours in the first place.

Given this knowledge of power, ought we not alter our concept of such power entities? Ought we not view the power entity with a certain *irreverence?* Ought we not take back the power we have abdicated? The bald-headed man with the pot belly and the thick glasses who sits mutely with his bored, dead-eyed wife at the local restaurant where he takes in his yearly supply of cholesterol in one greasy steak is just a man, although we call him "Your Honor." The priest is only a man, the teacher and doctor only ordinary human beings. They suffer, fuss, and wrestle with their own set of human problems and, in so doing, often abdicate their own power to other power entities—to religions and mythologies, to counselors, to anyone and anything who will take their power from them and from whom they can then beseech its return.

How to deal with the power against us: What do we do when parents or teachers or bosses use their power to control or injure us? By understanding power, we can make their power powerless against us. Their threats, their fearsome rantings and ragings, their pointing fingers and accusations, their sordid abuse—what is this about? It is about *their* infirmities, not their power. Everyone's personality is pockmarked with holes, much like a block of Swiss cheese. A hole may represent a place void of intelligence where wisdom should have filled it in. Still another may be a hole void of sensitivity while another a paucity of insight or empathy. A handsome man may compensate for his want of courage by filling in his holes with charm. If he is quick-witted, he may fill in his holes with quips and cleverness. If we are brainy, we will be quick to use our intelligence when we should feel instead. Good looks, a quick wit, cleverness, intelligence—all are forms of power. We use power to fill the holes in our personalities. When a power entity, a judge, for example, has no other asset with which to fill in his deficiencies, we will usually endure, instead, his ugly exhibitions of raw power.

Once we understand how power is misused by those in power and why, their power no longer intimidates us. We see it, shrug our shoulders and press on. We do not lend it reverence. We are not afraid of it. We do not worship it. For who would worship a squawking child, a screaming, aching, lonely man, a frightened judge, a stupid person with power?

There is a certain pity we feel for those with power, for usually they have been granted no special talent by which to effectively exercise it. Power in the hands of many is useless. A judge can have all the power the law bestows, even the power to sentence men to death, but without wisdom he cannot deliver justice. A parent can have all the power parents possess over their children, but the parent cannot, by the use of power, rear a child who will become a successful human being. The boss may have the power to fire the worker and injure the worker's record, but the boss, by the imposition of power, can never force his employee to work to his capacity or to create, nor can he cause the worker to be loyal or to excel.

Any discussion of power would be incomplete without acknowledging Lord Acton's immortal law: Power tends to corrupt and absolute power corrupts absolutely. That unalterable rule applies both to God and man.

The powerlessness of power: Responsibility is the symbiotic twin of power. Neither power nor responsibility can be effectively exercised without the other. They are like a binary star, two ends revolving around a center. The almighty judge is responsible for justice in his court. The all-powerful parent is responsible for the child's growth and welfare. The omnipotent boss is responsible for production at the plant. But the judge cannot obtain justice without the skill of lawyers who present him with the facts; the parent cannot form the successful child without the love of the child; and the boss is powerless to achieve production without the respect and aid of his employees. Are we not confronted with a paradox? Is it not apparent that power is finally vested in the powerless?

No parents are more grateful than those whose children understand the parents' struggle to be successful parents, whose children assist the parents in fulfilling their goals. No boss is more grateful than one whose employees understand the stress of his responsibility and respond accordingly. But the power to aid those in power, those who bear the responsibility, is, always, *our power.* Do you understand? And, when we exercise our power to aid those who have power over us, we invest ourselves with power, do we not?

The loneliness of power: Power is lonely. Power segregates. God must be the most lonely entity in the universe. No person is more lonely than a judge. No person needs a friend more. The boss was once a worker with many friends. Now he exists apart from them. He is lonely. Some of his old friends hate him. Others fear him. The parent is always separated from the child. Parents and children can be friendly. They can love each other. But rarely can they be friends, for they are never peers, which is the foundation of all friendships. Power, real or imagined, physical or psychological, isolates.

Understanding the neurotic need for power: Many in positions of power take up such posts in the fulfillment of a neurotic need to exercise power over others—prison guards, police officers, some judges, some deans, some teachers, some parents, almost all politicians—you understand. Insecure, afraid, those who must maintain control are, indeed, lonely and frightened. Their awful sense of vulnerability is a disease of the psyche. It is marked by a dark, smoldering misery. Such people most frequently treat their disease with massive doses of power that manifests itself in anger, cruelty, and aggression. I think of Plato, who said, "Access to power must be confined to those who are not in love with it." The old saying is old because it is true: "This will be a better world when the power of love replaces the love of power."

Understanding power and responsibility: On the other hand, those who are responsible are often fearful of their power. "What," they ask, "if I abuse my power? What if I use it innocently but wrongfully?" To these people, power is an entrustment often felt as a crushing load. For some of them it can be a hideous gift. In the First World War, those who made triage decisions that determined who would live and who would die were often unable to recover from the psychic scars. When I must turn down cases that are patently just in favor of other cases that seem equally as just, I anguish over whether I made the right choices for the right reasons. I know my vision is often opaque. I feel the doubt. Sometimes the guilt.

Power is often a burden. We cannot blame God. We cannot blame others. The power is ours. But so is the responsibility, for we know that power over others may be safely exercised without injury only when it is released in the form of love.

The blinding power of power: Power over others often lifts us into a deluding cloud where we are concealed from ourselves. In the fog we are sometimes dazzled and intoxicated, sometimes blinded, and blind tyrants cannot excel or succeed. I know of no great man or woman who ever thought himself or herself great. The realization of one's potential of greatness *ipso facto* destroys that possibility. I think of John Steinbeck's own judgment on his immortal *Grapes of Wrath*, when he said, "It isn't a great book. I had hoped it would be. It's just a run-of-the-mill book. And the awful thing is that it is absolutely the best I can do."

On the other hand, when we realize that we are the source of all power over ourselves, this recognition is divinely empowering. When we understand our power, we are freed from intimidation, delivered from fear, and provided with the magical wherewithal to realize our perfect potential.

Power, the pistol that fires in both directions: Power is like a pistol with barrels that point in both directions. When one with power pulls the trigger against someone with lesser power, one barrel fires in the direction of the intended victim while the other fires into the person who has pulled the trigger. As a weapon, power has little to offer. It germinates resentment and reaps hatred. It fosters the deep and abiding need for revenge. Power exercised without love releases an adverse Karma that returns to defeat us—where or when we never know. But it will return with all its destructive force, with all its gathered vengeance. Revenge is the bastard child of justice.

When I was a young lawyer feeling my power, my strategy in a certain case was to attack and destroy every witness the other side put against me. I took on the witnesses, old men with watery eyes who I knew were but company sycophants trying to keep their jobs. I took on the experts, scholarly actors who I knew were but paid witnesses attempting to earn their fees rather than reveal the truth. Cut them up, shredded them, pulverized them. The jury was out only fifteen minutes before it returned a verdict against my client. I was devastated. Hadn't I won every battle? Hadn't I destroyed the witnesses? Hadn't my power on cross-examination been over-whelming?

As the jury was filing out of the courthouse, one of the women approached me. She looked up at me with tears in her eyes. It had obviously been hard for her to turn my severely injured client out of a court of justice with nothing.

"Mr. Spence," she said quietly, "why did you make us hate you so?"

For many months her words haunted me. *"Why did you make us hate you so?"* Then one day I realized that not only had I destroyed the witnesses, I had mocked them, held them up to the jury in scorn and derision. I had been angry with the sweet old company men who had spent their lives smiling—smiling at their bosses and their customers all the while knowing the machine they sold was defective. I hated the hypocrisy. I hated the injustice. And I had attacked. I attacked everyone in sight. I attacked the nice company lawyer with the cryptic smile and guileful arguments. I attacked the scholarly experts with their unctuous ways and wily dissertations. In the merciless barrage that I leveled in the courtroom, I inadvertently attacked even the jury, for my cruelty forced them to the side of the defense. I had unleashed all of my power, and in doing so I had defeated myself.

Although I will preach that sometimes we must attack and that when one attacks, the attack should be relentless, yet the power one uses must not be used to bully and bludgeon the powerless. One does not attack mothers and children, not until it has been demonstrated that the mothers are deserving of an attack, a fair and appropriate attack, and that the children are, under the skin, rascals who have earned a stern comeuppance. Power can be safely exercised only in the service of that which is ostensibly good. Power is like gasoline. Spread aimlessly over the landscape, it can result in an inferno, causing untold harm. Correctly contained, it can cook supper or transport us to Boston.

Using power to intimidate: I have heard of books that purportedly teach how to win by intimidation. As a young lawyer I was intimidated by older, more skillful lawyers. As I gained power through my experience I began to intimidate other lawyers myself. I remember ever having challenged opponents to fistfights, believing that the threat would so befuddle them they would be rendered ineffective. I remember coming close to their faces, looking into their eyes and telling them fearsome, hateful things. I now remember such occasions with sorrow. I am sorrowful that I was so afraid of my opponent, so insecure in myself that I felt obliged to intimidate. I am sorrowful that I was not wise enough to recognize that when one attempts to intimidate one's opponent one only motivates the opponent to greater action, for no opponent is as dangerous as one who fights for his very life. I am sorrowful that I did not reserve my power to present my case in a quiet, open, compellingly honest manner. But I was afraid. I did not recognize my own power. Instead, I sought to usurp the power of my opponent by intimidation. The tactic of intimidation only confirms to all who are casual observers the piteous lack of power possessed by the intimidator.

AND SO: It is clear that we require power. But the power we need is our own. The power exhibited in the winning argument may not be overtly powerful at all, for power may be experienced as gentleness, as compassion, as love, as humility, as sensitivity.

We have come to understand that even sounds we thought powerful—the harsh voice of authority, the demanding dictates of the bully—are not sounds of power but the wretched noise of the insecure. We have come to understand that the application of excessive power often conceals cowardice or grave personality defects, that power is often useless to achieve what we want—to gain love or respect or success. And we have learned that power is deceptive, that at times there is no one more powerful than the powerless. So it has been throughout history. The Rockys have always been more powerful than the Apollo Creeds. The meek, unsullied by power, shall indeed inherit the earth.

We have already discovered that our power, and theirs, is born of ourselves. All power originates from us.

Only from us.

At last we understand: *We are power.*

All of the power.

4

The Incredible Power of Credibility

STANDING NAKED

THE LOCK: No one listens to me. Why should they? Who am I?

THE KEY: Anyone can be credible, but we must risk telling the truth—about ourselves.

One can stand as the greatest orator the world has known, possess the quickest mind, employ the cleverest psychology, and have mastered all the technical devices of argument, but if one is not credible one might just as well preach to the pelicans.

How often have we seen a child win an argument with simple language that innocently reveals the truth? We see everyday people win great encounters because they were believed. They offered no pretensions, no phony veneers of style. They made no attempt to charm or manipulate. We had a sense that what we saw was what we got, the *real person* with all of the blemishes—but real.

The first trick: The first trick of the winning argument is the trick of abandoning trickery. Most of us can talk about ourselves—a little—and zoom in on our feelings—a little. But most of us do not tell much of the truth about ourselves. We hold back our hurt, our anger, our deep dread. We fear to reveal our fear, our joy, our jealousy, our hunger, our ideas, our insecurities, ourselves. *Credibility* comes out of the bone—deeper yet, out of the marrow. We puff and swell, hoping to appear like a frightening Goliath. But do we not remember David? Great pretenses win nothing. The tears, the unctuous oratory—all are useless if, at last, we have no credibility.

To win, we must be believed.

To be believed, we must be believable.

To be believable, we must tell the truth, the truth about ourselves—the *whole truth*.

Winston Churchill once said, "What the people really want to hear is the truth—it is the exciting thing—to speak the truth."

The search for the child: We must argue from the place where the frightened child abides. We must argue from the place where the whimpers and wailing are held back, where the anger boils, where the monster rises up and screams, where the lover and the saint and the ancient warrior fuse. That is where we must focus, in that rare, rich place, that nucleus of our being. That is the magical place where credibility dwells.

Several years ago I was speaking to a group of sophisticated, stylish trial lawyers in Chicago, those who adorn themselves with expensive wool with those little blue stripes. After my presentation to the group, a young lawyer, appropriately besuited and bestriped, stopped me in the lobby.

"There's something going on with me," he said. "I used to win all of my cases. Back then I couldn't cross-examine. I couldn't argue. But I won. Over the years I've learned all the tricks they teach trial lawyers—I've gotten good, but I can't seem to win anymore. It seems the more I hone my technique, the more I lose."

Technique has little to do with credibility and therefore little to do with winning. The most articulate, greasy-lipped lawyer is not able to fool ordinary juries, at least not for long. But my two-year-old grandson, pounding the table with his rattle, is credible. He cannot launch a pedagogical argument brimming with splendid language. Yet, when the child cries, we know he is hungry or tired. Credibility is becoming the child.

THE LOCK: We are lied to every day—by the media, by politicians, by our employers, by everyone. Lying is a way of life. Isn't successful argument merely learning to become an expert at lying?

THE KEY: We can fool the *Other* for a while, but at last, their *credibility detectors* convey an irrefutable message: "This is not the truth." At that point every argument is lost.

We, of course, can achieve temporary credibility by acting credible. But not for long. When we argue, those who hear and judge our arguments extend countless psychic tentacles to detect the first hint of deception. The tentacles search out the phony and the fraud. The tentacles look for hidden malice, for danger that lurks in the interpersonal forest through which we make our way.

Our psychic tentacles: If we could see our psychic selves, we would look like a strange two-legged bug with feelers extending out in every direction. Our psychic tentacles wrap themselves around the speaker, palpate him, measure him, test him. Is he telling the truth? Together the feelers form an alarm system that measures and values all that is said, all that is heard, all that is seen. The system searches for that which is out of sync—a sound that is wrong, a word that is inappropriate for the idea, a movement that is slightly premeditated, a rhythm, a look, a twitch, a cough that does not quite fit.

We all possess such feelers. Like our immune systems, our invisible *credibility detectors* are constantly searching for the enemy, for the thin clank of the counterfeit. I am not speaking of intelligence here. Both the genius and the everyday person have such detectors. I am not speaking of intuition or of some mystical, far-off concept. I am speaking of the psychic mechanism by which we can recognize the ring of truth, by which we can protect ourselves from those who invade us with pretense and deceit.

Speaking with many tongues: As we shall learn in later chapters, we communicate not only with words, but with the various sounds of words and their rhythms. We speak with silences. We speak with hands, and bodies, with *physical* words—the way we pose or stand or move.

Take the smile: What do we make of the person who smiles when he speaks of sorrow or pain, who smiles through it all? See him? He is still smiling. What about those whose mouths turn down when they smile, as if they are fighting back the smile? What else do they hold back from us? What about those with the nervous tick of a smile who use it to punctuate every other phrase? You have seen them too. The mouth spasms into that nanosecond cookie-cutter grin that fails to suggest happiness, but instead leaves a clear impression of pain. Do we trust any of these?

And the eyes: the said "mirrors of the soul," what about them? We have all encountered those who never permit us to peer into their windows. We do not trust them any more than we trust the veneer of thin ice. I knew a judge who, when he spoke to me, focused on a spot about two inches above the convergence of my eyebrows. I thought, My God, do I have something nasty up there? More than once I wiped where he looked. I stood a little straighter. But he lifted his eyes so they stayed focused at the same place. Although I appeared before him on many occasions and knew him socially for many years, he never once looked me in the eye, or anyone else for that matter. Although through the years he must have shared something with me, I cannot remember a single word he ever said, for he never spoke to me, but to my forehead.

Still, sometimes, the eyes, like mirrors, can mislead us. In court I have encountered the worst of psychopathic killers. I have had them aim their eyes at me, vacant eyes that did not reflect their hate. These were eyes that revealed nothing, eyes void of life, like empty bottles. In the courtroom I have also seen loving eyes that concealed a vicious heart. I know an insurance company lawyer who, when he speaks, always gazes on me and everyone else with adoring eyes. Even though he had often been my hostile and devious adversary, I still find myself feeling friendly and warm toward him. It is hard not to feel kindly toward those with loving eyes. But when I turn away for a moment, I always realize something is out of sync. He is clever enough. His words are sweet enough—I call him "Sugar Lips." But if one looks and listens, one can always make out a slight deviousness in the air, the eyes too ripe with love, the lips too dripping. And if one innocently enters the trap, well, I have no doubt that he will be destroyed, and that as Sugar Lips drives his knife into the heart, his eyes would be as gentle and loving as his lips are sugarcoated.

The eyes of the credible convey a message consistent with the plain meaning of the spoken words. These eyes are in sync with the rest of the presentation. They are happy eyes, sad and sorrowful eyes, angry eyes, eyes that match the sounds, that support the feeling of the messenger and that are consistent with the message. And when the eyes do not have it, as it were, we know it.

Speaking with the body: The body muscles speak to us, sometimes more subtly than words. We can all identify the beginner who is painfully aware of his hands and sticks them in his pocket, or clasps them behind his back or stuffs them into stiff, straight casts at his side. Damn the arms! Damn the hands! As a beginner, I was terrified that I might have to speak without a lectern to hold on to. Women have it better. They have no pockets. But still, some buckle their hands in front of them as if their navels were at serious risk.

The accomplished speaker has forgotten about his hands and permits them to range freely with his feelings. But the speaker who has become comfortable with his body movements had also best tell us the truth, lest they reveal the speaker's contrary feelings. Recently I was shown a television pitch for the sale of an accounting service. The man on camera was dressed in the typical "trust me" gray business suit with an honest blue shirt and a subdued, respectful tie. His hair was nicely styled, and so far as I could tell there were no telltale dandruff flakes on his shoulders to irrevocably ruin him.

In accordance with those who teach sales, this announcer looked the viewers squarely in the eyes and began his pitch. At the point where we were to jump up and cry, "Yes, yes, tell me no more! I'll buy it!", his *physical words* contradicted his message. As he implored us with words to buy his service, he was vigorously shaking his head from side to side, as if to say "no."

We all know about body language, how people reveal certain truths through the movement and stance of their physical selves. A person may turn slightly away from those he does not accept; he may lift a finger to the side of his mouth when he is perplexed, or seal his lips with a finger when he is telling himself not to speak but to listen. But body language does not always tell the whole truth.

In a case I brought against Chrysler, a negligently designed seat installed in its vehicle had given way in a rear-ender and had seriously injured my client. During the trial, I became concerned that a juror in the back row, a farmer in bib overalls, had shut me out. In accordance with the theory of the body language experts, his arms, which were always folded across his belly, signaled he wanted no part of my argument. But I needed to convince him. In Wyoming the verdict must be unanimous. As the trial progressed, I found myself speaking to him more than to the others. But as he scowled down at me, his arms stayed folded. When the jury returned a record verdict in favor of my client, I was still wondering about the farmer. I caught him before he lumbered out of the court-room.

"You know," I said, "I was worried all through the trial about you. You had your arms folded, and I've been told that means you were against me."

"Oh, that don't mean nothin'," he said. "I got a big belly. A man's gotta put his arms someplace." He laughed. "You done good."

Our credibility detectors: My experience confirms that everyday people employing their natural credibility detectors can almost always recognize the disingenuous. Therein lies the great virtue of the American jury. In nearly every jury trial, lawyers on both sides hire experts to testify on issues that are beyond the ordinary knowledge of lay people. But everyday people judge the experts, and they do so with uncanny accuracy. An expert on ballistics may testify that the gunpowder residues found on the hands of the accused establish that the accused fired a weapon on the day in question. But the defense may call an expert who will tell the jury that the elements found in gunshot residues are found in common substances we touch every day. Ordinary car grease, for example, contains barium, one of the elements commonly associated with gunshot residues. And even if the substances removed from the defendant's hands were from a gunshot, the defense expert may testify that it is possible he became contaminated without having fired the weapon. He might have touched a recently fired gun. He could have touched the deceased's clothing after the deceased was shot. He might have been standing near the muzzle of the weapon when it was fired. And so the arguments of the experts go on. But which expert is to be believed?

Jurors are natural-born experts in judging credibility. And like jurors, the people we speak to every day are also experts. They test us with their credibility-feelers. When something in the communication string does not fit, they are alerted. They hear and see subtle differences, often subconsciously. They hear the difference in the sound of words. They perceive the subtle inconsistencies between the *chosen words*, the *sound words*, and the *physical words*. The polygraph attempts to analyze our physiological responses when we lie, but each of us is many times more sophisticated than that primitive device. Our senses record hundreds of signals over the course of a brief encounter, and, faster than any computer, we assimilate the information, and pronounce our judgments. While the lie detector with its operator may take minutes, even hours to complete its analysis of a single sentence, our minds, as rapidly as the words fall from the speaker's mouth, record split-second conclusions concerning the speaker's credibility.

Were we able to painstakingly analyze the signals we transmit in a few brief minutes of speech—a contradicting expression creeping over the mouth, the unconscious turning away, an errant eyebrow, the discordant word-sounds in disharmony with the message, the giveaway body language, the eyes that betray—we'd begin to realize how impossible it is for us to intentionally, simultaneously, perfectly coordinate this whole string into a harmonious presentation. If we concentrate on the words we choose, our sounds and gestures will likely be wrong. If we try to bring our bodies into sync with our words, we become self-conscious, stiff, unbelievable. Trying to control and synchronize the scores of signals we send in a given communication is like trying to harness a flock of wild turkeys. We may be able to get one under control, but we'll lose the flock—and we will have lost the argument as well.

The biological advantage of truth: There is a valid biological explanation why all cultures past and present hoist honesty to the top of the moral totem pole. Those who lie to us put us in jeopardy. We can protect ourselves from an assault, but not from the undiscovered lie. In a jury trial, I can present my arguments to honest jurors and accept their honest responses. But I cannot protect my client when a juror has a hidden agenda against my client, for that juror will surely rise up, usually by ambush from the safety of the jury room, and do my client in.

Several years ago I defended a sheriff who shot his undercover agent between the eyes while two other deputies looked on. The dead man had been scheduled to testify the following day before a statewide grand jury that presumably was investigating the sheriff, among others. The case was highly publicized. Dan Rather had aired the story on *60 Minutes*. The grand jury had been asking questions about organized crime in Wyoming, and now the murder of this undercover agent on the eve of his testimony to the grand jury became a scandal on the lips of everyone. People were outraged. Even I, though trained to afford the defendant the presumption of innocence, believed the sheriff had assassinated the witness who was to testify against him. Later, after I agreed to talk to the sheriff, I became convinced that he had actually shot the undercover agent in self-defense. But soon I was in the courtroom facing a venire of Wyoming jurors who had been bombarded with the same information from the same media that had so convinced me of my client's guilt.

Did I dare trust the life of my client to jurors who sat in the jury box and insisted, under oath no less, that despite what they had read or heard they could be fair? I remember turning to the sheriff and saying, "Well, Ed, shall we keep the ones who say they haven't made up their minds against you, or shall we keep the ones who've told us the truth and think you're guilty as hell?"

"Let's go with the ones that'd hang me," he said. "At least they're tellin' the truth."

We chose a jury of men and women who, without having heard a word of testimony, had already deprived my client of his most precious constitutional right, the presumption of innocence, people who admitted they believed my client was guilty. But when the state failed to prove the charge of murder beyond a reasonable doubt, twelve jurors who had been honest enough to admit they thought my client was guilty were also honest enough to return a "Not Guilty" verdict. We can usually trust those who will tell us the truth. That is why, in the course of human history, truth-telling has been designated as the highest of virtues in every culture, and why the credibility that results therefrom is always so powerful.

THE LOCK: Don't tell me a person can't be fooled. I've been taken in more than once.

THE KEY: Everyone has. But when we are "taken in," our *credibility detectors* have usually been overridden by our wants.

I know, as do you, that we can be fooled. But the signs, the signals, the alarms were all there to be seen and heard if we simply looked and listened. Most often when we are taken in, it is not because we are incapable of detecting artifice, but because we do not want to detect it. We have grown up on Santa Claus and Superman. We want to believe the myths. We have been taught that in America there is liberty and justice for all. We want to believe the prosecutor in the courtroom and the anchorman on the evening news. We want to believe we are loved. We want to trust our neighbors and our friends. We want to feel safe. We want to eat the food and drink the drinks that taste good. We want to get rich quickly. We *want* more than we want to pay attention to our credibility detectors.

I believe most people tell me the truth—the truth for them. I believe most people want to do good—good as they see it. I believe most people are honest—as honest as it is comfortable for them to be. I believe that most people will do me no harm—at least not intentionally, at least not viciously. I do not argue here that we should distrust all who come before us. I argue only that we should look and we should listen. The ability to listen and to see must be twice as important as the ability to speak, else why would God have given us two eyes and two ears and only one mouth?

THE LOCK: I try to tell the truth most of the time, but people don't take me as seriously as I wish they would. Something's missing.

THE KEY: Openly revealing our feelings establishes credibility. We are what we feel.

How do we feel about our child's conduct, our mate's plan to change jobs, the boss's hiring policy, or the city's proposed zoning ordinance? Our willingness to openly reveal our *feelings* in our argument nearly always builds our credibility. But many of us refuse to express our feelings because we fear we may become angry. "I keep mum so I don't blow a fuse," says someone. But often our anger shields fear. Our child's conduct may make us angry, but we are *afraid* our child will get into serious trouble. Our boss's hiring policy may cause us to rage, but behind it we are *afraid* the boss's policy will put our job in jeopardy. The city may make us furious when it rezones to permit a business in our neighborhood, but underneath we are *afraid* the city's zoning decision will affect the value of our property. Argument may be combat, and like any combat it ultimately gives rise to fear—our fear of losing the argument and the resulting consequences of our loss.

Fear, the fuel of successful argument: I cannot remember an argument I've ever made that did not in some way engender some fear. If I lose my argument, even a minor argument, I will at least

feel disappointment. Disappointment is unpleasant, and the operative avoidance mechanism, even to escape disappointment, is fear.
Small doses of fear as well as large ones move us to avoid the
pain—small or large—that constitutes the risk we assume when we
argue. Even a small amount of pain is still pain, and even a small
amount of fear of experiencing pain is still fear.

Credibility and the confession of fear: I have made the simplistic
but correct argument that to be credible we must tell the truth. We
have already discussed the notion that it is all right to be afraid and
that we should feel that fear. But should we go so far as to confess
our fear to the *Other*? I say that acknowledging the truth, even the
truth about our fear, perhaps *especially* the truth about our fear,
creates credibility.

Recently I was about to make my final argument to a jury in a
widely publicized trial, the defense of Randy Weaver, who was
charged, among many other crimes, with the murder of a United
States marshal. The assistant U.S. attorney had just concluded what
many said was the best argument of his career. My client's life
depended upon how convincingly I could make my own arguments. The court had called a five-minute recess before I was to
begin. I was pacing up and down, my belly tight, my nerves tangled
and raw. A friend of mine, an attorney with whom I had tried
another murder case, called me over to where she was sitting in
the courtroom. She had seen my pain.

"Let me tell you a new joke," she offered.

"Don't tell me a joke," I replied in my preargument agony.
"Tell me how to be real." Then suddenly I knew once more how
to be real. I had to feel the fear—again. Always the damnable pain
of fear. I could cover the pain of fear. But what could I cover it
with? Could I cover it with bravado? Who loves a swaggering cock
on the walk? Could I cover it with a cold, unemotional blanket?
Who cares for the callous, the insensitive, the apathetic? Who
would believe them? Could I withdraw like the turtle into its shell?
Who trusts those who hold back from us? Could I attack the way
the lion attacks? Who is open to such a fearsome beast? Could I
run for my hole like the rabbit? Who believes those who hide? The
turtle when it retracts into its shell, the lion when it charges, and
the rabbit when it scurries into its hole all react to the same emotion: fear. I watched the jury march in.

I heard the judge speak those fateful words I had longed for, and dreaded. "Mr. Spence, you may begin your argument." I glanced quickly at the jury. They were watching me as I walked toward them, waiting to hear me, waiting to judge me. Could I answer the U.S. attorney? Would the jury believe me? Would I measure up? I felt like running. Trapped, I, like the lion, felt like charging. My heart was racing. I was afraid. God Almighty, I am always so afraid!

Then I looked down at my feet and I tried to feel where the fear actually lay. There it was, where I always found it, pressing at my ribs on each side, up high. I looked up at the jury. "Ladies and gentlemen of the jury," I began. "I wish I weren't so afraid," I heard myself saying. "I wish after all these years in the courtroom I didn't feel this way. You'd think I would get over it."

Some of the jurors looked astounded. Here was this lawyer who had fearlessly guided the defendant's case through the cross-examination of over half a hundred mostly hostile witnesses—the FBI, the marshals, the experts. Here was this man who seemed always able to prevail now confessing his fear. They watched. They waited. Their tentacles were out—feeling, probing.

"I'm afraid I won't be able to make the kind of argument to you that Randy Weaver deserves," I said. "After nearly three months of trial, I'm afraid I won't measure up. I wish I were a better lawyer." As always, the fear began to slink away and the argument began to take its place, one that was to consume nearly three hours. It was an argument that was honest, and angry and humorous, one that was punctuated with defects and false starts and syntax that would horrify any self-respecting English professor. It was an argument that was as real as I was able to be—an argument that, in the end, was to free my client.

After the arguments were over and the jury had retired to deliberate, a young lawyer came up to me as I was leaving the courtroom. "Mr. Spence, how come you started so rough?" he asked.

"What do you mean?" I asked back.

"Seemed like you were all hung up to begin with, but then you got going and, boy, it was hell to pay after that." He laughed. "But you started rough."

"I started 'rough' because that's the way I was," I said.

"Oh," he said. But he didn't seem to understand what I meant. He had experienced the credibility of my argument, but he did not understand that the argument's credibility was the product of a lawyer who was afraid he could not measure up, and was willing to admit it.

Credibility and the white lie: The wheels of society are lubricated by the so-called white lie. We tell a friend he looks wonderful when he looks like he's been mangled by a herd of gorillas. We may exclaim about the food at dinner when it has been ghastly. We tell people to whom we are introduced that we're glad to meet them when, in truth, we don't give a damn if we ever see them again. Most social intercourse is pretending. But we provide each other a mutual permission to engage in these social lies. Sometimes we need to believe them.

Recently a man walked up to my table in a café where I was having lunch with Imaging. I hadn't seen him since he was a young upstart. He was no longer young. His hair was graying. He'd put on weight, and I was fortunate to have recognized him at all. "You're looking good," he said, which, loosely translated, meant, "After all these years you have sure grown old." But he stood there at the table insisting, shaking his head, his body words betraying his spoken words, "You sure look good."

But what was he supposed to say? Was he to walk up and say, "My God, man, I haven't seen you for twenty years—you look like a truck just ran over your face? Why, you can see the tread marks. And your hair—it used to be a kind of dirty blond, and now it's damn near white. But, in spite of all the damage, I was still able to recognize you." And what was I supposed to say? "Why, when I saw you last you were a young, good-looking kid, and now I couldn't tell you from any of the run-of-the-mill, paunchy, seedy, middle-aged bastards who are always coming up to my table, interrupting my lunch and telling me I look good"? Was I supposed to say that? No. I said, "By God, you're looking good too, man!" And when we left he was probably thinking, "That old boy is on the way out for sure," and I was thinking, "Old Father Time-Bomb sure took his toll on that kid," and neither one of us thought much about how we really looked. It was all right for us to lie a little to each other. It was our gift, one to the other. It had nothing to do with the issue of credibility.

THE LOCK: Acting. That's what I think argument is really about. You're either a good actor or you're not. I never was good at acting.

THE KEY: *Acting is simply revealing the truth.* **And to be a good actor, one must be credible.**

The most frequent question people ask me is, "When you're in court, do you act?" The question really is, "Can we trust you? You seem genuine enough. We want to believe you. But you must be a skilled actor who can fool juries and who, therefore, can fool us," which, of course, brings up the question of acting. What is it?

Acting is being. True acting is never pretending; it is, instead, the process of revealing the truth of the character in the situation in which he finds himself. Acting requires the actor to get in touch with the truth of his feelings, his anger, his joy, his surprise, his sorrow, his pain. When Al Pacino played the blind, retired, curmudgeonly army officer in *Scent of a Woman*, he was blind in his mind's eyes. He did not pretend to be blind. When he was deep into his performance, he lost the ability to see. Of course, it is possible for us to pretend, but actors who pretend rather than act rarely bring home the Oscar.

Even so, the most flawless performance on the stage, rehearsed for days, lasts but a couple of hours. Not only do movie stars practice their lines until they become the lines, but the scenes are shot over and over until they are as perfect as possible, and the test of success is, "Was the scene *believable*?" The director's search, like ours, is for credibility. When we argue we do not have the luxury of repeating our performance until it is flawless. We cannot ask our wives or employers to disregard our last three performances and to stand by until we get it right. If we are pretending, no matter how skillfully, how convincingly and well-rehearsed, at some point the *Other* will perceive that something is awry. At that moment we have lost the argument. We are believed and the *Other* is convinced because we tell the truth, the truth about the facts we know and the truth about the feelings we experience.

THE LOCK: So how do I tell the truth? Maybe I don't know how.

We have been admonished from childhood to tell the truth and assured through every stage of our lives that "honesty is the best policy!" Yet over a lifetime we've developed few skills in truth-telling. Strangely, our society does not encourage truth-telling. I know of no college courses on "How to Tell the Truth." I know of no Liars Anonymous organizations. I have never met a person who professes to be an expert on truth-telling, and if I ever meet a man who tells me he always tells the truth, I most likely will turn and run.

Our earliest experiences have taught us that when we tell the truth we are often punished. If we tell the truth, we often lose or we're rejected or banished. If we tell the truth about the wrong we've committed, be it ever so petty and innocent, we are often punished. If we tell the truth about how we feel, about our fear, we are scorned. If we reveal our yearnings, we are mocked. If we admit our love, we are sometimes rejected. If we expose our dislike, we are ostracized. If we reveal our anger, our opponents strike back with anger. We learn to shy from the truth. We build around it. We create myths that blind us from its glare. We avoid the truth like the god-awful pox. We have been taught that truth-tellers are naive—suckers, fools. To us, truth has become a bad word. Truth: God save us from it! Especially the truth about ourselves.

THE KEY: Learn to stand naked.

Despite what we have learned to the contrary, I say we must all learn to disrobe our psyches. But before I can persuade you to take off your psychic garments I must take off mine. Pursuing the metaphor, I admit I am afraid of what I might expose were I to disrobe—my sagging middle, my pale, unenvied chest, my whatever else that might not measure up. But still I say we *need to speak as if we were naked.*

I once wrote the following parody to illustrate the frustration of judges who are unable to extract the truth from the lawyers who appear before them.

When I awakened, everyone in the courtroom, including the witnesses, was naked except for his stockings. The prosecutor was naked, his hairy potbelly proclaiming the peculiar sort of pregnancy most men suffer at fifty. Strangely, the prosecutor seemed comfortable enough. He leaned back and scratched at his armpit, slowly parting his sparse underarm hair with absent-minded fingers. A pair of garters grabbed his scrawny hairless calves. He wiggled his toes inside his black silk hose. I looked down. I was naked too, and—horrors!—my socks didn't match! I pulled the lectern closer to cover my front.

"My God, Your Honor, everybody's naked!" I screamed.

"How observant, counsel," the judge replied in a bored voice.

"But why?"

"Simple, counsel. I ordered everybody to take off their clothes—all but their socks. Feet are ugly."

"But why in God's name, Your Honor, with all due respect, did you order everybody to take off their clothes?"

"I'll tell you why, counsel! I'm sick up to here with all the cover-ups and snow jobs I get from fancy Brooks Brothers pin-striped suits. Lawyers who present their cases naked are more likely to tell the truth."

"But you're not naked, Your Honor. That doesn't seem fair," I protested.

"Judicial privilege, counsel. We judges hide many a secret thing under these black robes." Then he laughed as if he had made a very great joke.

We wear our psychic clothes so we can conceal who we are. We have become a society that rewards not who we *are*, but how we *appear*. It is more important to look good than to be good. Our image, as opposed to our substance, our mythological persons as opposed to our real selves, are presented and marketed like so many nicely packaged peaches at the supermarket. And what we see is not what we get—at the supermarket or elsewhere. We are so confused, so confounded by our own disguises and theirs that we no longer know who anyone is. Therein lies the great power of standing naked, for we all know when the *Other* stands naked before us. We recognize that he or she is real. At that point another dynamic comes into play. That the *Other* has trusted us sufficiently to disrobe his psyche in front of us confirms that the *Other* is trustworthy as well.

Sometimes when I'm seriously struggling to discover how I feel, I imagine that I've stripped off all my clothes and that I'm standing naked before my audience. Sometimes the fear of it seems too much. To stand naked? To reveal those raw, seldom visited, unprotected psychic places! Yet behind our psychic shrouds lies the great power of credibility that permits us all to argue, to be heard, to be understood, and to win.

THE LOCK: If I tell the truth, if I tell the *Other* what I really want, I will suffer from it. I've already learned that.

If we tell our neighbor that we want his land, the price suddenly goes up. If we tell our friend that we covet his wife, his possessions, his manservant or maidservant as in the Ten Commandments, our friend becomes defensive, hostile, aggressive. If we express our true desire to the opposite sex, well, we can be in a lot of trouble. We all know that. But . . .

THE KEY: Revealing our honest desires, asking for what we *want*, makes it difficult for the *Other* to refuse us.

When we honestly communicate our wants to the *Other* we exercise a great power. People do not want to say no, not to us, not to our face, not when we have plainly asked for what we want, not when our request is reasonable, not when it is just.

Telling the truth to sell: When Imaging and I were in London, we visited Burmansy Market where the farmers brought their produce to sell each day. The street was lined with carts and booths offering every variety of fruit and vegetable indigenous to the British Isles. Most of the vendors sat at their stands like wooden Indians with dull glass eyes waiting for someone to buy. But one old grizzled salesman hollered out as we walked by, "Buy me vegetables, sir. I *need* the money."

Before I realized what I was doing, or why, I'd walked up to the old boy and bought a bundle of carrots. I wasn't hungry. I'm not even very fond of raw carrots, and my hands were already filled with other packages. Yet I made the purchase, captivated by the *ring of truth*, by the simple winning argument of the old man who told us plainly what he wanted. He didn't tell me how carrots were rich in carotene or about their value as roughage. He didn't tell me how fresh they were or how they were grown without chemicals. He didn't try to convince me I was getting a bargain. He just told the truth: *he needed the money*. Because he communicated truthfully and openly, he was credible. Because he was credible, I bought his forthright argument, not to mention his carrots.

Freeing one's client by revealing one's wants: In my argument to the jury in the Randy Weaver case, I used a similar strategy. I told the jury straight out what I wanted. I said, "At the end of this case I want us to walk out of this courtroom together—all of us." I pointed to my client. "I want you to free Randy Weaver. I want

Randy Weaver's children who sit over there"—I pointed to them—
"to walk out with us—right out the front door of this courthouse
with him and with you and with me." I walked slowly toward the
children and as I did the jury watched the children, saw their faces,
saw them listening, waiting, hoping. Then the jurors looked back
at me. "I want your verdict to free us all."

Weeks after the jury had returned its verdict, I talked to one of
the jurors who had fought very hard for the acquittal of Mr. Weaver.
"You told us what you wanted," she said. "That's what I wanted
too. I was glad you were up-front about your wants. It made it
easier for us to understand you. We wanted to give you what you
wanted." The power of the argument was in telling the jury about
my dream, the truth for me—what I wanted for me.

Getting the big money by asking: Wherever I go, lawyers ask, "How
do you get those big-money verdicts?" I reply that I simply ask for
the money. I tell the jury what I want. It seems that the more we
want something, the more we are hesitant to ask for it. Have you
ever noticed how people who want to be with each other seem
afraid to simply say, "I'd like to be with you tonight," but, instead,
often talk about everything else and go home alone? The fear that
inhibits is the looming, dreadful fear of rejection.

People are afraid to tell others what their services are worth.
They are afraid to ask the doctor what the doctor expects to be
paid. In a civil money case, I tell the jury outright that I want them
to give my client money, and how much. When the jury retires to
reach its verdict, it knows exactly what I want. Such openness also
serves my credibility. How can we feel comfortable with someone
who we know wants something from us but who will never be
honest about it?

Money seems to be difficult to ask for. Although the legal system, reflecting our society, measures most things human in dollars,
it still seems wrong for lawyers to talk about human life, human
worth, human pain and suffering in terms of money. The idea
seems to prostitute justice. How do jurors give money to parents
whose little girl was smashed into a dead, bloody mangle of ripped
flesh and broken bones? I might begin my argument to the jury by
asking if the jury could return the dead child to her parents. That
brings us to the truth. The jury cannot return the child.

"We are here for justice. Well, their child was taken from them.
Can you give her back?" I look at the jurors, each of them. I wait.

"So you cannot give me justice? You cannot return their child?" I let the silence underline my question. "So what sort of justice *can* you give?" Again I wait for the jurors to think about it. "The law says when we are injured by another we are entitled to be made whole again. How can we be made whole? With all the power that a jury has, with all the power of the law, we are nearly powerless to do justice. Isn't that true?

"The court has instructed you that you may award damages. That is the only justice you can give. Damages! That means your power to do justice is limited to awarding money for a little dead girl. That is not much justice, is it? Mere money, mere dollars for a child? What parent could take money as justice? Yet in a case such as this it is all that any jury can give. It is all that you can give."

Then the argument builds on a simple truth. "If you have only the power to give money for justice, if money is all that can stand for justice in this case, if only money stands for these parents' horror, their unspeakable loss, if money stands for their child, then should these parents receive only *part* of what they are entitled to? Should they be further injured, this time by the law, this time by a jury that returns to them only *part* justice?" I still leave large quiet spaces in which the jury can weigh my words. "Justice in this case is that which stands for the *whole* child, for these parents lost a *whole* child, not part of a child. I ask you for *whole* justice, not part justice. Do not give them back part of this little girl. Do not give them this child's small hand with her little chubby fingers. Do not return to them only that which stands for the sound of her darling, tiny voice. Do not give them just her smile or the velvet touch of her cheek when these parents kiss her good night. Do not give them just part of her. Give them back *all* of the child that justice can give.

"This was a million-dollar little girl. Give them all of her. *I want it all, for them!*"

How do I get the large money verdict? I get it because I tell the truth, because my clients are entitled to it, because it is just. *I get it because I ask for it.*

Winning a raise by asking: I will discuss how to argue with the boss in a later chapter. But how do you ask for a raise? I say, simply ask for it.

"Mr. Jones, I've been wanting to talk to you. But I've been afraid to. This morning it finally came to me that you'd *want* to hear me out because you're a fair man."

Both of these statements ring true. You have been afraid. And, indeed, the boss sees himself as a tough but fair employer. The boss now occupies the comfortable trap you created. "I'd like to talk to you about a raise. Could I have a couple of minutes?"

Take your time. Look the boss in the eye. Now describe the work you've done, the loyalty you feel and have demonstrated. Identify the one thing you can do better than anyone else. Go slow with it. Why are you unique? What quality, trait, or talent, what skill do you have that no one else can match? Do people especially like you? Are you easier to talk to than the others? Do you have the ability to see a problem and find its solution before damage sets in? Are you a better organizer? Can you produce more? Speak out of your own authority. Ask for what you *want*. And be exceedingly straight about it. Ask for the money you want, for the money you deserve. You might add, "I know times are hard for you. I know, because times are hard for me." Give him time to absorb what you have just said. The boss knows you have heard his prior argument about tough times. Now you have asked him to hear yours.

The no-risk risk of asking: But what if the boss is not receptive to your argument? He might say, "Well, we've been thinking about thinning out your department, and if you're really not satisfied with the salary we're already paying you, maybe we should put you on the cut list." But you win either way. What's more risky than selling your life, an hour at a time, a day at a time, a year at a time, to a company that converts you to a cut-rate, throwaway product? The greater risk is that you might work for the next year or the next twenty for an employer who is dead to justice and dead to you.

AND SO: Throughout our lives we must all face our juries—our fellow workers, our bosses, our spouses, our children. We all have cases we must win. But fancy words and gilded phrases usually don't prevail. Always the argument is more in the person than in the words, more in *being* credible than in *appearing* credible.

The problem of credibility, of course, arises when what we say is not what we mean, when we speak of caring but do not care, when we feign deep beliefs but our soul is empty. The problem of credibility arises when we fail to tell the truth—when we fail to tell both the factual truth and the *emotional truth*, when we fail to tell the *Other* how we feel.

The form and content of the winning argument may stem from the logical, intellectual, linear progeny of the mind. But the energy, the power, the stuff that excites and moves, that makes us credible and eventually convinces, is born of the soul. Because an argument from the soul is truthful, it bears the ring of truth. When we fail to tell the truth, our communication string will always be out of sync. It is as though a platoon marches down the street, but one of the soldiers is left-footed. The slickest of prevaricators cannot keep the entire platoon in step for long. But when we truthfully reveal our feelings, the *chosen words* are released in sync with the *sound words* and *physical words*. When we tell the truth factually and emotionally, all the elements of communications, physical and verbal, automatically come together.

Successful argument unfolds when we have regained the ability to reveal ourselves, to expose our feelings, and simply ask for what we want. In the end, we must undress our psyches and stand naked before those to whom we make our arguments. Ah, the power of the honest who will but tell us *who they are* and *what they want!*

5

The Power of Listening

HEARING THE PERSON BEHIND THE NOISE

THE LOCK: They argue and I argue back. But I never seem to win.

THE KEY: Listen—just listen, and you'll start to win.

I f I were required to choose the single essential skill from the many that make up the art of argument, it would be the ability to listen. I know lawyers who have never successfully cross-examined a witness, who have never understood where the judge was coming from, who can never ascertain what those around them are plainly saying to them. I know lawyers who can never understand the weaknesses of their opponent's case or the fears of the prosecutor; who, at last, can never understand the issues before them because they have never learned to listen. Listening is the ability to hear what people are saying, or *not saying* as distinguished from the words they enunciate.

Listening for what is not said: "How do you feel about a widow who is asking you for money for the death of her husband?" I once asked a prospective juror in a case in which I represented the widow.

"I don't know," the juror replied. "I don't know" did not mean that the juror didn't know. It meant he didn't feel comfortable telling me. If he felt all right about money for justice, he would have said, "I feel fine about it."

"Do you have some feeling about this kind of a lawsuit?"

"Not really," the juror replied. "Not really" did not mean "not really." It meant probably. The juror did not want to get into a public argument with the likes of me. If he were at home with his wife he would have said something quite different. I followed with this question:

"If you were home and were talking about this case with your wife, is it possible you might say something like this to her: 'I don't think people should sue for their dead husbands. All the money in the world can't bring the man back. I think those kinds of lawsuits are wrong.'?"

"I don't talk about things like this with my wife," he replied. Now he was obviously refusing to answer the question at hand.

"If you and I were best friends and were talking about this case over a beer, what would you tell me?"

"I don't drink beer."

"How about coffee?" I gave him a big friendly smile to assure him I wasn't trying to push him around.

Suddenly the juror blurted it out: "My father was killed and my mother never got a cent." There it was! You could immediately feel all the pain—a boy without a father, a mother struggling to rear her family without a husband.

"It must have been pretty hard on your mother trying to raise a family by herself." (The words *It must have been* are magical words that say to the *Other*, "I understand how it was.")

"You bet." Now the juror and I were on the same side.

"And it must have been hard to grow up without a father."

He looked down at his hands.

"If you could have had the power as a boy to get help for your mother, would you have done so?"

"Sure. I did everything I could for her."

"Is it all right with you if I try to help Mrs. Richardson get justice in this case for herself and her children?"

"Yes," he said. And that was the end of it—the magical product of listening.

Our desperate need to be heard: If we step into the kitchen where a couple is engaged in a typical domestic shouting match, if we listen, we will often discover that all the noise is nothing more than evidence of a dire need to be heard. For if we are never heard, if we are never understood, if we are never loved, we find ourselves alone even when we are with someone. In short, *there is usually a need to be heard behind the racket*, usually pain behind the rage. I see Van Gogh who in his desperation to be heard first cut off his ear and, when still no one heard him, committed suicide. Oh, the crucial ear—the ear to hear us!

When we hear the shouting, the anger, both ours and the *Other's*, *if* we are skilled listeners, we will step back to hear not the tirade but the weeping, not the cloying racket but the loneliness, the disappointment, perhaps the fear that smolders beneath the noise. When we hear all that pugnacious racket it is a time to ask a simple question quietly: What *pain* drives this ugly cacophony?

Surrogate rage: Many times in the courtroom lawyers encounter judges who seem bent on venting their anger on someone, usually us. Often the judge's anger is not the product of our misconduct, but the result of a painful experience outside the courtroom. I have seen judges attack lawyers when someone has caused them pain at home or when something in the trial causes them to revisit a painful part of their past. And the judge will attack, not the wife who may have poked him at breakfast with an emotional prod, not a fellow judge who may have angered him, not the appellate court that may have recently reversed him, but some wide-eyed frightened lawyer who just happens to be handy. The judge, who is himself a victim, now wants to make a victim of someone else.

Have you ever seen two dogs standing nose to nose, hair bristling on their backs, tails wagging in those short, stiff wags? Then someone pokes the larger of the dogs with a stick, and the larger dog attacks, not the person who poked him, but the smaller dog. People are like that. Both dogs and humans search for scapegoats. The parent often takes out his pain on the helpless child, not on the spouse who caused the pain. The foreman takes it out on the hapless worker, not the vice president who has just read him the riot act, who in turn was threatened by the president of the company, who was himself embarrassed by the board of directors, who had seen the company's stock go to hell on the big board. It reminds me of the biblical lepers who believed that if they could pass on their disease to another they would thereby be cleansed. It is important to understand this process of *surrogate rage*, this anger vented not on the person responsible, but on a substitute, usually powerless person.

On the other hand, we ought not argue with those who are chronically abusive, pathological—whether they are in the judiciary or elsewhere. With them we retreat to take such steps as may be necessary to protect ourselves. But always the powerful key is listening, for retaliatory anger closes the ears, turns off the brain, and drains the soul. Its appearance leaves us tensed and ready for combat, but not ready for effective argument. Not ready for winning.

"Ver llegar:" The Spanish matadors had a phrase for dealing with the onslaught of the beast—*"Ver llegar."* Hemingway explained the meaning of the phrase in *Death in the Afternoon*: "the ability to watch the bull come as he charges with no thought except to calmly see what he is doing and make the moves necessary to the maneuver you have in mind. To calmly watch the bull come is the most necessary and primarily difficult thing in bullfighting." So it is when one faces a charging *Other*, a judge, an opponent, a witness, a boss. By sheer concentration one watches the charge calmly with one's ears. If we choose, we can observe the *Other's* aggression come spewing out, and, *at our will*, we can also permit the noise to bounce off the walls like rattling cans.

Listening to the *soul's ear*: Endless knowledge lies like hidden treasure to be gleaned if only the *soul's ear* will listen. Let the *soul's ear* tell us what it hears. Then trust it. I am not speaking here of something mystical. I am merely giving full faith and credit, as it were, to the vast storehouse of knowledge with which we were born and have gathered in a lifetime. As we proceed through life, our reservoir of knowledge fills, gradually, steadily, imperceptibly. Words are chosen, usually unconsciously. And how they come together—the syntax, the tone, the inflection with which the *Other* flavors the words—carries more information about what is being said and who is saying it than the words themselves. When I was a small boy, my mother used to say to me, "You can tell who a person is the minute he opens his mouth."

We have the ability to call upon the mind's reservoir almost instantly, to sort through the billions of items of information stored there, to select that which is relevant to our decision, and to present the decision in the form of a feeling, usually a negative or positive one. People who listen to the disclosures of their *soul's ear* are said to be intuitive. But we all possess a *soul's ear*. And it will report to us if we listen. Listening and believing what the *soul's ear* tells us—that is the trick.

How can we believe such an unverified, unsupported report from within? We are taught to be logical and to demand proof. But the conscious, logical mind can gather only a few facts, wrestle with only a few concepts, and even then we are never sure of our logic, for logic is often a perilous gift. On the other hand the *soul's ear* listens to whole libraries of data from which it constantly constructs its bottom line, *the feeling*.

There is no operator's manual to explain how the *soul's ear* works. But one does not need explanation of how to operare the *soul's ear* any more than one requires an explanation to the secrets of the beating heart. The heart beats. The *soul's ear* hears. We can tune into the heart and hear its beat. We can tune into the *soul's ear* and hear its wisdom as well.

The meaning in music: If we listen we can also hear the music that *carries the words* of those who speak to us. Everyone plays a certain music with their personal musical instrument, the vocal cords. Do they play alive and happy sounds or sad and depressed ones? Do they sound as if their throats are closing on the words to hold them back? Is their voice strong and affirmative or weak and tentative? Do we hear music or the sound of the deadly monotonous machine? Do we hear sounds of anger, of aggression, of sorrow? Do the sounds match the words? Sounds from the voice are like light that is shown through a filter. The light takes on the color of the filter, and the sounds of the person take on the substance and mood of the person who authors them.

Sometimes when I am listening to the final argument of my opponent, I lay my head back, close my eyes, let the words drift by and focus only on the sounds. The sounds always carry the argument better than the words. The sounds betray the urgency, the sense of caring, the anger, the ring of truth, the power that can change the jury. If the sound of the words, no matter how powerful the words may be, does not move me, it will not move the jury. Sounds carry the meaning. It is only when the sounds penetrate and prod and awaken that I take a note for rebuttal.

Delivered orally, the greatest written speeches in the history of the world containing the finest syntax and the most eloquent verbiage can pass through the mind of the listener like empty radio waves unless they are accompanied by the sounds of a committed soul. The Gettysburg Address, a speech we've been taught to revere, derives its stature as writing, almost as poetry. But the speech was said to have gone nearly unnoticed by the audience who actually heard it.

Listening with our eyes: I have already spoken of the emerging science of kinesics commonly called "body language." We can often tell how someone feels about us when the person does something as simple as shaking our hand. Have you felt the person let loose a fraction of a second before the handshake was complete, a dead giveaway that he or she is anxious about the meeting, or repulsed? Have you noticed whether a person chooses to shake your hand or give you a hug? When you are hugged in a social setting, have you noticed the way the person holds you, how some withhold their bodies? Do you notice when you pull back from the hug whether the person looks you in the eyes, and, if so, what the eyes are saying?

Body language is words heard with the eyes. Bodies reflect fear, boredom, interest, repulsion, openness, attraction, caring, hatred. Bodies will speak to us, if we will carefully listen with our eyes. And the easiest way to discover what the body language of another is telling us is for us to mimic the *Other* and then ask ourselves how *we* are *feeling* when we take on the *Other's* body positions.

If, for instance, we see a person listening to another with his index finger pressed firmly against his lips, we can put our own finger in the same position. When we do, we realize that with our finger hard against our mouths we are warning ourselves to remain silent and to listen attentively. When mimicking the *Other* with our index finger extended and touching our lips lightly we realize that the meaning, loosely translated, is, "I wonder if what he is saying is true?" So, too, when a woman crosses her legs tightly, when a person throws his or her arms firmly around the body and holds on to himself, the message usually is apparent. The combinations are endless. So are the exceptions.

One can also listen with the eyes by observing what the *Other's* dress is saying to us. What about the flashy tie? A touch of the maverick, perhaps? I know a woman who wears old sloppy bib overalls and a T-shirt for every occasion, even a formal affair. What does that tell us about her? Once I observed a defendant who took the stand in his own defense. He wore an immaculately tailored suit. He sported a perfectly tanned face. His shoes were expensive, shined and spotless. His shirt was stiff with starch and bore his embroidered initials at the pocket. The cuffs were French, the cuff links gold with his initials engraved in Old English script. When he took the stand he crossed his legs, looked down at his pant leg, fastidiously picked off a small piece of lint, and, with an arrogant flip, cast the lint into the air. Then he looked over at his attorney, his nose slightly elevated, awaiting his attorney's first question. The jurors didn't need to hear the first word from him, and they disposed of him in short order in their deliberation.

We can listen with the eyes by observing the way people walk. Do they slump? Do they walk as if they are carrying the weight of the world on their shoulders? Is there a sprightly bounce, a swagger? See how they pound the floor with their feet as if they are angry at the very earth beneath them. When I am in court I always have an associate keep notes so that I am freed to watch the jurors walk to the jury box. The manner in which jurors carry themselves is a stamp that life has placed on them. I see people who walk as if they are trudging uphill. I see women hop about as if they are sparrows about to take flight. I see young men prance like stallions in the ring. I see people shuffle, slither, slink, creep, glide, tiptoe—the way people move is their autobiography in motion.

AND SO: We cannot argue until we understand what the argument is about. Arguing into the air is analogous to the fighter who throws a hundred punches during each round and never manages to hit his opponent. Daily we see people contending, battling, struggling with words, with everybody about everything. For some, life has become one everlasting, never-ceasing argument. For others, for those who win—well, they listen.

6

The Power of Prejudice

EXAMINING THE GARMENT, BLEACHING THE STAIN

THE LOCK: Prejudice locks the mind. Nothing can enter. Nothing true can escape.

Peeping into a prejudiced mind is like opening the door to a room packed to the ceiling with junk. Nothing whatsoever can get in, and when the door opens, the junk comes tumbling out.

Those whose minds are jammed with prejudice have room for little else. Growth is dead. Learning is gridlocked. They may understand our logic, but logic makes no difference. The word root of prejudice, *praejudicium*, implies *prejudgment*. People are prejudiced both for and against a philosophy, a religion, a belief system. They are prejudiced for or against a political party, the make of an automobile, a race, a person—you name it. If a person hates Jews or Catholics, probably nothing will ever change him. You can drown the prejudiced person in reason, scream, weep, and beg, but your pleas of fairness and justice will go for naught. You had just as well sing to a bag full of jelly beans.

Understanding prejudice: Our prejudices—we all have them—are part of our personality structure. The problem is that our prejudices may lie lurking at the bottom of the subterranean mind where they slowly ooze up and color our thinking without our knowing it. Prejudice can be derived from a cruel or neglectful father, from a sick or jumble-headed mother, from having been locked in a closet. Prejudice can grow out of one's terror, from being forced to do loathsome tasks, from having endured undeserved punishments. It can emerge from having been lost, from getting sick on a certain food, or from having one's young brain washed and rewashed with the lye of hatred. Prejudices, like phobias, are so deeply set that even if we become aware of them we are usually helpless to do much about them. If we are aware of our prejudices we can guard against their danger to ourselves and to others, but our prejudices are there as surely as the birthing scar we call our navel. Arguments do not erase prejudice any more than arguments erase scars, whether psychological or physical.

Religion as prejudice: Are not all religions prejudices? Or are we too prejudiced to acknowledge this? Indeed, should one wish to, what chance would one have in convincing a Baptist that Christ was not the son of God, or a devout Mormon that Brigham Young was a pariah with a penchant for the ladies? If you close this book at this point, it will have something to do with your prejudice.

Try to convince a business tycoon that hoarding more than his share of the common wealth is driven by greed and is evil. Instead, he will point to his freshly audited financial statement as evidence of his success, an accounting that makes mention of his struggling workers only as "cost of labor." The notions that children ought not starve, that the sick should be cared for, that our young should be educated, that every man, woman, and child should have a roof over their heads are seen not as notions of humanity, but as the evil tenets of socialism. That we have more concern for starving puppies in the street than starving children under the bridge can only be attributed to a blinding prejudice.

The law and prejudice: The law understands the implacable nature of prejudice. It acknowledges that prejudiced judges ought not sit on a given case, although most prejudiced judges are too prejudiced to recognize or admit their prejudice and to remove themselves. To get a prejudiced judge off a case is like prying a tooth out of a rabid gorilla. The law also permits a potential juror who has been shown to be prejudiced to be excused from service on the case. But, absurdly and paradoxically, as soon as the prejudice is discovered, the juror himself, the opposing party, and usually the judge all conspire to keep that prejudiced juror on the case. But that is another subject.

The ubiquitous nature of prejudice: The question is not, Are we prejudiced?, but, What are our numerous prejudices? We are prejudiced even against the word *prejudice*, for we are taught that it is socially and "politically incorrect" to be prejudiced. I myself am prejudiced against racists, bigots of all types (except those I agree with), bankers, and to a lesser degree golfers. I am also prejudiced against sour cream on my Mexican food. I don't like bankers because legally they rob people. I call them, as some have in the past, "banksters." I respect Dillinger more than I respect most bankers. Dillinger did not rob poor people. He robbed those who became rich by robbing poor people. Bankers are also very snooty. Snooty as hell, and usually quite ignorant of anything except money, which is per se boring. I am also prejudiced against bankers because of their spite toward the poor, which is a reflection of their own deep, abiding, and ugly prejudice. They will pass a starving man on the street, but give generously to the socially correct symphony (but only if their names appear on the evening's program as major contributors). I am prejudiced against golfers because any given group of golfers is likely to include a lot of bankers, or friends of bankers, and because golfers, on the whole, are as boring as bankers. They offer little by way of enlightenment other than their golf scores. I argue (through my prejudice) that if on any given day God should strike all golfers on all golf courses dead—all at once—the world would likely go right on without missing a beat.

I am prejudiced against sour cream because as a child my grandmother churned sour cream into butter. It smelled bad. She fed the sour milk to the chickens. This in turn created a prejudice against chickens because I wondered how anybody could eat anything that ate something as stinky as sour milk. That prejudice never rooted itself fully. But once in a while my grandmother would demand that I drink all of my milk, even though it was beginning to turn, and that formed my lifelong hatred of sour dairy products.

My son hates nuts—I mean, nuts of every kind and character: peanuts, walnuts, cashews, Brazil nuts—any nuts, which is nuts. As we have observed already, prejudices grow out of early experience, as when one's parents hate blacks, or cops, or preachers, or whatever parents hate—be it the Boston Red Sox or the Republican party. Prejudices also stem from our life experience, as when someone is mugged by a Hispanic and thereafter tends to hate all Hispanics. The problem is that prejudices spread out like a bad stain on the tablecloth. The person who was mugged by a Hispanic may also now hate all who display any pigment in their skin whatsoever. I know a man who suffered horribly as a child from poison ivy. He now hates not only any plant that looks like ivy, he even hates any plant that crawls up buildings, he hates forests where poison ivy abounds, he hates all things living outdoors, he hates the mountains, the prairies—he, in fact, hates the living botanical world.

Worse, people who are prejudiced are often not only ignorant of their prejudices, they are usually quite comfortable with them. To them, prejudices are the truth—their truth. My truth is that bankers are empty-souled robots who are morally and socially disadvantaged, who kick poor people out of their houses when they miss a payment, and who haven't read a decent book since they graduated from Harvard Business School. Probably didn't read one then. And although I am aware of my prejudices, I am perfectly comfortable with them. I like my prejudices. I wouldn't be without them.

THE KEY: Information is the key to protect ourselves from prejudice. But how?

So how do we discover the prejudices of the *Other*—whether the *Other* be a juror, a customer, a city councilperson, or our next-door neighbor? One thing we do know: their prejudices will be obvious *after* they decide against our perfect argument. But it would be nice if we could learn of these prejudices to begin with. *Information*. Ah, information! But how do we get information?

Sometimes we can ask jurors if they are prejudiced against a cause or a client and they will admit that they are. Most often they will admit it to avoid jury duty, or, worse, manufacture a prejudice to avoid jury duty. But most jurors will not admit their prejudice. They think their prejudices are simply well-founded opinions. They know in their hearts that they are prejudiced, but they think it is perfectly swell to be this way. Besides, why should they reveal their prejudices and get thrown off the jury when they want to sit on the case and send our client to the frying pan? Moreover, a courtroom full of people is no place to be confessing one's idiosyncrasies, one's antisocial views, or one's politically incorrect attitudes. What banker is going to tell us that he is prejudiced against blacks or Hispanics or the poor? What personnel director is going to admit that he will not hire people over fifty? What homophobe is going to admit, at least to anyone but another homophobe, his prejudice against homosexuals? So, with a nice smile on his face the juror denies his prejudice, simply denies it—just like that. And so what are we going to do about it?

Identifying personality clusters: I often rely on the "cluster concept." People's personalities, their likes and dislikes, their attitudes, their viewpoints, their prejudices come in *clusters*, as grapes come in bunches. If you examine one grape you will know pretty much what the rest of the grapes on the cluster look like. If you taste one you know how the others will taste. There may be minute differences from grape to grape, but you can bet that the grape you didn't taste does not taste like beefsteak.

For example, take the banker: If you know the *Other* is a banker, you also know he does not live in a ghetto, and likely never did. He does not drive an old junker of a pickup with some fence posts, a roll of bailing wire, and an old cow dog in the back end. He most likely does not belong to the Pentecostal Church, nor does he subscribe to the *Daily Worker*. His friends are not likely members of the Communist party. He probably doesn't smoke pot. He has never slept on the street overnight, not once. He has likely gone to a good prep school, and he probably has a college degree. It is a good bet that his parents had money. He will likely vote the Republican ticket. He does not buy his suits from J. C. Penney and he has never been out of work for any substantial period of time. He has never written a poem. He has never painted a picture. You can point all day to exceptions to the above, for there are always many.

What about the banker's attitudinal clusters? He probably thinks that if you are unemployed, you are lazy. He will tell you, "There are plenty of jobs out there. Why, I can't get anyone to wash my windows. I can't get anyone to fix the furnace. It takes two weeks to get a plumber down here to the bank. Those who don't work simply don't want to." His views on welfare, although widely shared by others, are absolutely predictable. He will tell you a story you have heard a hundred seventy-five times about how women on welfare have babies simply to get a bigger dole—"Why, those welfare women make money having babies. It's their business"—although he has never taken to dinner, not once in his life, a poor, uneducated woman with seven kids who lives in a third-story three-room walkup, a flat that is cold most of the winter, and he has never asked her why she has so many children. Why should he?

The banker's views on the black community are also easily charted. He will tell you he is completely without prejudice against black people, but when you press him, you will discover that black people make up about .00067 percent of his borrowers. His view about the homeless is that they are on the street because they want to be there. His answer for the problem, although he will not likely confess it, is laissez faire. We have to "let nature take its course," which is a euphemism for ridding ourselves of the remnants of society by letting them starve to death.

You can predict his political views without asking him the first question. He is for free trade, he is against any more taxes, no matter how small. He thinks government should be totally out of our lives except that he thinks government should generously underwrite industry and banking. The savings-and-loan crisis is mostly a governmental hoax. Government should protect us against crime on the street, but not against the crimes of bankers against their depositors. The borders of the country should be closed, tight: "We don't need any more Mexes here" (although he will never use a pejorative word except to fellow bankers in the sauna). The death penalty should be extended, not eliminated. In other words, society should kill more of its members, not fewer. Society shouldn't be required to house killers for the rest of their lives. We should hang bank robbers and thieves, especially bank robbers. Those who write bad checks should be tattooed on the forehead so we can identify them more easily. In the prejudicial aspects of his personality, if you have met one banker, you have met them all. Exceptions can always be held up to your nose, but if you examine a cluster of purple grapes, you can usually find one that is off-color. I am talking about the clusters, the fifty-seven purple ones, not the one brownish little grape on the back side.

Another example: What, for example, are the personality clusters of the black railroad worker? His views on some subjects are poles apart from the banker's. Yet on others, you could hardly distinguish them. They both look down on the unemployed. They both resent paying higher taxes. Their viewpoints on welfare are likely identical. But the black railroad worker knows that 70 percent of prison inmates are black, and he suspects that racism is responsible for this disproportionate number. He doesn't like bankers. (He also doesn't like golfers.) He is politically correct with respect to his fellow workers, gets along with them, eats with them in the lunchroom, and considers many to be his friends. I am speaking of *clusters*, now, don't forget. Every person has his or her own cluster, but his or her cluster will most often look pretty much like the clusters of those with similar backgrounds and experiences.

The preacher: Take the preacher as another example—here's one that may surprise you. Many, perhaps most, support the death penalty. Many preachers, although they profess to follow Christian doctrine, suffer from "dislocated love," that is to say, they love God but hate man, although God has played more dirty tricks on them than any single person they can point to. It wouldn't surprise me, considering the wide support the clergy have given to our various wars, to see bumper stickers popping up on the cars of preachers that read KILL FOR CHRIST. In short, preachers are becoming politically more and more aligned with the far right, which paradoxically means they harbor less and less love for the human race. When preachers want money they tell us to give of ourselves, as Christ gave. But when some poor twisted soul whose psyche was mercilessly traumatized as an innocent child commits a crime, the preacher is likely to refer to the law of Moses—"An eye for an eye . . ." Or are we dealing once more with my prejudices?

Others: The clusters for ranchers and blue-collar workers are similar to the clusters of government employees and utility workers. The clusters for writers, actors, musicians, and artists belong in the same group, but be careful. Look at Charlton Heston, who leans so far right one looks to see if his right leg may not be a foot shorter than his left, while Jane Fonda once had a left-leg problem. The clusters for schoolteachers, mountain climbers, nurses, and secretaries are more vague and unpredictable. The second-generation born-rich are dangerous to predict. The best of them often feel guilty for all their undeserved affluence and seek to make amends for this crime of birth, while others, like the Menendez brothers, are as void of moral content as an empty Coors can on the beach. Older housewives will more likely reflect the clusters of their husbands than will younger working wives. And as you read my views of clusters, which are tainted by my own prejudices, you will react as a result of your own. If we see eye to eye, neither of us will seem prejudiced. If we disagree, you are prejudiced—don't you agree?

The danger of ignoring the cluster: It is dangerous, perhaps wrong, to lump people into categories by reason of race, ethnic background, sex, economic status, or profession. But if we are to act in any responsible way to protect ourselves from the ravages of prejudice, the concept of clustering is an available tool. Although it may not be "politically correct," it is significantly better than reading the cards.

Let me tell you a story: Some years ago I was defending a banker in Louisiana in a criminal case in which the banker had been charged with various federal banking frauds. I had been up-front with the banker, who had traveled all the way from Louisiana to Wyoming to convince me I should take his case.

I said, "Listen, I don't like bankers. You look like a nice man and all, but I have never represented bankers and, frankly, I don't know why I should make an exception for you." I tried to say it with a pleasant tone of voice.

"Mr. Spence," he said. "I am a good son of a bitch." That got my attention. He looked at me with extremely sad and serious eyes.

"Well, when I put a lot of my life into a case, I want to get something in return for it. I like to believe that the person I defend will make a contribution to society. Otherwise I have wasted my life. And I don't want to waste my life."

But the banker explained to me that the reason he was in trouble was because he had actually done too many good deeds. He had made loans to the poor that had turned sour, loans he ought not to have made because they did not meet certain rigid government requirements. He had come from a poor family himself. He had worked his way up from nothing. He despised the standard business of banking that operated on the premise that if you don't need the money the bank will loan you all you want, but if you do need the money you can't get it, even if you mortgage your wife and kids. He had tried to help small businesses get started. He had been loyal to his friends, who were not bankers. He had made many contributions to the local black community, including large donations to a black university. As a consequence of his viewpoints and his aggressive stance, he found himself at odds with the regulators and eventually, as he vigorously defended himself, at odds with the United States attorney who had vowed to get him.

He did not fit my banker cluster. Even so, I didn't want to represent him. I discussed the case with Imaging.

"I don't know why you don't represent that poor man," she said. "Bankers are human beings."

"Right," I said. "But so is every other social deviant."

"Bankers are entitled to the presumption of innocence," she said.

"So is every other accused."

"Bankers are entitled to a defense."

"So is every other person who is charged with a crime."

"You are prejudiced," she said. "This would be a good chance for you to work through your prejudice."

She was right, as she usually is. The more I got to know the man, the more I admired and liked him. Something shines in nearly every human being, even bankers. Finally I agreed to take the man's case.

When we got to court I was confronted with an issue I had never faced before: How would Louisiana blacks feel about a white Louisiana banker? As the jury selection process went on, and without being conscious of it, I began to select jurors I felt comfortable with. Although I was born in Wyoming and had little experience with blacks as a child, I feel comfortable with blacks. I maintain a healthy distrust of the dominant white society. I feel the injustices of that society as it imposes itself on the disenfranchised and the helpless. I grew up poor. At school I was rejected by the social elite, the fraternities. I was a pariah who was often willing to incur banishment as the price for independence. Yet I often felt lonely and unwanted. By the 1960s I found myself empathizing naturally with blacks.

As jury selection continued in the banker's case, I decided, if possible, to seat an all-black jury. I thought I understood blacks. If I liked them, they would like me, and if they liked me, they would hear my arguments. And if they heard my arguments they would free my client. That was how my logic went. The banker agreed. He liked blacks as well and was perfectly willing to entrust them with his fate. Moreover, a black jury would surely understand that the banker had chosen them, that he trusted them, and therefore they would more likely trust him. Trust begets trust. I preach that all the time.

The prosecutor, for his own reasons, thought black people would favor the government, so when the jury was finally selected we went to trial with ten blacks and two whites. I had even tried to get the whites off the jury—a white farmer and a white housewife—but I had run out of challenges and, much to my disappointment, they were seated.

The case lasted several months. And, as in every trial, a leader on the jury began to emerge, in this case a young black man who sat on the far left in the front row. Among my colleagues I referred to him as "the Dude," because he kept a very large ego on display and he had that certain bouncy swagger that told the whole world that he was in charge. And the Dude liked me. When I would make a point he would give me a big grin, sometimes a wink, sometimes a vigorous nod.

As the trial wore on, I came to the conclusion that the Dude would not only be the foreman, he would likely lead the jury to an acquittal of my client. Moreover, we had placed before the jury the fact that my banker client had supported many black causes and was obviously a friend of black people. My cross-examination, so they said, had been stunning. By the end of the trial I had reduced the government's case to reveal little more than a bunch of government bureaucrats trying to show my client who was boss by prosecuting him. They wanted to get even with him for his intransigent refusal to buckle under.

I gave a marvelous final argument, one that exemplified all of the ideals and notions, techniques and skills that I write about in this book, and I hung the jury. The judge declared a mistrial and the jury went home. As I was walking out the front door of the courthouse, I saw the Dude drive by, and he saw me. He gave me a big wave, a big smile, and tossed me a vigorous *V* for victory signal with his fingers.

Later the judge himself polled the jury, and, to my bewilderment, I discovered that the ten blacks had all voted against me while the two white jurors I had tried to get off the jury had voted with me. I had ignored the cluster phenomenon. It was true: I liked the black jurors and the black jurors liked me. But their deep and abiding prejudice against bankers, especially white bankers, especially those who tried to patronize them by giving large sums of money to black institutions (which none of them could afford to attend) was the controlling dynamic in their decision. Their prejudice, similar to my own, was fully predictable. I simply paid no attention to it, arguing, as I did to myself, that the blacks would be more prejudiced against the authority of the United States attorney and the United States government than against this banker. I should have known better. I did know better. I was prejudiced for the black people on the jury, and my own prejudice nearly did me in.

The white jurors voted predictably in accordance with their cluster. The farmer had had it up to the tip of his gullet with government regulation. He liked me and he liked my client, who was more generous in his loan philosophy than most bankers with whom the farmer had to do business. The housewife, otherwise alone, followed the white farmer. It was that simple. Any reasonably thoughtful lay person who had never read this book could have predicted the outcome.

In fine, the clustering concept is *prejudgment,* a prejudice itself concerning people who share similar backgrounds, ethnic origins, needs, experiences, values, goals, and occupations. It is the process by which one applies one's own prejudices to predict the prejudices of the *Other.* The process is rife with pitfalls and exceptions. It can never claim more efficacy than to put one on notice—and one must be on notice—that if one finds one grape one is most likely to find others like it. One of the great joys of learning about people is to find the grape that surprises.

Learning about people: I am often asked by young people what courses they should take in school to prepare themselves to become trial lawyers. The question is better put, what do we need to learn to become human beings? Whether we want to be successful trial lawyers or successful in any other calling we must become proficient in understanding our brothers and sisters who occupy this earth. But how? How do we become experts in simply knowing people? Unfortunately one does not learn how to become a person in school.

Those from moneyed parents often are sentenced to private schools where they are dunked in old ink, soaked in Latin and Greek, and suffer the education of the elite. I know the arguments for a classical education. However, the point I labor toward is this: our perception of the people we deal with every day depends upon who we are *ourselves.* When our cluster of experiences matches those of the *Other,* we are more likely to understand and predict the *Other* than if we had not been so enriched. The working man understands another working man better than the scholar understands the working man. Nothing is sadder, yet more amusing, than to watch a lawyer who has been given a stiff Ivy League education arguing to a jury of ordinary people. His choice of words, the syntax he constructs, the metaphors he chooses, his ideas of what is persuasive to a judge and jury all reflect the pool of experience from which he operates. Often he comes off as snobbish or patronizing. It is hard for the jury to empathize with him or to trust him because its members are not familiar with his clusters.

I tell young people that if they want to be fine trial lawyers, indeed, if they want to be successful in any calling, they should learn as much as possible about every aspect of the human condition, hopefully by experience. I argue that young people, as a part of their education, as a part of preparing for a lifetime of play, should work a lot. They should learn what it is to pinch a penny, to worry about coming up with the rent, to come home at night tired, to do without, to experience the joy of completing small tasks. I want my children to know a wide variety of things: how to clean a latrine, how to frame a house, how to carry hod, to lay a brick. They should know how to attend the sick, to irrigate a pasture, to climb a mountain, to write a poem, to sing the songs of people, to lie by a stream and dream, to know the joy of love and the pain of loss. I consider the young who have never had to work, worry, or struggle to be seriously underprivileged in much the same way that young people who grow up in the ghettos are underprivileged.

Affluent parents most often make the mistake of sending their children off to some safe place where they are isolated from the rest of the world, after which these children are expected magically to become fully operative individuals in the adult real world. One does not prepare for a fight in the boxing ring by becoming an expert in the highly formalized techniques of ballet (although, I admit, any boxer could improve himself by learning to be a better dancer).

THE LOCK: So having discovered prejudice, how do I deal with it?

Having discovered how prejudice lurks, we must remember what we have already learned—that arguing directly into prejudice is like hollering at the kitchen sink. I have seen many lawyers argue their cases to prejudiced judges or prejudiced jurors, and when they lose, they ask agonizing questions: "Where did I fail? Where was I deficient? I thought I made a perfect argument." Their failure, of course, was not in their argument. Their failure was in not uncovering the prejudice and learning how to deal with it.

THE KEY: The key here won't unlock many doors once they have been jammed with prejudice.

Self-interest, the impenetrable wall: When the *Other* realizes that his self-interest is at stake, no winning argument is possible. This is so because the core prejudice of any living creature, man or forest fern, is for its continued existence. *No matter how skillfully we may argue, we cannot win when the* Other *is asked to decide against his self-interest.*

A winning argument that loses: Take, for example, an argument one might be called upon to make to a lumberjack to save the old-growth forest when the lumberjack's livelihood depends upon the availability of trees to cut. Understandably, lumberjacks are prejudiced against the spotted owl, that innocent little bird whose plight is to have become the hated symbol of the environmentalist. To illustrate the insurmountable difficulty we encounter in making an argument directly into prejudice that is rooted in survival, let us, hypothetically, empower our lumberjack with the absolute power to say "yes" or "no" to the cutting of the old-growth forest in question.

The best argument one can make to the lumberjack begins by acknowledging his prejudice. He has a need to survive:

To the lumberjack: "We both understand, of course, that your livelihood depends upon cutting this old-growth forest."

"Right. That's how I make a living. What do you want to do, deprive my kids of supper in favor of some damn hoot owl?"

"You have a point. But you've agreed to listen to my argument against cutting the forest and to try to make an impartial decision about it—that's our agreement, isn't it?"

"Right. I'll give you a fair hearing. Then I'll shoot the little spotted bastard."

One then confronts the lumberjack by inquiring how he intends to put his personal interest aside:

"How you are going to put your personal interest aside so that you can be totally impartial and fair?"

"What do you mean?"

"Well, how are you going to make sure that your decision isn't based on your own self-interest? After all, feeding your family comes first, doesn't it?"

"You bet."

"It even comes ahead of being fair, don't you agree?"

"Maybe."

"Well, how are you going to be fair under these circumstances?"

"I don't know. I can try. That's all I can do."

"Under these circumstances it's really not fair for me to ask you to even try to be impartial. If our positions were reversed I don't know how I could be impartial either. Maybe no one could be when their livelihood and their family's welfare is at stake."

He doesn't answer.

"Could I give you a suggestion on how you might try to be impartial?"

"Yeah, sure."

"Try to pretend you are the 'ultimate authority in the universe.' You have absolute power over all living things on the earth. Pretend that your desire, as the one with absolute authority, is to render pure, perfect justice. Do you think you could imagine this—just for the moment?"

"Well, I don't know. Do you want me to play like I'm God?"

"That's the power you have here, isn't it? But this old forest is a universe itself that took billions of years to evolve and, to millions of plants, animals, trees, and other living things, your decision will be the decision of God to them. Do you think, as God of this forest, you could render a fair decision?"

"You're putting a lot of pressure on me."

"Yes, but as God of the forest you have a lot of responsibility. It isn't easy to be God."

At this point in the argument the lumberjack has been fully *empowered*. He understands that he alone makes the decision. Moreover, he has been forced to see that his interest is in conflict with the interest of the many living entities that make up the forest universe. He has agreed to try to set aside his personal interest, and although he acknowledges that this will be hard, he probably understands something else: if he holds in favor of himself and his family, his decision will be seen not as an impartial decision but as one tainted with self-interest. He's on the spot in deciding the fate of the spotted owl.

Now I might shift my argument to storytelling. "Let me tell you a true story: By 1800, somewhere in the neighborhood of ten to fifteen million Africans had been transported to the Americas as slaves, which represented only a third of the men and women who had been seized in Africa by the slave traders. Two out of three blacks who were seized died. Blacks were packed into the holds of the slave ships like fish. One observer reported that a slave-deck was 'so covered with blood and mucus that it resembled a slaughter house.'

"In 1637 the first American slave ship, the *Desire,* sailed from Marblehead. Its holds were partitioned into racks two feet by six feet and they were equipped with leg irons and bars. Authorities estimate that Africa lost roughly fifty million human beings to death and slavery in the centuries that followed the discovery of America."

"Well, what's that got to do with the friggin' spotted owl? The spotted owl isn't a human being."

"Right. But the spotted owl, like African slaves, is a living creature *without rights.*"

"But the spotted owl is a damn bird. The slaves were human beings."

"I admit that. But do you leave room for the proposition that the slaves were *seen* as things, mere wild creatures that once captured became property, and as such they could be bought and sold or killed at the will of the owners?"

No answer.

"And trees are also wild things, which, when they are cut and taken possession of, *become* mere property, isn't that true?"

"Trees are trees."

"So, whether a slave is property or a tree is property is purely a matter of what we humans *designate* as property, isn't that true?"

No answer.

"I mean, whether human beings are treated as property *without* rights or as citizens *with* rights is purely a matter of who wields power. Isn't the same also true with the forest? Property and power are inextricably interconnected, wouldn't you agree?"

"What do you mean?"

"I mean, since we no longer have power over the black man we can no longer convert him into property. And if you had no power over the forest you could not transform the forest into property either. In the end, whether the forest is or is not property is simply a matter of power."

"So?"

"So today we view old-growth trees as our property, not because they *are* property but simply because we have the *power* to declare them property."

"So?"

"So you have the power. Will you declare the old-growth forest as property, or would you be open to seeing the forest in some other way?"

"Maybe so, maybe no."

"Could we agree on one thing—that mere ownership in itself does not dictate what is right and what is not. I mean, merely because the slave owners had the power to own slaves did not make such ownership right."

"We're a long ways from the spotted owl."

"The power of ownership does not establish what is morally right or morally wrong. What is right and what is wrong exists independent of ownership, isn't that true?"

"I suppose so. But I don't like where you're going."

"So merely because one may own a forest does not provide an excuse or a reason for destroying the forest, wouldn't you agree?"

No answer.

"I mean, if you decided to cut down the forest, you couldn't say it was right simply because you owned it or had the power to decide its fate, isn't that true?"

"You're getting a little far out there."

"With ownership goes responsibility, wouldn't you say?"

No answer.

"If you own a horse, you can't let it starve to death and excuse your conduct on the basis that since you own it, you can do with it as you damn please, right?"

"Right."

"Let me give you another example. Suppose I own a great painting, say, an incomparable Van Gogh. Do I have the duty to preserve it or could I destroy it if I wanted to?"

"Well, it's your painting, but it's no horse."

"But wouldn't you agree that the whole world has an interest in the preservation of that great painting, and that the rights of all the people in the world to the preservation of the painting is greater than the right of a single individual, under the rules of ownership, to do with the painting as he pleases?"

"I'm not sure about that."

"Well, let's think about it further. Where does the right of ownership come from? Is it a divine right? Does it come from God?"

"I don't know. I doubt it."

"It is merely a rule of man, is it not?"

"I suppose."

"And being a mere rule of man, is it not possible that the rule can also be changed by man for his greater benefit?"

"Sounds right."

"Do we not also believe that rules should be made to benefit the greatest number of people?"

"That's what a democracy is about."

"Applying these ideas to the forest in question, if saving the forest would benefit all of mankind by preserving that unique universe of flowers, trees, birds, and beasts, do you not agree that we might change the rule of ownership so that one man, or a few men, cannot destroy a whole universe for their private gain?"

"What about my job?"

Here it comes!—the impossible wall that stops all reason and justice—the wall of self-interest. No matter how we batter at the wall, no matter how we attempt to climb over it, it remains impenetrable and insurmountable. The survival instinct is stamped in the genes. It overrides every thinking brain cell of the species.

"You agreed not to consider your self-interest, remember?"

"Well, I have rights, too."

"Of course. But as an impartial judge, you would have to set your rights aside and decide this case on reason and justice, isn't that true?"

"I think I have more rights than a friggin' spotted owl."

"Who gave you those rights?"

"They are my rights as an American citizen. As a human being."

"You were born with them?"

"Yes."

"What rights are the creatures of the forest born with?"

"They have no rights."

"Why not?"

"Because trees and bugs don't have rights."

"Who said so?"

"*I say so!*"

"Are you making your decision as the impartial 'ultimate authority in the universe' or are you making your decision as the lumberjack with a family to feed?"

"In this case, I guess they're the same."

The above argument, when presented to a schoolteacher in Sioux Falls, or to an artist in New York (where neither have close family or friends affected), might succeed. It is possible that both might find my argument against destroying the old-growth forest both logical and just. But even with them the result would likely be the same. I suspect that most people believe that humans have more rights than spotted owls. That is the prejudice of our species.

Shifting the argument to win: The thrust of our argument can, however, be shifted slightly, so that a winning argument can be made. The shift will be made so that the *Other's* self-interest is addressed. It could now go like this:

"Being a lumberjack is dangerous work, is it not?"

"You got that right."

"Men are killed or injured in the forest every year, and their families have to get by with a pittance, isn't that true?"

"Right."

"And the work is hard. I mean, a man is pretty well done in at the end of a day, isn't that right?"

"Right."

"And the work isn't always steady. Sometimes there's work and sometimes not."

"That's right."

"Do you like the work?"

"It's all I know. I like being in the woods."

"Would you support a plan that would permit us to save the old-growth forest if we could also provide you with safe, steady work that you would like and that pays as well?"

"I'd sure give it consideration."

"Would you become a member of a planning committee to try to work out such a solution?"

"Certainly. Actually I don't like cutting those big old trees. I hate hearing them fall. Sounds like they're crying all the way down."

Placing the lumberjack on the committee is the necessary act of empowering the lumberjack, remembering, as we must, that we cannot win an argument when the *Other* has no power to accept or reject the argument. But suppose he and others like him can be hired by a pharmaceutical company to gather samples of plant growth in the forest to study possible new cures for human disease. Suppose he can obtain work as a guide, or he can get better pay in a plant that produces building material from other sources. Under these circumstances we will likely hear the lumberjack, who truly loves the forest, now adopt the arguments I have made to save the forest and its symbol, the spotted owl. "Why, that's a pretty little bird," we would likely hear the lumberjack argue. "There's just a few of them left. And there's a lot of us. Human beings can make their houses out of something other than those old trees. The spotted owl can't."

I read the above arguments to a friend of mine. When I had finished he said, "Well, I'll tell you what I think. I think that a single spotted owl is more important to the earth than a single human being, because the spotted owl is near extinction while the human race is so pervasive it is starving to death all over the world."

"That's a good point," I said. "But *which* human being's life would you trade to save the spotted owl?"

"I don't know," he said. "But we have plenty of people hanging around, crowding up the earth, destroying it."

"But the question is, *which* human being would you trade to save a spotted owl? Would you trade a starving child in New Delhi?"

"Probably be better off," he replied.

"Which child in New Delhi?"

He didn't answer.

"How about your child?"

"Come on," he said, "let's go take a good run."

When we are faced with a prejudice, logic and justice are impotent. Still we may have an obligation to argue directly into the face of the prejudice, even though there is no chance to win. If someone argues that all Irish are sloppy drunks or that Hispanics are inherently lazy, or that women, because of their emotional nature, are less qualified than men to hold responsible positions, we incur, as an obligation to ourselves, the duty to argue against the prejudice with all our skill and our power—whether we can win or not. But the *Other's* prejudice—a stain on the cloth of the *Other's* character—will likely take more than an argument to remove. The stain of prejudice is often indelible.

A personal case: Some years ago a very close friend of mine, his wonderful wife, and his eighteen-year-old son, an outstanding athlete, were blown up in their home while they were sleeping. The man responsible for the explosion was a longtime criminal—a dope peddler, who hired a local thug to do the job. Later, after I was appointed special prosecutor in the case, the killer ordered our principal witness murdered just before that witness was to testify before a grand jury we had convened to investigate the first murders.

I have always been adamantly opposed to the death penalty. It has been my heartfelt belief that we cannot stop the killing in our streets until our government stops slaughtering people at home and around the world. Killing is killing, and it is no more defensible when committed by a government, a conglomerate of individuals— of us—than when the killing is committed by a murderer.

But when it came time to argue my case against the killer who was responsible for the four senseless deaths of people I knew, I found myself following the law and, as a special prosecutor, arguing for the death penalty. The killer was convicted, and after more than twelve years of appeals, he was executed. I can vividly recall the pain of those years, when my moral conviction clashed head-on with the law.

It is easy to remain high and aloof, to remain uninvolved, unconnected, to pass judgments, and to stand up and preach and holler self-righteously in the abstract. It is easy to argue one's strong moral convictions, as I have just done, for the preservation of the old-growth forest so long as it is not my job that is lost or my family that suffers. It is easy to argue that the life of the spotted owl is more valuable than the life of a human being so long as it is not my life, or the life of my child, that might be given in exchange. And it is easy to argue against the death penalty until it's my wife who has been murdered, or my child, or my friend. Only saints can evade self-interest, and even they evade it to preserve themselves—their great and compelling personal need to bring about justice in the world.

Recognizing and dealing with social prejudices: As a member of any social system, we encounter its prejudices, be they noble, principled, evil, or corrupt. We are prejudiced for a profit system and against a regulated economy. We are adamant for democracy and recoil from totalitarian ideals. We think good Muslims are suspect and good Christians upstanding. We accept our prejudices as the norm of the society. Our social attitudes are mostly known, predictable, and controlling.

The forces that dictate that which is politically correct and that which is not can be both beneficial and destructive to a society that struggles for justice. The "politically correct" thinking of Nazi Germany led to the most abhorrent abominations in the history of mankind. Yet, were it not for social coercion brought on by politically correct thinking, we could make little advancement against the invidious blight of racism and the scummy injustice of sexism. But for the power of political correctness, we would still be slogging along in the muck and mire of former, infamous times. The point I make is that social attitudes, like individual prejudices, can be both good and bad.

The Marcos case, and conventional wisdom: I have already mentioned my defense of Imelda Marcos in the federal court in New York City. The case became a classic example of the operation of prejudices that become the conventional wisdom of an entire culture. Following the overthrow of Ferdinand Marcos by the Aquino regime, both Marcos and his wife faced scores of indictments that included nearly every conceivable charge known to the FBI in the field of racketeering and fraud. By the time the case got to court, it had become conventional wisdom that Mrs. Marcos, the former friend and benefactor of several of our past presidents and their wives, had suddenly become an avaricious criminal bitch who ought to be strung up by her toes in Times Square.

Conventional wisdom demanded that Mrs. Marcos would and should be convicted, that she should be sent to some ugly place where she could wear none of her three thousand pairs of shoes on her evil feet. Rudolph Giuliani, mayor of New York, then the United States attorney, was aware of the universal prejudice against her. He guaranteed the government a conviction, and his guarantee was in writing. Yet few who condemned her had ever met her.

I took the case, for despite conventional wisdom, I believed the government of the United States had no right to stick one of its many noses into the internal affairs of the Philippines by prosecuting the wife of its deceased president. In the end, her most serious crime turned out to be her undying loyalty to her husband, both before and after his death.

The trial went on for three months before a jury. Not burdened with conventional wisdom, the members of a carefully selected jury returned a verdict of acquittal on all charges. The government's case was so weak I wasn't required to call a single witness in Mrs. Marcos's defense. I didn't even call her to the stand. The government had focused its case on what the government believed the jurors' prejudices must surely be—her alleged wild spending sprees, her alleged association with the money schemes attributed to her husband—matters calculated to outrage poor New York jurors, many of whom had a hard time paying the phone bill.

During the trial the press, believing its own stories and having fully adopted as true the conventional wisdom it had created—that Mrs. Marcos was an extremely evil woman—continued to belittle and berate her. Every morning I picked up the several New York newspapers to read their stories about my trial. I was bewildered. Reading the news accounts, I thought the reporters must be watching a different trial from the one I attended. One would have thought that the prosecution had won with every witness and had won every skirmish, while in the courtroom witness after witness left the stand without having connected my client to a single act of wrongdoing. As a matter of fact, witness after government witness vouched for the kindness and decency of Mrs. Marcos. As the case progressed, even the trial judge began to wonder aloud what the case was doing in his court.

During the trial, one newspaper sent its reporter around every morning, not to interview Mrs. Marcos, not to gather any newsworthy news, but simply to take a picture of the shoes Mrs. Marcos was wearing. They were all black, very proper pumps, and there is no doubt that she often wore the same pair day after day. Yet this paper intentionally played into the nation's prejudice against this allegedly villainous, depraved woman who owned three thousand pairs of shoes. I stopped the reporter once to tell him that my client owned so many shoes because there are many shoe factories in the Philippines, and, as the first lady, Mrs. Marcos received hundreds of shoes each year from companies who wanted to claim that their first lady wore their shoes. Mrs. Marcos confided in me that most of the shoes didn't fit, but she stored them away in her closet anyway. But this fact, the truth of which collided with conventional wisdom, was never reported.

One particularly cynical member of the media was so captured by his own prejudice that when Mrs. Marcos collapsed in the courtroom, her head falling to the table and blood gushing from her mouth—the result of a ruptured vessel in her stomach—he rushed up to ask me where I got the phony blood capsule for my client to bite at that precise moment. She was rushed to the hospital, where she remained under medical care for several days before she was able to continue in the trial. Today, whenever I am faced with the conventional wisdom that Mrs. Marcos is a bad person, the conversation goes like this, after the usual opening volley:

The person who knows she is evil: "I used to admire you a lot, Mr. Spence, before you took on that Marcos case. What got into you anyway? Was it the money? Just tell me it was the money. I could forgive you if it was just the money."

"I take it you don't like my client."

"You got that right."

"You must have spent a lot of time with her and got to know her really well."

"Never met the woman in my life."

"That's very strange. I know you to be a fair person. You must know a very reliable source then who knew her personally."

"Can't say as I did."

"Could it be that you have read something about her that you didn't admire?"

"Damn right. I read the paper every day."

"That's it, then! You've discovered a basic principle upon which you have relied: If you read it in the paper, it's the gospel."

"I don't buy that."

"I may be the only person in the entire world you have met who knows Mrs. Marcos personally, and who has spent many a day with her under the most difficult and trying circumstances. Sometime, if you're interested, I'd be happy to tell you what I know about her." But such arguments are mostly for my satisfaction. I've never yet had a person confess that after my argument he set aside his understanding of conventional wisdom.

How (sometimes) to argue into social prejudice: How do you argue into the storm of social prejudice? You usually do not steer into it head-on. You tack into it like a sailboat heading into the storm. If, for example, I were called upon to argue against the conventional wisdom that criminal defense lawyers manipulate things so that their guilty clients escape through loopholes in the law, I might argue in this fashion (the conversation always begins with this question, which is truly an assault in disguise):

"Tell me, Mr. Spence, did you ever represent someone whom you knew to be guilty of the crime charged?" (The question sets up a no-win answer.)

"Interesting that you should ask such a question. If I answer 'yes,' I am immediately adjudged a scoundrel. If I answer 'no,' you would adjudge me a liar. How do you wish me to answer the question, as a scoundrel or as a liar?"

"That was a very clever answer. You deserve your reputation."

"Well, let me ask *you* a question. When you see your doctor, does your doctor ask you whether the illness you complain of is the possible result of your having committed a crime?"

"Of course not."

"Wouldn't your doctor treat you whether you had ever been guilty of a crime or not?"

"Of course."

"I take it he wouldn't judge you before he agreed to try to help you?"

"You're getting cute on me."

"You must certainly agree with me that you have a right to be treated without first being morally judged by the doctor."

"Obviously."

"My client has legal rights as well. Until he is proven guilty beyond a reasonable doubt before a jury of his peers, he is *presumed innocent.* Most of us forget that—it has something to do with some stodgy old instrument called the Constitution."

"Now you *are* getting cute."

"Yes. But I am simply trying to establish that my client, like you with your doctor, has the right to be assisted by his lawyer—without first being judged."

"So you have represented people who you knew were guilty, right?"

"If you were charged with a crime and came to me, would you expect me to set up a confessional booth in the rear of my office to hear your confession before I took your case?"

"You are still being cute."

"But you see, the proper question to ask is, What rights does every accused have, guilty or not, that every honest lawyer should defend? If you will ask me that question I will answer it."

"All right. Consider the question as asked."

"Every lawyer understands that before a citizen in this country can be convicted, the state must prove its case against him according to the rules, the most important of which are guaranteed protections under the Constitution. These rules preserve our rights as American citizens and protect us from the tyranny of the state. Every honest lawyer has the duty to see that every person accused of a crime, guilty or not, is not convicted unless the state fairly and lawfully follows those rules. This very noble ideal is what distinguishes our country from nearly every other country in the world."

"Quite a speech."

"Think about it."

"How about the loopholes you lawyers always find?"

"What is a 'loophole' for 'those criminals' will become *your* sacred constitutional rights if, God forbid, you or a member of your family is ever charged with a crime."

"Oh, well, then who do you think is going to win the Super Bowl?"

The prejudice set in stone: Finally, there are those occasions when one is confronted by sincere people who suffer from prejudices that are set in stone. With them, no argument can be made, none at all. Winning may be simply listening politely. For example, try to convince one who construes the Bible literally that we are the product of eons of evolution, not the creation of the Lord on the seventh day. The great lawyer Clarence Darrow attempted to argue against such prejudices set in stone in the Scopes trial of 1932—the "monkey trial." He failed. I would rather have a mind opened by wonder than one closed by belief.

Winning, as I have previously defined it, is getting what we want. What we *want* in the long run is to preserve our supply of productive life for use in fruitful endeavors. We do not want to be wasted. I reserved for myself the right to determine what wars I will fight, what battles, what arguments I will make and to whom. If I were a general, I would never launch my army into a battle in which the enemy was so entrenched it would be suicide for my troops. We should care for ourselves as much as that general cares for his soldiers. Winning, therefore, is not always winning. Winning is sometimes appreciating the wisdom of a tactical withdrawl, especially in the face of immutable prejudice—in the face of this impenetrable vault that locks the mind.

AND SO: There are always arguments that may be made in the face of insurmountable prejudice. But usually they are made because we must make them. Sometimes, when the self-interest of the *Other* is properly addressed, the argument will win. Sometimes, rarely, the argument will serve to sensitize the *Other* to his or her prejudice. Sometimes the argument will be heard by people other than the one to whom it is addressed, and it will do great good.

Sometimes we grow strong by making arguments we cannot win, but, at the end of the day, arguments rarely change prejudice. Christ was said to have changed the world with His arguments, but His were addressed to man's greater self-interest of eternal salvation and were, at last, supported by the ultimate fear of eternal damnation if rejected. With such power working behind our arguments, we too could change the course of history.

And so, beware of prejudice. Understand that every argument cannot be won with every person. Were it otherwise, the title of this book notwithstanding, the world would have been conquered long ago by logic and justice, and those of us who strive for their triumph would be out of work, would we not?

7

The Power of Words

GILDING THE SOLILOQUY

The best arguments shimmer with wit, the best arguments dazzle with metaphor. When we describe the bore at the podium, we could turn to a handy bromide and remark, "That guy is as exciting as watching wallpaper peel off the walls." But by long overuse this cliché has become boring itself. Worse, when we use such we become slowly peeling wallpaper ourselves. A better description of a boring person might have been what Dorothy Parker remarked on hearing that Calvin Coolidge died—"How could they tell?"—or to quietly complain, as did Denis Healey, former chancellor of the exchequer, in 1986 in response to the droning of a pompous dullard, "I feel like I've been savaged by a dead sheep."

The creative gifts of others are always there for the plucking; as Montaigne said, quotations are "other men's flowers." Indeed, is it not true, as Emerson observed, that "every man is a quotation from all his ancestors"? But might I not have said something better myself, like, "the quotes and quips of others provide raisins for our oatmeal"?

For me, if one must quote others, the best sources for quotes are the everyday people around us. We will always encounter something more amusing, more visual, more witheringly lucid out of the mouth of an oil-field worker who recklessly maims the language than from the deadly austere pedagogy of an English professor who speaks the language with brutal perfection. I agree with Nietzsche, who exclaimed, "I have left the house of the scholars and I have slammed the door behind me. Too long I sat hungry at their table."

I remember sitting in a saloon some years ago after a long day in court. I began listening to the working men, who sat on the stools next to me, describe the mental acuity of the local sheriff.

"That sheriff is so dumb he could fuck up a two-car funeral," a cowboy wearing a baseball cap said. You could tell he was a cowboy because of his bent-over boots, and his drawl was one that had tumbled in from Oklahoma and had got caught on some Wyoming fence.

"He's so dumb he couldn't find his ass with a six-cell flashlight and a mirror," the oil-field hand said. He wore a steel helmet and you could smell the wellhead grease from where I sat.

"He's so dumb he couldn't pour piss out of a boot if the directions was wrote on the heel," the other cowboy said. This was a real cowboy. You could tell by the ring from the Skoal can that faded a circle on his blue denim shirt pocket. Only drugstore cowboys carry their Skoal in their hip pocket. A real cowboy sits in a saddle all day, and no cowboy I know is going to sit on his Skoal can.

One could, if one chose, quote no less than Oliver Wendell Holmes for the characteristics of a dolt. "The last one to find himself out" is how the great judge put it. But still I prefer the trenchant sarcasm of the working men. I will never see that sheriff again without a vivid image of his trying to read directions from his boot heel (and already I have forgotten Holmes's dictum). And I remember one guy's quip about the mental agility of a candidate for the U.S. House of Representatives: "Why, it takes that guy two hours to listen to *Sixty Minutes*."

I listen to the arguments and language of working men. They speak indelicately, but straight from the heart with a simple wisdom that intellectual patricians often seem to have missed. When I want to discover how to argue a point, I often discuss the issue with a man who has calluses on his hands or who lives inside of aching bones. Take the infamous Imelda Marcos case again: I broached the subject of her defense with the New York cabby who was hauling me to court.

"What do you think of the Imelda Marcos case?" I asked.

Without so much as glancing back at me in his mirror he said, "I don't get why they're so upset about her shoes," he said in a deep Brooklyn accent. "My wife's got a hundred pairs of shoes and I'm only a cab driver. Who gives a shit?" With a slightly altered choice of words, I successfully argued the cabby's point to the jury.

More than ever we are a visual people. Television, with its preponderance of sound bites, has become the means by which many, perhaps, sadly, most, obtain the bulk of their information. Some educators claim we have evolved to the place where if we can't see it, we can't learn it. Thus, today clear visual images become the stuff of successful argument. I once wrote of having witnessed the first bulldozers lumber into a pristine old-growth forest. We stood in silent horror as if we were watching a giant crocodile devour a lamb. Here is how I described it—out of the feeling of the forest:

"By then the noise of the bulldozers had grown louder, and the ground began to tremble, and the great pines began to shudder. And when I looked up I saw that the slender needles on the trees were shivering. Towering firs that had bravely stood against four hundred years of fire and lightning, against flood and drought, against pestilence and windstorms, giants that were already tall trees when Patrick Henry lauded the virtues of liberty, began to groan and to tremble. The forest's throat was seized in terror. The jays ceased their chattering. The crickets, the frogs, even the mosquitoes, were silent as dry stones. The faces of the people were clenched fists."

Yet I preferred the earthy description of the dozer operator who drove the first tractor into the forest, because I could understand the human experience more readily than the experience of the collective forest to which I had ascribed human attributes. The driver's came out of his pain and was more credible. The driver's name was Billy Joe Wheeler. Billy Joe was struggling to explain the human dilemma he faced as the first man to strike out at the helpless forest. He began to weep.

"Good people work growin' tobacca and makin' cigarettes, an' good people work in them whiskey distilleries an' in bars an' all. Good people work makin' A-bombs. And there's good people that drive them Cats into the woods, too." He stopped to gather his composure. "Ya oughta try raisin' a family once. If I didn't drive that tractor somebody else woulda. It's easy ta have them high ideas when ya got money." He wiped his nose in his red bandanna. Finally he whispered, "You should hear the sound of one of them old firs hitting the ground. Some of 'em is over four hundred years old, ya know. It's horrible ta hear 'em come crashing down. It's a sound a man never fergits."

Then the driver of a logging truck who also took part in the massacre chimed in. His name was Cap. "Us humans ain't the only ones killing trees ya know. Bugs kill trees and porcupines kill trees. Sometimes me and Georgia haul logs. [He was referring to his truck, which he called Georgia.] Man's gotta make a livin'. I met Jimmy Hoffa once. Now there was a *true* fuckin' criminal. But I'll say one thing fer Jimmy. We had jobs! If them 'viormentalists had their way we'd all be on welfare along with them."

"What about the old-growth forests?" someone asked.

"The way I got it figgered, man is like a tree beetle. He's gonna eat himself outta house an' home an' keep fuckin' things up, an' after the human race is gone things'll get good again. Ya can't talk no sense inta tree beetles, an' ya can't talk no sense inta human bein's neither. Me—I'm gonna get my share while the gettin's still good."

"We have brains. Beetles don't," somebody else hollered.

"Brains just make a man do crazy things," Cap said. That's all Cap said. On the other hand, one need only listen to the argument of the venerable James Watt, former secretary of the interior, to prove that Cap was right. Watt, an admittedly brainy man whose apparent mission was to deliver the national forest treasures over to corporate America, was asked by a reporter what value he personally placed on the trees in old-growth forests. "How many trees do you need to look at, anyway?" Watt replied. "If you've seen one, you've seen them all."

The orthodoxy of Watt and the bum in the park were remarkable. A reporter was making the rounds after Watt rendered his immortal judgment. He happened to ask the bum sitting next to him on a park bench what the bum thought of those old trees. "Well," the bum is reported to have said, "you make newsprint outta trees, right?"

"Right," the reporter replied.

"And ya make newspapers outta newsprint. Right?"

"Right."

"And ya know what ya do with newspapers?"

"Why of course," the reporter replied. "You read them."

"Wrong," the bum said. "Ya wrap yer ass up in 'em at night to keep yer ass warm. That's what ya do with newspapers. So I say cut them trees."

Another story in point, the truth of which I have not verified, concerns the eloquent argument allegedly made by a small group of environmentalists to Mr. Watt. I am told they invaded his Washington offices where, without a word, they dumped five fresh elk fetuses on his desk, lately aborted after Getty Oil Company cut roads up Little Granite Creek and frightened the herds from their calving grounds.

Choosing the words: As we become, shall we say, "more educated, more sophisticated," we often adopt signposts intended to tell the world who we are. We no longer speak the language of the common man. We begin to favor larger words that affirm that we are, indeed, more learned than those around us. Having begun to live more in our heads than in the *heart zone*, we begin to think out our sentences, one fancy word at a time. We have also learned that words can protect us from other people. We can render ourselves quite impenetrable, as surely as if we wore a fine steel net to shield us. How do they get through to us when we are so magnificently protected behind the steel net of fancy words?

Of course, the net of words works in both directions. The steel net also keeps us from them. It is like trying to make love with all of our winter clothes on. The argument has already been made: when one protects one's self with words, one also shields the *Other* from one's argument.

Words that do not create images should be discarded. Words that have no intrinsic emotional or visual content ought to be avoided. Words that are directed to the sterile intellectual head-place should be abandoned. Use simple words, words that *create pictures* and *action* and that *generate feeling*.

I am not as concerned about choosing the right words as I am in letting the words flow naturally. Word choosing is a mental process, a process clearly on the conscious level. When one chooses one's words, one is involved in sorting through the mental dictionary, where one picks the words, one at a time, which is not a very good way to communicate. It is something like eating vegetable soup with a fork. I mean, one forks a piece of potato, and stabs a pea. Then one looks around for a hunk of carrot and—you get the idea. It would be a much more satisfying experience if one just ate the soup, a spoonful at a time. The ingredients in the soup were made to be eaten together as they are spooned. If I am real, if I am speaking from the *heart zone*, the right words will come. They will come, a spoonful at a time, in the proper mixture.

When it comes to plain talk, lawyers are the worst. Most speak and write as if they live in a repository for dead bodies. When they write briefs that some poor trapped judge must read, they fill them with heavy, gray, lifeless, disgustingly boring word gravel—piles of it, tons of it. When I read most briefs I want to scream. I want to throw the brief out the window and jump. If I could find the author, and had the power, I would make the villain eat the thing a page at a time without salt or catsup.

I once filed a brief in the United States Court of Claims that consisted solely of a few pages of cartoons my brother had drawn for me. The brief did not contain a single citation to the reported cases. To the amazement of my opponent, and probably the judges, it turned out to be a winning brief. I think lawyers' papers, and everyone else's for that matter, should be fun to read. Unless we wish to condemn His Honor to cruel and unusual punishment— and what is more cruel than a life of eternal tedium?—we have a duty to entertain the judge, at least not to bore him, at least not to bury him alive under a mountain of gray word gravel. There are no rules in the law that say lawyers must bore the judge. There are no rules against originality. There are no rules that say lawyers cannot write or speak from their heart. Passion has never been formally outlawed, although it is a little-known experience among most lawyers and nearly all academicians.

Since we have been considering old-growth forests, I remember having drafted a complaint against a mammoth multinational-national corporation that had made a timber purchase of an old-growth stand. I wanted to stop it. The document alleged that our government had sold this stand of timber on the upper reaches of a certain creek to this corporation, "for a dirt cheap price—less than it cost to administer the forest in the first place." I alleged, in easy, understandable language, "The sale was a giveaway. The drainage of that small stream is a favored habitat for the grizzly, and the dense groves of lodgepole and spruce provide cover for moose, blue grouse, snowshoe rabbits, the pileated woodpecker and thousands of species of high forest flora and fauna. Logging the forests would demolish the homes of these creatures. Moreover, new roads would be carved through the woods, and lumberjacks with chain saws and logging machines would rip the air apart, and hollering men would drive crushing wheels and indomitable steel tracks over the forest floor until the very bones of the earth would shake, and all the inhabitants of the forest would tremble in terror." This does not sound like a legal paper. But it contains a better-understood allegation of injury than the usual "the introduction of vehicular travel into the aforesaid described area would cause irreparable harm to the inhabitants thereof."

I continued in the complaint as follows: "The forest would erupt into a war zone where the dead would be piled up and hauled out in great semi trailers and pulverized in monstrous pulping machines, and what was once the forest dwelling of the Steller's jay and the brown wood thrush would be transformed into disposable diapers and millions of chopsticks for the Japanese." That says it plainly enough.

I continued: "After the roads have been cut through the forests, a second wave of invaders will descend upon the dead, the dying and the terrorized. Hunters driving bumper to bumper pulling long trailers loaded with horses and supplies and enough firearms to drive the Russians from Afghanistan will overrun the forest. They will build large bonfires and drink beer and sing rowdy songs, and in the morning the men and their horses will trample the land digging deep trails, and they will scatter their garbage and defecate wherever the urge strikes them. The elk and the moose and the brown bear and all the other creatures will flee for their lives as the hunters comb every foot of the terrain for any creature that moves. The forest will be transformed into a living hell, and the sounds of hell will echo across the canyons until every creature that hides therein will run from its home, and some will run into the sights of the hunters and some into treacherous canyons and into high barren places where they will grow lean in the summer and lie down in what is left of their hides and bones to freeze in the winter."

Complaints, as they are called, are formal legal documents that are usually bereft of a single alive word. They are a pernicious exercise in intellectual perversion. In a typical complaint one can read about a horrid mutilation of a child as if someone merely forgot to put the dressing on the salad. But there is no law against aliveness or animation, even though the law seems mostly dead.

I once listened to the speech of a man who was known to us only as Jethro. He spoke eloquently for the cause of this same forest. He was not a handsome man to look at. A sparse brown beard grew over most of his pointed, pockmarked face. He was bald on top and his side hair hung down to his shoulders in scraggly clumps. I thought he looked like a molting vulture. Yet something attractive seeped through, perhaps in his eyes, something fierce and yet deceptively gentle, and his speech moved me both to anger and to tears. As you listen to his words, hear them as delivered in a high, strained voice. Yet observe his choice of the words I have emphasized:

Jethro began with a bomb. "A *blitzkrieg* has been launched against the earth. The ecosystems are being destroyed for profit. The life-support capacities of the planet are threatened. The world's climate is being *altered,* the oceans *poisoned,* the ozone layers *torn* while the earth is *doused in acid rain* and *radioactive fallout* and *drowned* in *carcinogenic pesticides.*

"Today, all life faces the *most critical moment in its three-and-a-half-billion years on this planet.*" I remember his voice reflecting a deep and painful love. "Never before, not even during the extinction of the dinosaurs at the end of the Cretaceous period sixty-five million years ago, has there been such a drastic reduction in the biological diversity of this planet."

"Hear, hear!" somebody hollered.

At times Jethro clutched at his hairy, scrawny throat. His beak of a nose protruded over thin lips that seemed perpetually wet at their corners, and his chin jutted out like a dislocated elbow. But the people were fixed on the face and feasted on it.

"Within the next twenty years *a third of the earth's species* will be lost," Jethro shouted. A long limp leather belt clutched at his sunken belly. He looked up at the great firs and his eyes turned sad, and he raised his palms to the heavens. "Our *forest brothers and sisters* are at risk, and this *great old forest has been sentenced to the saws of the executioner.*" He jabbed his head in the rhythm of his phrases. "This is not a war for an owl. This is not a war just for a forest, or for pretty flowers and pristine meadows and easy mountain trails for strolling. This is not a war to save fishing streams for fathers and kids. This is a desperate engagement for Mother Earth herself, for *when any species dies a part of our Mother dies too.* And there's no better place to fight this war than here and now. And there's no better time to lay down *our lives for our Mother than now.*"

I remember how Jethro paused, how he waited for the stream of his words to fill the pond of his listeners. Then he continued. "When they *murder* the living forest *they murder us all,*" he said sententiously. "It's a shrunken view of ourselves when we see ourselves separated from the earth. The air we breathe—is it part of us? Hold your breath a single minute and answer me. This stream—is it part of us? Do without water a single day and then answer me. This living forest, too, is part of us. When it's destroyed we are all diminished."

Then his voice became very quiet. *"The law has abandoned the people."* He looked at the people almost accusingly and bared his crooked teeth. "The law will not protect this forest, nor the spotted owl. "However"—his pause was perfect—"in the end, *the people are always the law*, and the people are here today!"

Despite Jethro's stirring oratory, the simple metaphor of a plain little woman standing next to me moved me the most. She spoke softly, as if speaking to herself.

"The earth is like my womb. We, the children, live in the womb. If we destroy the womb that nurtures us, all future generations will be stillborn!"

Another woman with an open face and a sleeping child bundled in a cradle board on her back produced another powerful visual: "Yes," she said, "and every species is like a spoke in a wheel. When we lose enough spokes the wheel will collapse."

And a postal worker still in his blue woolen uniform said, "Letting them log these woods to make plywood and toilet paper is like using a Rembrandt to wrap fish in."

And the carpenter standing next to him said, "Yeah, there oughta be a law against anybody cuttin' down a tree that's older'n him."

Still another at the same gathering referred to conventional environmentalists as "dildos with dead batteries." To this gathering of activists, membership in the Sierra Club was like going to Sunday school to fight crime. To them the milquetoast sweetpeas of the Audubon Society were "voyeurs with a Bambi-and-buttercup mentality."

The language, the metaphors, the stories of everyday people! I say listen to them if you want to witness the wholesome, serviceable, often brilliant use of the language. I say listen to the words chosen by ordinary people if you want to see the sun shine on the language.

At this same meeting I heard Jethro's interview with the media.

"Have you no respect for those who have acquired by legal means the right to log this forest?" the reporter asked.

"Man acquires his rights from the same source as the pollywog," Jethro replied. "Man's rights are no more sacred to Mother Earth than the rights of her other children, no more blessed than the fiddling cricket on the edge of the pond or the frog sitting on the lily pad like a small green bud."

One can see a man and frog and pollywog all on equal terms. His visuals were indelible.

"Are you telling me that a frog is as important as a man? A snail as important as your child?" The reporter seemed incredulous.

"It depends on whether you are the mother of the child or, as the Mother Earth, the mother of all children."

"I thought the rule of nature was survival of the fittest," the reporter snapped.

But Jethro had an answer for that argument as well. "In that case, brown sewer rats and cockroaches, both of whom can survive the radiation of an atomic holocaust, will become the chosen species."

"How about 'Might is right'?" The reporter was playing with him.

Undaunted by the mockery, Jethro came forward with this magnificent prose: "Man cannot create one small cricket in the lily pond. He can only rip out the lilies and drain the pond and silence the singing of the forest fiddlers forever. Man has the greater power to do both good and evil. Therefore his responsibilities to the Mother Earth are also greater."

"Who are you?" the reporter asked in gathering awe.

Jethro gave no answer.

Then from behind Jethro I heard a small clear voice: "He keeps faith with those who sleep in the dust. That is who he is."

That is where Jethro's argument ended.

And so, there too shall I end mine.

PART II

Delivering the Winning Argument

8

Structuring the Winning Argument

BUILDING THE HOUSE THE WOLF CAN'T BLOW DOWN

THE LOCK: I couldn't write an argument if my life depended on it.

THE KEY: Don't write. All you need to know is what you already know—how to tell a story.

Every argument, in court or out, whether delivered over the supper table or made at coffee break, can be reduced to a story. An argument, like a house, yes, like the houses of the three little pigs, has structure. Whether it will fall, whether it can be blown down when the wolf huffs and puffs, depends upon how the house has been built. The strongest structure for any argument is *story*.

"Let me tell you a story."

Storytelling has been the principal means by which we have taught one another from the beginning of time. The campfire. The tribal members gathered around, the little children peeping from behind the adults, their eyes as wide as dollars, listening, listening. The old man—can you hear his crackly voice, telling his stories of days gone by? Something is learned from the story—the way to surround and kill a saber-toothed tiger, the hunt for the king of the mastodons in a far-off valley, how the old man survived the storm. There are stories of love, of the discovery of special magic potions, of the evil of the warring neighboring tribes—all learning of man has been handed down for eons in the form of stories.

We are, indeed, creatures of story.

All varieties of creatures inhabit the planet—grazing creatures, hunting creatures, flying creatures, water creatures, burrowing creatures, and parasites that attach to and live on other creatures. But we alone are story creatures. Telling stories and listening to stories are the activities that most distinguish our species. The stories of our childhood remain with us as primary experiences against which we judge and decide issues as adults. They are forever implanted in both our conscious and unconscious. We are entertained by the drama of movies, television, and theater—highly developed forms of storytelling. The most effective advertisements on television are always mini-stories that take little more than half a minute. Jokes are small stories. The great teachers of the world taught with stories. Christ's parables are stories.

When the foreman in the plant discovers that a machine has broken down, the first thing he is likely to ask the people huddling around who are attempting to repair it is, "What's the story here?" When the cop pulls us over and pushes his pugilistic face into the front seat, his first gruff question is likely to be, "What's the story, buddy?" Your response to the boss or to the cop is usually in story form, that is, you tell what happened. "This roller," the factory worker answers the foreman, "was moving along just fine, and then I heard something, and I ran over, and the roller was clogged, and it started grinding itself up. I'm glad it happened while we were over there. Somebody could have gotten caught in it. And I've been thinking about how we can fix this so it won't happen again," which becomes the rest of the story, the argument for proper safety devices in the plant.

Storytelling is in the genes. Listening to stories is also in the genes. It follows, therefore, that the most effective structure for any argument will always be *story*.

The German philosopher Hans Vaihinger, in his important but, in America, little-known book, *The Philosophy of 'As If,'* proposed that in addition to inductive and deductive thought, there exists an original thought form he calls "fictional thinking." Myth, religious allegory, metaphor, aphorisms, indeed, the world of legal fictions and analogy are examples of fictions we use every day in thinking. An ordinary road map is actually fiction, for nothing like the map exists. Yet we can move accurately, assuredly in the real world as a result of our reliance on the fictional representation of the map. An argument that depends upon "fictional thinking," as Vaihinger called it, is the most powerful of all arguments—the parables of Christ, the stories of tribal chieftains, the fairy tales and fables that are the very undergarments of our society. Jorge Luis Borges, who won the Nobel Prize for literature, Gabriel García Márquez, and Joseph Campbell have all made the same argument, that "fictional thinking" is the original form of human thought, that it harkens to our genes.

Before we can tell an effective story to the *Other*, we must first visualize the picture ourselves. Begin to think in story form. Suppose we want to petition the county commissioners to construct a new road to replace an existing dangerous one. You could argue that the county commissioners have the duty to provide safe ingress and egress for the taxpayers, and that the present road is inherently unsafe and does not conform to minimum highway standards. You could quote the standards and cite the specifics of how the road is in violation of those standards. Or, you could provide the commissioners with the following argument that takes the form of a story.

"I was driving down Beach Creek Road today. I had my four-year-old daughter Sarah with me. I strapped her as tightly into the seat as I could, because I knew the road could be very dangerous, and I strapped myself in as well. Although this was a dangerous road, it was the only one Sarah and I could take to town.

"As usual, I drove very slowly, hugging the shoulder all the way. As I was coming to that first blind curve, I thought, What would happen to us if a drunk comes around that corner on the wrong side of the road? What would happen to us if a speeding driver came barreling around that curve and slid slightly over the center line? There would be no escape for us. The shoulder is narrow. There is a deep drop-off. I looked at my little daughter and I thought, This isn't fair to her. She is innocent. Why should she be subjected to this danger?

"And then when I was well into the curve I saw the approaching vehicle. A lot of thoughts flashed through my mind. I recalled there had been four deaths on this road in the past ten years, and I don't know how many wrecks that resulted in serious injury. I thought, based on the number of deaths per thousand persons in this war zone, a person would have had a much better chance to survive in Vietnam.

"As you can see, this time Sarah and I made it. This time the driver wasn't drunk. This time the driver was attentive. This time the driver was in control of his car, but there wasn't much room to spare when we met. I could have reached out and touched the side of his car. The question is, when will Sarah and I become just another statistic on this road? Will you remember us? Will you remember me standing here, imploring you to do something about this? Especially for her? Please?"

The argument creates word images of innocent people trapped in inescapable danger. It touches the emotions of the commissioners, who have the power and therefore the responsibility. "Will you remember me standing here imploring you to do something about this?" are powerful word weapons that will not be forgotten.

The story is the easiest form for almost any argument to take. You don't have to remember the next thought, the next sentence. You don't have to memorize anything. You already know the whole story. You see it in your mind's eye, whereas you may or may not be able to remember the structure and sequence of the formal argument.

When you explain the facts to the production engineer at the plant without telling a story, you would probably begin by citing to him the figures that reflect the decrease in worker production. You might reel off the numbers that establish the loss of profit this troublesome situation has created. You could then suggest your remedy. This is the typical argument production engineers hear every day. No word pictures come up. The argument possesses no emotional content. Nothing feeds the imagination.

The argument could better be told in story form:

> I went over to Z Area today. The workers looked dead. Their faces were empty. I thought, My God, have I just walked into the morgue? I walked up to a mechanic and said, "How you doin'?" He didn't even look up. He mumbled a reply I couldn't hear. The other people in Z Area were hardly moving. Finally I pulled the mechanic over, stuck a fresh stick of chewing gum in my mouth and offered him one, and said, "What the hell is going on here?" At first he shrugged his shoulders. Finally he said, "Do you really want to know?" That was the first time I saw any life in his eyes. And when I said, "Yeah, I really want to know," he said, "Okay, you asked, so I'll tell you." Here's what he told me. . . .

The argument goes on to outline the cause of the breakdown, the poor communications with the other areas, the feeling of futility the workers experience from trying to get the flaws in the machinery corrected, the endlessly stymied production and the resulting worker apathy. From the story, the production engineer can see the workers plodding listlessly. He can see their discouraged faces. He can hear the mechanic's story, out of which emerges a clear remedy.

The other day I was reviewing a reply brief written by one of the younger members of my law firm in response to one that had been filed by the other side. The opposing attorney was asking the judge to certify questions of law to the Supreme Court of Wyoming. The brief of our opponent was long and tedious and filled with citations.

Our young lawyer adopted the same lifeless approach as his opponent. He had begun by repeating the several questions that the opponent had already identified. The questions were as interesting as cold cornmeal mush.

"Suppose you were the judge," I said to the young lawyer. "Be him for a moment. Realize that he faces stacks of these briefs, that they are piled to the ceiling, these boring, god-awful briefs he must read. No wonder he hates lawyers. He is drowning in their paper excrement. Can you see him? He wants to burn the piles up. Suddenly something snaps. He goes mad. He grabs the top brief, rips off the cover sheet, lights a match to it and now, laughing, drooling, he feeds the little fire, a page at a time. He drops the burning brief to the floor, and adds other briefs to it until he has a large fire blazing away in the center of his office. You can see him madly feeding the fire with brief after brief until he comes to yours. He picks yours up. This is the last legal paper left. By this time, the drapes in the room have caught fire and the place is turning into an inferno. He stops for a moment to read the last legal words he will ever see. And what does he read?

> This response is made in response to the respondent's assertion that the matter in question constitutes a meritorious question for this court's consideration under Rule 3039 (b) (2) (a) (ii) subpart (zz).

"Can't you see that poor judge? With your brief in hand, he lets out a last horrible scream, throws your brief into the fire, and is about to jump in after it when, just in time, he is rescued by his clerk. Why not save the judge's life in the first place by beginning your brief with a story, perhaps like this:

> This story begins with the respondent standing there, looking up at you judges, and what do you suppose he is doing? He is *thumb-*

ing his nose at you. He is saying, "I can do as I please. I will destroy the land and violate the law, and by the time you judges discover what this case is about, I will have raped the land and taken my profit. And then you will hear me, as the saying goes, laugh all the way to the bank while you are still reading my lawyer's laborious brief."

I could have said to the young man, "Your brief is a bit too formal and traditional and somewhat bereft of original verbiage," which criticism he would likely forget the next time he sat down to write a brief. But he will never forget the story of the mad judge. Moreover, if the young lawyer will start his argument with a story, the issue in the case will be immediately identified, and the judges themselves will never forget the word picture of the respondent standing there thumbing his nose at them.

Why is the story argument so powerful? It is powerful because it speaks in the language form of the species. Its structure is natural. It permits the storyteller to speak easily, openly, powerfully from the *heart zone.* It provokes interest. It is an antidote to the worst poison that can be injected into any argument—the doldrums. We are moved by story. A story touches us in our *tenders*, in those soft, unprotected places where our decisions are always made.

Where do we begin a story? Sometimes I begin a story at its ending. If I want the jury to understand the devastation of defective brakes on a vehicle and the responsibility of the car manufacturer for having loosed such killing monsters on the road for profit, I begin the story with a picture of my client driving along on a pleasant Sunday afternoon.

It is one of those fresh spring days when we are glad to be alive. The sky is a deep Wyoming blue. The sun is warm and the wildflowers are on stage. Suddenly a cow jumps up out of the barrow pit and Sammy slams on the brakes. The rear brakes—something is the matter with them! Sammy's veins are suddenly flooded with adrenaline. His heart is in his throat. His brand-new car begins to swerve and the rear of the car begins to come around. He is trapped! If he takes his foot off the brake, he will hit the cow and be seriously injured or killed. If he doesn't, his car will careen out of control and wreck. He realizes he is about to die.

By starting the story at its ending I have created a two-pronged suspense: Will the driver be killed? And what was the cause of this horror? The listener's interest will be held until the entire story is told—how the manufacturer's engineering department had discovered this danger the year before, but management chose not to correct it because it was cheaper to defend the lawsuits and pay for the injured and the dead than it was to recall thousands of cars and correct the defect. I will tell how this same nightmare was experienced by countless other innocent drivers who, when they bought their new cars, were entitled to believe they were not inherently dangerous. Then I will bring the jury back to the scene, to the terrible crash, the steel frame and body of the car crushing in on the driver, and tell how his mangled body had to be cut out of the wreckage.

I will tell the jury who Sammy was, where he grew up, the schools he went to. I will show them how he was as a little boy, what his ambitions were, his loves, his triumphs and failures. I will tell the jury how he and his wife had saved for their new car, how proud they were when they brought their new car home to their children. Little did they know that what they saved and scraped for would become the trap that would kill their husband and father. Finally I will introduce his family, the little innocent-faced children, and the frightened wife sitting next to them. This is a story people will not forget. Sammy will be alive in the jury room when the jury deliberates the case for his wife and his children.

Preparing the story—the thesis: The story is always built around a *thesis*, a point of view that is advanced by the argument. Ask yourself, "What do I want?" I want the commissioners to widen a dangerous road. The thesis that forwards my want is that the commissioners have the duty to protect the people. I want the judge to throw out my opponent's case. The thesis is that my opponent's case is brought so he can rape the land before the court can get around to deciding the case. I want justice for the family whose father was killed by defective brakes. The thesis is that the manufacturer's greed is responsible for the death of my client. We obtain what we want with the core argument, the thesis.

The simple questions of structure: And so, when we begin to prepare our argument we ask these simple questions:

- What do we want?
- What is the principal argument that supports us?
- Why should we win what we want? That is, what facts, what reasons, what justice exists to support the thesis?
- And, at last, what is the *story* that best makes all of the above arguments?

How to get started: Suppose you are dissatisfied with your job and want a change. "What do I *want?*" you ask yourself. Maybe you dream of running a little diner in a small town in Wyoming. Maybe you see yourself making fresh wheat bread every morning and serving a hearty breakfast to the local workers who become your friends. Maybe in your mind's eye you see your kids pedaling down a nearly vacant street with their fishing poles over their shoulders. Maybe this is your dream—to live in a place where your kids are safe, where they can learn to trust, where they can grow up away from the experiential grime of the cities that leaves indelible stains on their tender souls.

And what is the *thesis* for your argument? Begin by writing your thoughts as they come to you. "I'm entitled to be happy and I'm not happy where I am. Life is going past very fast. This morning I squeezed the last out of the toothpaste tube and suddenly I realized that life is like that—the tube was full a short time ago. I don't want to squeeze all of my life out on this job where I feel I am being wasted." In short, the thesis seems to be, "I am entitled to live my life in a more satisfying way."

Looking into it; finding the facts: Before you make your argument to your family, you should also know something about diners. Perhaps you should visit one, get to know the owner, learn about such things as food costs and equipment, about licensing, insurance, and rent. Perhaps you should do a shift or two at your expense to see how you like it. It all has to do with *preparing* your argument.

Go to the library and look up all the articles in the periodicals that deal with restaurants, diners in particular. You will want to investigate where to relocate. Call the Chamber of Commerce to find out what the competition would be. What about schools? Churches? What else?

Selecting the net from the gross: Although you will never read your argument, writing down the facts as you learn them and assembling this rambling pile of often unconnected ideas provides a fund of *gross thought* from which you will begin to arrive at the *net*.

Tightening, outlining: Now review what you have written. Strike out those ideas that no longer fit. Rearrange the ideas, tighten them. Outline them.

—I'M ENTITLED to live my life in a more satisfying way (the thesis)
  —Not happy where I am
  —Life is a toothpaste tube
    —little more squeezed out each day
    —soon empty
    —*wasting myself*

Go on with the rest of your outline—about the money you need to earn, a better school for the kids, a place to live where they can have more meaningful primary experiences than television and crime on the street.

—I'D LIKE TO BE MY OWN BOSS
  —I'm thinking about a diner
    —Nine or ten stools
    —Small Wyoming town
—THE COST:
    —equipment: used, $2700
    —can finance with Jako Restaurant Co.
  —rent: $700 a month, etc.

What about the other side of the argument? What about the fact that you will be giving up a job that provides security, and, some day, a pension? What if you get sick and can't run the business? What if the competition is too severe and the diner loses money and fails? What if, after a year or two, the work is too hard, too restricting, and you end up hating the damn place? What if it becomes your prison? I suspect that many an empty diner stands as a peeling, rotting monument to owners who once lived in the rhapsody of their dreams rather than in a reality revealed by a competent, thorough investigation of the facts. So what are your answers to these questions?

Judging the argument (like a trial marriage): We can readily see that preparing our argument also prepares us to make an intelligent decision for ourselves. Preparing the argument is like a trial marriage. I sometimes fully prepare my argument only to discover that I don't want to make the argument at all. Better that I discover this state of affairs on the safety of the written page in my study. The rule, therefore, remains constant. *Every argument begins with us.* If we have not prepared ourselves to make a credible argument, we ought not make it. On the other hand, if our preparation has been thorough we will know it is founded on fact, including the most important fact of all—*that what we argue for is what we want.*

Now we are ready to tell our story: The husband might take his wife out for dinner and, when the time grows ripe and she asks what the occassion is, he might say, "I took you to dinner tonight because it is a special occasion. I want to tell you a story."

"A story?"

"Yes. A story. Would you let me tell you a wonderful story?"

"I guess so." His wife nods.

"The story goes like this: Once upon a time there was a man who had a dream. He dreamed that one day he could leave his inhuman, mind-numbing job in the city and take his beautiful wife and children to a small place in the country where they could live happily ever after."

Although the wife soon knows where her husband is going, she will listen to the story when she might not listen to his ranting and raging at home.

"The man felt as if he were wasting his life," the husband continues, "as if he were dying. He was unhappy. He saw his life like a toothpaste tube that was squeezed every morning, and already it was almost empty. He thought, 'If only I could be my own boss.'

"Suddenly the man realized what he should do. 'I love to cook,' he said to himself. 'And I'm a good cook. I could start a little diner.' And he began to look into it. . . ." Now he tells his wife the rest of the story, about the small town in Wyoming where the kids could go to school. His wife is a teacher. He has already looked into the possibility of her getting a job in the local school system. He tells her the rest of the facts, and when he is finished, he says, "Could I tell you the end of this story?" And before she can answer, he says, "The end of this story is that this man and his beautiful wife and their wonderful children moved to their dream town. They shared their dreams together. He opened a small diner, made pot roast and great chili, and she taught school, and," and he raises his glass to a toast, "they lived happily ever after."

More on preparation: Preparation calls into operation a simple and obvious rule of physics: Unless there is something in the reservoir, nothing can flow from it. "Nothing in, nothing out," as computer people say. To prepare for an argument to a jury on how to survive as a partial quadriplegic (that is, partially paralyzed from the waist up and totally paralyzed from the waist down) and how a jury might translate that devastation into a dollar amount in its verdict, I might spend several days with my client, live in his house, get up with him in the morning, see him struggle to get out of bed, see him fight to get his pants on, see him exhausted before the day begins from performing the tasks we complete automatically every morning. How does he move his bowels, change his urine bag, how does he bathe? What massive part of his life is consumed each day in the enormous effort it takes just to get up, to bathe, to dress?

I'll have talked with him about his most tender feelings: what has happened to the romance in his life; how he can no longer make love; how he feels a black sense of helplessness; how he resents having to enslave his mother into his service; the sense of self-hatred he fights every day; the deep, dark pit of depression into which he sinks and from which he can emerge only by pulling himself up and out by the bootstraps of his injured body and psyche. I'll have learned of his propensity to disease, to kidney and bladder infections; the cost of special medicines and continuous medical attention; the cost of attendants, of equipment—wheelchairs, a specially rigged van he must learn to operate and drive for transportation, ramps to his house, extra-wide hallways for his wheelchair, a bathroom specially designed so he can wheel into the shower. I'll know all about muscle spasms, about the hyperthermia from which he will suffer if left in the heat because he cannot sweat. I will have read the medical literature and interviewed the experts until I find I have begun to double back on myself by learning the same things all over again.

More about writing the argument: Yet after all this preparation, I will still write out the story. Writing is the process by which the computer of my mind is loaded. Writing one's argument in longhand, on one's word processor or computer confirms that the argument is important enough to devote the time and thought to the proposition one wishes to forward. Such an act of preparation is an affirmation of one's self and of the importance of one's argument. It also confirms our respect for those to whom we will deliver the argument so that both we and the *Other* are acknowledged as persons worthy of the effort, for we do not take the time to exquisitely prepare an argument to those who mean nothing to us, or spend our lives preparing arguments on meaningless or empty issues. The fact that we have shown the *Other* respect by careful preparation will be revealed in our immediate possession of the most intimate details of the argument, in the clarity of our thought and the depth of our passion. That we are committed to our argument will be proven by our preparation, and, in return, our preparation will cause the *Other* to respect us. Respect is a wondrous mirror.

Still more on the magic of writing: I prepare by writing my argument for yet another reason—to explore what I know. We never know what is hidden in our psychic cracks and crevices until we search for it. As I began to write my thoughts about why writing our arguments is so important, I began to consider the relationship of the physical act of writing—the use of the fingers and the hands—to the creative act—the use of the right brain. Without having thought of it beforehand, I found myself writing the following: *The fingers and the creative portion of the brain are somehow joined by ancient connections, for creativity was always tied to the hands—the shaping of spear points, the fashioning of scrapers and awls, the weaving of baskets, the drawing of petroglyphs on rock walls, the fashioning of pots—all man's creativity seems to have been tied to his hands. And so I think it is today. When we engage in the physical act of writing, a connection is struck between the hands and that portion of the brain where our creative powers are stored, so that we are more likely to produce a new idea while we write or type than while we engage in the simple act of thinking alone.*

How the mind works: Over the years, as I have prepared my arguments, I have discovered a remarkable similarity in the way the computer and the human mind seem to work. Since the former is the product of the latter, it is not surprising they should mimic one another. Data is stored in the mind in such a fashion that it can be sorted and retrieved in various ways. But the computer is able to retrieve merely that which it has been fed, while the mind can not only retrieve whole sentences, but reconstruct them as it pleases, gild the words with emotion, and play back the words with lyrical sound and oratorical fury, calling into service the entire body to support the argument. It can cause the hands and arms to provide appropriate gestures, the face to take on the correct expression, the eyes to gleam in sync with the message being delivered, and it can do all of this automatically.

The bullshit artist: But if we do not prepare, if we do not know the facts intimately, our only alternative is to fake it or admit we don't know. Those who peddle bullshit (there is no more descriptive word for it) are fixtures of American society. The bullshit artist often occupies important positions, from the White House to the television studio. He abounds on Madison Avenue. His stock in trade is hype, rhetoric, and the verbal mirage. He is sometimes accepted, sometimes adored—but not for long. He is always exposed, and in the end he can win no arguments. He victimizes himself when he fills in factual voids with specious constructions. Eventually he cannot identify fact from fiction, and since the first rule of argument still prevails—that *every argument begins with us*—his argument will finally prove to be as incredible as he.

Bullshit, as some insist, may grease the machinery of society, but it does not ultimately win important arguments, for to the same extent that the bullshit artist may have become expert in delivering it, we have also become exquisitely capable of detecting it. That only 32 percent of eligible Americans go to the polls is proof enough of the malaise from which the electorate of the nation suffers. A kind of numbness has set in. We have become smothered in the bullshit. We feel impotent and angry. In the end bullshit deprives us of the vital political arguments and as a result, we have withdrawn from the critical dialogue.

Selecting the theme: Now that we have written out and outlined the argument, let us go over it again, not once but many times. Let us rearrange and edit it. Let us circle in red crayon the key words. Then let us write a descriptive phrase or metaphor that symbolizes the soul of the case—a refrain, perhaps—and let us call it the *theme*. *The argument's theme supports the argument's thesis.*

In the Silkwood case, I wanted to argue that, despite the fact that Kerr-McGee had not been negligent, it was nevertheless liable for having contaminated Karen Silkwood. My theory was the old common-law idea that if one brings an inherently dangerous substance to one's premises, something such as plutonium, and if it escapes, causing injury to others, the company that possessed the dangerous instrumentality is liable. I told the jury the story of a case in old England in which a citizen brought a lion onto his property and, although he had taken all precautions to keep it caged, it somehow escaped and mauled his neighbor. The old common-law court held that the lion's owner was liable, for the beast was inherently dangerous as the owner well knew, and the owner, not the innocent neighbor, should therefore bear the risk of injury from the escaping lion.

In preparing the Silkwood case I outlined the story, but on the opposite page in the notebook I wrote a few words, a slogan of sorts, that stood for the entire argument, my *theme: "If the lion gets away, Kerr-McGee has to pay."* I played and replayed that theme like the recurring refrain in a song. And the jury played the theme as well by returning its verdict in favor of Ms. Silkwood's estate for $10 million.

In a case that I argued for a small ice cream company against McDonald's, the hamburger corporation, which had breached an oral contract, I chose the *theme, "Let's put honor back in the hand-shake,"* the message, of course, being that a handshake deal should be fully honored by honest businesspeople. In fact, I argued, a handshake deal should carry more honor, more weight than a contract reduced to writing by clever lawyers, for honor must finally become attached to the soul of American business. The jury honored the theme and my client with its verdict: $52 million.

Several years ago I defended a young man charged with stabbing a fellow worker at a school for the mentally disadvantaged. As I investigated the case, I came to see the victim as I thought the young man must have seen her—a sex goddess, a beautiful young seductress who, to amuse herself, taunted him mercilessly, even to the extent that she made blind dates with truckers over her CB radio. One morning the people on the day shift found the woman's partially nude body in the basement of the school. Her body had been punctured with numerous knife wounds. My client was arrested immediately.

Stab! Stab! Stab! Stab! It was as if the young man had attacked her with the only effective phallus he possessed—his knife. The prosecutor, a man I had trained as my assistant when I was the county's prosecuting attorney, had obtained my client's confession. Prosecutors always secure a confession. From my perspective, the prosecutor, to show his old boss who was the boss now, wanted to do in not only my client but me as well. Trials are often gunfights with words.

My client was a skinny, frightened sparrow with glasses that looked like the bottoms of Coke bottles. He froze a queer little smile on his face, and when you looked at him you felt nervous and strange.

But in the course of the trial we proved that the boy was innocent and that the murder had likely been committed by an unknown, nocturnal intruder.

By the time of the final argument I was referring to my client's plea for justice as *"the cry of the sparrow."* That became the theme. In my argument I turned to the prosecutor, a handsome man in many ways, a good man, but one who possessed an aquiline nose. He reminded me of a hawk. "This is a little sparrow," I said, pointing to my client. "The hawk wants the sparrow. The hawk wants him!" Then I turned back to the jury. "Well, I say give this little sparrow to the hawk! Pay no attention to the cry of the sparrow. Give him to the prosecutor!" I waited and looked each of the jurors in the eyes. The woman in the back row shook her head, no. Then I spoke to her. "No? He is only a sparrow. Who cares for him? Surely we should reserve our caring for someone more important than a mere sparrow." I saw several of the jurors cross their arms. After that, the argument was easy. For although he was a sparrow, he had become the jurors' sparrow. My argument, with its chosen theme, underlined the truth. The kid was small and helpless and unimportant. But justice! What about justice? The feeble cry for justice from the mouths of the innocent is deafening.

Let us select a phrase, a theme, a slogan that represents the principal point of our argument. The theme can summarize a story that stands for the ultimate point we want to make: a saying, as it were, that symbolizes the heart of the issue. In a recent case in which I sued an insurance company for its fraud against my quadriplegic client, a case in which I sought damages for his emotional pain and suffering, I created the *theme*, "Human need versus corporate greed." The jury responded with its human verdict: $33.5 million, to which a human judge added interest amounting to another $10 million.

If you are going to argue for a raise in pay, you might use as your theme the Thirteenth Amendment prohibiting involuntary servitude. Given in good humor, the theme might be, "Slavery has been officially abolished in this country for over a century." (Humor can be one of the most devastating weapons in your arsenal. But, used inappropriately, humor can also be dangerous, as we shall see later.)

If you were going to argue at a city council meeting that a proposed industry would be harmful to the environment, you might borrow as your theme a key phrase from Chief Seattle, who said, "We do not own the earth. The earth owns us." In arguing for a little diner in a small Wyoming town, I might choose the theme "Free at last." The selection of a theme aids us in understanding the nucleus of the argument and creates a mental image more moving than all the words we so carefully choose to describe it.

The magic, the joy of preparation: Ah, preparation! There is where the magic begins! Yet young lawyers seem disappointed when I tell them so. They yearn for an easy formula that will permit them to bypass the stodgy stuff called work. I wish I could explain to them that true preparation is not work. It is the joy of creating. Preparation is wading into life, languishing in it, rolling in it, embracing it, smearing it over one's self, living it. I doubt you could have gotten Mozart to admit he ever worked. But his life, his breath, was his music. His argument, rendered with immortal notes, was the product of intense preparation—preparation that consumed him every day of his life. I would rather be a regular person who has eloquently prepared than a person with an extraordinarily high IQ who hasn't been bright enough to prepare. Preparation is simply the nourishment of the *heart zone*. At last, genius is not some fortunate arrangement of brain cells. Genius is energy, only directed energy. Genius is preparation.

I do not work when I prepare my arguments. I am not working as I write this. I am in play. I am my child when I prepare. As child, I never tire of my play. As child I am self-centered, focused—greedy for the pleasure of my play. As child I am enthralled, delighted, curious, joyous, excited like bees and butterflies and birds busy in the business of play. As Chief Smohall of the Nez Percé proclaimed, "My young men shall never work. Men who work cannot dream; and wisdom comes to us in dreams."

So you want to convince your associates to change a company policy, and you want to win? So you want to talk your spouse into agreeing to a career move, and you want to win? So you want to convince a jury of the justice of your case? I say research it, learn it, live it, prepare it. I say, go play. Go prepare your argument. Write out your thoughts. Watch new ideas come popping out from magical depths. Learn how it feels to discover not only what there is to know about your argument, but also what there is to discover about the most uniquely interesting person in the history of man-kind—namely, you.

Still, lawyers ask me, "What about the magic, the spell you cast in the courtroom, Mr. Spence? Once I was accused of hypnotizing juries by a leading member of the defense bar. His argument to the judge was that I should be enjoined by the court from engaging in this trickery. He argued that he had, in the history of an entire career in court, never seen juries so eager to return verdicts for plaintiffs as were the juries in my cases. He had actually investi-gated my win-loss record, claimed it could not have been accom-plished by proper methods of argument, and, to prove his argument, pointed to the fact that I used my hands in rhythmic ways and employed compelling, authoritative, musical sounds with my voice, arguing that this was nothing more than a cheap trick, now uncovered by him, one that should be barred by the court.

My opponent, of course, did not understand preparation. He mis-took me for a Svengali. He had prepared to attack me rather than to learn and prepare his own case. He had little idea of the weeks, indeed, sometimes the months that I spend in lonely isolation pre-paring my case. What he saw, without knowing it, was a lawyer who had been freed by acquiring a fund of eloquently prepared facts. The judge understood the process and, of course, denied the lawyer's motion. When it came my time to argue to the jury, the lawyer rose on many occasions to interrupt me with objections, hoping to destroy the effect of my argument. Instead, he made himself obnoxious to the jurors who wanted to hear me. The jurors were out only long enough for it to appear that they had not been hasty before they returned a hefty verdict for my client.

My arguments are always powered by my stories, stories laden with fact. I try to make them rich with the emotional commitment of a lawyer who cares. In the end, my arguments are the product of my evolution in whatever case I am preparing. Indeed, I have watched the reflection of the rising sun on my computer screen many a morning while my opponents have slept their lives away peacefully, so peacefully. "How much should we prepare?" That depends on the volume of one's appetite. I can remember a huge pink porcelain cup from which my grandfather always drank his morning coffee. It showed the smiling face of a fat man under which were written the words, "I'm not greedy, I just like a lot."

I visualize my arguments: I don't intellectualize them. I don't choose the intellectual words like, "My client suffered grave emotional distress as a result of the evil fraud committed against him by the defendant bank." Instead, in my mind's eye I see my client coming home at night and I tell the story: "I see Joe Radovick trudging home at night to face a heap of unpaid bills sitting on the kitchen table. Nothing but the cold bills greets him in that cold, empty place, the pipes frozen, the heat turned off by the power company. I see my client, a tired man, worn-out, exhausted, a man without a penny, without pride, without hope. An empty man. The bank had it all. Even all of Joe Radovick."

By visualizing the argument in human terms, we tune in to the power of the *heart zone* and avoid dull and empty abstractions. Abstractions are on a second level, a level beyond the action. Let me show you what I mean: If I say, "The blacksmith engages in a variety of physical activities with a variety of tools, all of which result in the product he is making," I am using an abstraction. What I have said is true and accurate, but we know little of what the blacksmith does. On the other hand, I may say, "The blacksmith picks up his heavy steel hammer, and lifts it above his head as if to strike a killing blow. In his other hand, with a pair of tongs, he holds the red hot iron flat against the anvil. Down comes the hammer with a vicious crash. Down it comes, again and again! Down it comes still once more! Now the blacksmith turns the iron with his tongs and strikes it again, blow after blow. The iron begins to surrender, to flatten and to take shape, until at last the blacksmith has fashioned the iron shoe he will fit on old Ned, the dairyman's horse, who stands patiently waiting at the door."

Action verbs, action pictures—the man trudging home to an empty house, the blacksmith fashioning the horseshoe for old Ned—avoid the abstract that tells us so little. When people explain things to me in the abstract, I grow impatient. Give me an example, I most often say. Show me how you do it. Don't tell me. Draw me a map. Draw me an illustration, a chart. Show me a time line of the events that have occurred. Let me *see* what happened and when. Don't tell me the man was hurt and suffered a broken femur. Show me a picture of his broken leg. Show me the X ray. Don't say he suffered pain. Tell me what it felt like to have a broken leg with the bone sticking out through his flesh. Tell me how it was! Make me see it! Make me feel it! Make me understand! Make me care! If I cannot care, I cannot make anyone else care.

Action, not abstraction: *Stick with the action—avoid the abstraction,* that is the rule. When you prepare your argument, ask, "Am I abstracting or am I *showing* and *telling* as we once learned to do as children?" Remember, the power of the story is in its ability to create action, and to avoid abstraction. When someone abstracts in his argument to me, it requires me to supply the mental images on my own. Often I do not understand the abstraction sufficiently to create a mental image. Often I do not care. Often the words pass through my ears without leaving a trace. But at best, I must translate the abstraction into action and, by the time I have accomplished that, the argument has likely gone on to other abstractions, and I am lost. And so is the argument.

Concession—the power of confession: Concession is a proper method both to establish credibility, as we have already seen, and to structure a successful argument successfully. I always concede at the outset whatever is true even if it is detrimental to my argument. Be up-front with the facts that confront you. *A concession coming from your mouth is not nearly as hurtful as an exposure coming from your opponent's.* We can be forgiven for a wrongdoing we have committed. We cannot be forgiven for a wrongdoing we have committed and tried to cover up. A point against us can be confessed and minimized, conceded and explained. The *Other* will hear us if the concession comes from us. But the *Other* retains little patience for hearing our explanations *after* we have been exposed. Presidents should learn this simple rule. Nixon could have avoided Watergate by simply admitting, "I knew about this whole messy thing. It got out of hand when zealous people, who believed in me, did the wrong thing. I wish to God it had never happened. I hope the American people will forgive me."

An easy example of the power of concession: Many years ago I had a case in which my client George was drunk. He staggered across the street and was run over. But he crossed the street with the green light and was hit by a speeding motorist who ran the red. I conceded my client's drunkenness in this fashion:

George had been to a party and he had had a pretty good time. He was, to put it plainly, drunk when he left the party. And he was drunk when he crossed the street. But George was one of those persons who knew when he was drunk. You have seen them—supercautious, superslow people. Well, we can all tell such people are drunk because they are overly cautious and overly careful.

And so George came to the crossing and the green light was with him. There is no question about that. More than half a dozen witnesses saw him crossing with the light. And, when he was helplessly trapped in the center of the street, Mr. Majors here, the defendant, came careening and screeching around the corner at a high rate of speed, nearly tipped his car over, ran the red light, and ran poor George down like a mangy cur.

Now, George was drunk all right. But the laws of this country were passed to protect both the drunk and the sober. One does not lose one's rights as a citizen because one crosses the street with the green light while drunk. As a matter of fact, if you think about it, a drunk man like George needed the protection of the law more than a sober man would under the same circumstances.

I would not have achieved the favorable result in the case for George had I held George's drunkenness back, tried to cover it, and objected like hell to the introduction as evidence of George's blood alcohol level of .18 taken in the emergency room a half-hour after the accident.

For fun—how to run for president and be honest at the same time: As John Madden, the famous football coach and sports announcer, says, "The higher up the flagpole you climb, the more your underwear is exposed." People who run for public office (their campaigns are nothing more or less than arguments in support of their candidacy) should be up-front about their past. If I were a candidate I might write my opponent a letter that would read something like this:

Dear Henry:

Since we are opponents in the race for the presidency of the United States, and since you may be interested in the major indiscretions and scandals of my life, I thought it only proper to advise you of them myself. I do this because it will save you a lot of time, energy, and expense in finding out about them on your own. We both know that these campaigns are expensive enough. You will also have the first opportunity to decide whether these disclosures should remain a part of my private life, or, on the other hand, whether the public should know these facts in determining my fitness to serve as president. If you believe these disclosures are matters the public should know and consider, then you are at liberty to disclose them.

On January 6, 1962, I had an affair with Mary Lou Jordanson, my secretary, while I was still married to my first wife. This is commonly known as adultery. I was thirty years old. I offer no excuse for this conduct. Mary Lou was very pretty and very kind. I would hope her name would be kept out of this. She has honored this as a secret all these years. Hope you have never done the same, but if you have, I hope it was with a woman as kind and loving as Mary Lou.

On June 7th, or thereabouts, 1972, I was at a party of young people, some my friends, who offered me a drag off a joint. I took it. And I *inhaled*—not once but several times that night as the cigarette was passed around. Interesting experience. Haven't done it since.

I had an interest in the Peabody Savings and Loan Company. It went broke. My son was the manager. I gave him advice. Told him he had done nothing wrong and to tell the whole truth to the investigators. He did. And he was subsequently indicted. Hurt him a lot. His family, too. I cried with them. God bless the American jury that acquitted him. Hope you have never gone through such an agony.

I left my first wife, gave her half of everything, and married my true love Betsy. If you ever fall in love as I have fallen in love, I hope you never have to also go through the pain I went through to leave my first wife and my family. It was hell. It hurt them a lot, too. But my love for Betsy endures. It is the one monument in my life of which I am most proud.

I have committed other sins. From time to time, as a matter of fact frequently, I use outrageous vulgarities. I have probably been guilty of various forms of political incorrectness. I hope I have fully reformed and have, from my sincere struggle to be properly sensitive to all human beings, become a good, decent, and caring person.

I have tried not to lie, but I probably have from time to time.

I have tried not to be a phony. But a phony streak appears in me occasionally. I am not always brave. I have not always done what was right over what was expedient. But I have been able, over the years, to do the right thing most of the time.

So, Henry, there you have it. I may have forgotten some wrongs, some indiscretions, some scandalous things, but if any come to my attention, you will be the first to know. In the meantime, if you are so inclined, I would be happy to receive a similar letter from you, which, I'm quite sure, I would light a match to. I therefore enclose a match so that you will have one handy should you choose to use it on this letter. If not, I will understand that you release the same to the public not for your benefit in your candidacy but for the good of the American people.

I offer you my best wishes for a clean and relevant campaign that is directed to the important issues that face our beloved country.

> Respectfully,
> Bill Peabody
> Candidate for President
>
> (One kitchen match enclosed.)

If Henry decides to make the letter public, or if it is leaked, well I have a hunch the people will forgive Bill a lot quicker than if these facts were made public, one painful disclosure at a time.

AND SO: Prepare. Prepare. Prepare. And win.

9

Opening Them Up

BRIDGING THE GAP TO BE HEARD

THE LOCK: How do you get them so they'll at least listen to you? How do you open them up?

THE KEY: The key is too simple. Give them all the power. Tell the truth. Be who you are.

Howling at the moon: If argument is a gift, a gift of ourselves, a sharing of our thoughts, our feelings, our desires with the *Other*, how then can the gift be realized unless the *Other* is open to receive our gift? Successful argument, like successful lovemaking, requires two participants. And, like successful lovemaking, the desire of one cannot be forced upon the other.

Yet how often the *Other* is closed off to us! When we begin an argument, the *Other* will often take a defensive stance. Anticipating the argument from our word choices and the intensity of our voice, the *Other* closes off. Seeing the muscles of our faces tighten and our bodies growing rigid, the *Other* prepares to defend against us, to fight back as if the *Other's* life depends upon it. Our budding argument calls up in the *Other* all the traditional emotional forces of self-preservation and retaliation. These forces burst out of primal sources, out of the very place where the species has, for eons, responded to life-threatening assaults. When these defenses manifest themselves, the *Other* closes against us fully and for good. We lose before we begin.

If we could but open them up to receive our arguments!—for whenever the *Other* *wants* to hear us, the simplest argument will win. On the other hand, we can deliver the most skillful argument yet conceived by man and, until the *Other* is willing to hear us, we had just as well join the coyotes howling at the moon. So how do we open the *Other* to receive our arguments?

The phrase "He will not hear of it" reveals the operative dynamic where most arguments begin. When the *Other* is closed to us they do not hear us. Their hearing mechanism is, in fact, shut down as surely as if they were wearing ear plugs. When I am lecturing to lawyers and suspect that, for some reason, I am being shut out, I may suddenly stop in mid-sentence and ask the audience, "Did you hear what I just said?" I wait for a response. And when there is none, I select someone in the audience and ask, "Please. What did I just say? Repeat it for me if you will." Often what I suspected proves true. There was nothing wrong with the structure of my argument, nothing wrong with its delivery. I had simply failed to open ears that were closed in defense against some conscious or unconscious threat.

Why am I shut out? Is there something wrong with me? Am I some ghastly specter standing before this audience that so repulses, so frightens that its members cannot hear me? Most often the mind's ears are shut down when one is frightened. If we or our argument is perceived as a threat, we will never be heard. Underlying the difficulty lurks our old friend and enemy, *fear*. If the *Other* is afraid of us, the doors will remain locked. We will lose without having spoken the first word.

What fears skulk in the mind of the *Other*? You name the fear and we shall find it there:

"If I accept your argument, will I feel as if I have given in?"

"I am afraid I will be seen by you as weak."

"Will I lose your respect if I accede?"

"Will I suffer some sort of loss of self?"

"What else might I lose? Will I lose money, stature, power, position?"

"Will I have to admit I am wrong?"

"Will I feel as if I have failed?"

"Will I find myself in an uncomfortable, even untenable position?"

"Will I be expected to do something I do not want to do?"

"Will I suffer loss, any loss?"

"Will my power be diminished?"

"Will my giving in renew old, painful memories of a previous capitulation?"

"Will I have to take the risk of thinking about something new?"

"In short, does your argument in appearance or in fact threaten my well-being?"

If the answer is "Yes" to any of the above, the *Other* may not hear our argument. He may argue back. He may shout and interrupt. He may scream and fill the air with logic or illogic, with epithet and insult, but he will not hear us. And so, before the *Other* will open to our argument, we must deal with *his* fear.

The power of empowering the *Other*: The key to opening the *Other* to our arguments is to *empower* the *Other* to reject us. The key is putting our power in the *Other's* hands. By relinquishing power to the *Other*, we avoid the *Other's* fear of us or our argument. If the *Other* retains the power, the clear, acknowledged power, to accept or reject our argument, there remains nothing against which the *Other* need defend.

Raccoon pie: How do we respond when someone uses power to shove an argument down our throats? Suppose a friend of mine has lately returned from a hunting trip and has just baked a pie from the raccoon he bagged. He takes the pie from the oven, obviously proud of his culinary effort, and he wants me to eat a generous helping of it. I'm repulsed to the toes. Raccoons have little hands that look like human hands and they wear masks and do cute things, including killing the farmer's chickens—which they take to the creek and wash thoroughly before they eat them. That's the wholly irrelevant truth about raccoons. Now suppose the conversation goes like this:

"Hey, look at my coon pie! And look at my crust!" My friend doesn't look at me to see the horror on my face. "Man, is that something or what?"

Silence from me. I'm closed down—fear. I'm going to be asked to eat something as loathsome to me as a raw liver milkshake. Finally he looks at me.

"Well, what's the matter, don't you like coon pie? Here..." He's cutting the pie into big dripping pieces, hacking away at it with a huge butcher knife. A brown gravy oozes up.

"Look at the gravy! I got that old coon all spiced up perfect. Look at the onions and carrots and potatoes!" He reaches in with a fork and spears a hunk of meat, shovels it into his mouth and chomps the meat with wide, gaping movements that put me in mind of Jerry Lewis chewing on a softball. Brown drool runs down the left corner of his mouth and his lips are covered with the gravy.

He spears another hunk of meat and shoves it into my face. I shy back. "Hey, for Christ's sakes, whatsa matter with you? This is coon pie, man! Anybody in this part of the woods with any class likes coon pie. You going to act like some puny-assed foreigner?" My manhood has now been put at issue.

"They eat dogs in China," I finally blurt out.

"Well, this ain't China and I ain't a dog eater." Then he turns his back on me and says, "And if you're a friend of mine you'll eat my pie."

"Friendship ought not turn on the basis of shared coon pie," I say.

"Here. Eat this! This is for your own damned good. Make a man out of ya." My supposed friend grabs me, friendly-like, and tries to stuff a bite down my throat.

Under this circumstance not only may I consider giving up his friendship, but from now on I will likely despise anything that has to do with coons, including coon dogs, coon country, coon caps, and coon hunters.

We cannot stuff an argument—nor a coon pie—down the throat of anyone. On the other hand it might have been possible for my friend to empower me to try coon pie. Suppose as he stood over the oven door and had remarked as in passing, "I remember the first time someone thought I should eat coon pie. Revolted me beyond words, but once I tried it, I was hooked."

"It's not the taste, it's the idea," I reply.

"I know," he says. "I have a hard time eating a little pig. I was at a party the other night and they brought the little fellow out on a platter, head and all, with an apple stuffed in his poor little scorched mouth and . . ."

"I love roast pig!" I say.

"Really?" He seems surprised. "At least this raccoon isn't watching while we eat him."

"While *you* eat him."

"Life is opening yourself up to new experiences," he says as he pulls the pie out of the oven.

"Why not eat cats, then?" I reply, my riposte quick and biting.

"You have a point," he says. I have to admit the pie looks delicious, the crust pretty and brown. And there's that tempting aroma filling the air. My friend has engendered no hostilities and has empowered me to win the argument. He cuts a small piece and puts it on a plate. The steaming carrots and potatoes and pieces of green pepper are mixed with small chunks of meat and look marvelously appetizing. He takes a small bite, chews it, relishes it, shakes his head in quiet approval, smacks his lips, and takes a second bite. "I wouldn't think of asking anybody to eat something this strange that tastes this good," he says, grinning at me.

"Well, don't ask me to, then," I reply.

"Wouldn't think of it, so long as you don't ask me to eat one of those little pigs that is mercilessly choked to death when someone stuffs an apple down his innocent little throat."

"Ah, damn it," I might then say, feeling like I'd been left out, "give me a little bite of your pie." Then picking up his fork and spearing a bite of meat along with a piece of onion, I might have said, "I'll be damned! Tastes sorta like chicken!" Then looking over at the cat: "And so, speaking of new experiences, shall we have cat stew for supper tomorrow night?"

Whenever I begin an argument, I try to remember that I cannot make the *Other* eat coon pie. By empowering the *Other* to reject our arguments, by acknowledging that the decision rests solely with him, we take a no-lose position, since if we do not so empower the *Other*, he will always remain closed and protected against our arguments and we will always lose.

Discovering the fear, placating the terror: We can see this dynamic more graphically in the following parable: A hunter had been lost in the mountains for many days and was exhausted and nearly starved to death when he stumbled onto a small cabin in the woods occupied by a hermit, an old devil who was infamous for his aggressive hostility toward anyone who intruded into his territory. But the hunter's hunger forced him to confront the hermit.

The hunter could have adopted one of several strategies: He could walk up to the hermit's front door with his loaded rifle, demand the hermit's surrender, and while holding the hermit at gunpoint, he could attempt to rob the hermit of his food. In such case the hunter would later be called upon to answer in a court of law for his crime. On the other hand, the hermit might make a run for his own gun which would result in a gunfight. If the hunter shot the hermit, he would be guilty of murder. If he got shot himself, he would have lost as well.

The hunter settled on a much wiser solution. He knocked on

the door, and when the hermit opened the door the hunter greeted him with a "Hello," and handed his rifle to the hermit, butt first. Surprised, the hermit took the gun.

"I was wondering if I could trade you my gun for a little something to eat?" the hunter asked. "I am very hungry." And with that, the hermit, feeling quite safe with the hunter's weapon in his own hands and also gratified at being acknowledged and respected, invited the hunter into his cabin, prepared him a meal, and, when the meal was over, handed the hunter's gun back to him and gave him directions out of the forest.

Empowering of the *Other* to accept or reject our arguments removes the *Other's* fear, the fear that always defeats us. You could, for example, go to your spouse and say, "I've had enough of this work. I am going to go on a vacation next week. You can either get time off from your job and go with me or I'm going alone," in which case you may well go alone. Or you might say, "Honey, I am really tired and I know you must be too. Whenever you can get time off from your job, the sooner the better, I'd like to take a little vacation."

"Yes," she replies, "where?" and she is open and ready for your argument on your dream trip to Argentina.

When the son wants his parents to understand why he and his bride want to run away rather than submit to a big expensive shindig at home, the argument by the son could go like this:

"I hate big weddings. We are going to run off to Reno and get married in a small chapel."

"But you know how much your father and I have been looking forward to your wedding. It means a lot to us," implores the mother.

"Right," the son says. "Big weddings are just an excuse for you and Dad to show off to your friends. It's our wedding, not yours." After which, no matter how contrite, the son will be mending broken hearts for the rest of his life.

Instead the son might have argued, "Mom, we have been planning our own little wedding. We think, with your and Dad's blessing, we will just run off to Reno and get married."

"But you know how much your father and I have been looking forward to your wedding. It means so much to us."

"I know, Mom. And if you really want us to have our wedding at home, we will. But that isn't what Betsy and I want to do." Most mothers want their children to be happy. This mother now has been empowered to cloud with unhappiness an event that is designed to be the epitome of joy. Given such power, mothers usually will not use it against their child. But if the boy had not given his mother the power, the encounter might well have become a seed-bed of resentment for years to come.

On the other hand, the mother could have empowered her son. She could have said, "Well, son, this is your wedding, yours and Betsy's. It's not ours. Whatever you decide to do we will support—all the way." The son, with the power, will better hear his mother when she tells him how much it would mean to her to have the wedding at home where the whole family would be together and be included in this most important of all events to mothers. And even if the son's decision is unchanged, the mother will know she was not shut out—that she was heard.

When a good doctor wants his patient to undergo a necessary operation, he empowers the patient to exercise his or her own judgment. "See another doctor. Read this literature. Consult other patients who have faced and recovered from the same ailment. The decision is yours," the doctor says.

The employer, who wants his employee to work more hours for less pay, might begin his argument in this fashion: "George, we have a problem. I'd like to talk to you about it."

"Yeah, what?" The employer invites George into the office. After he takes a seat, the employer hands him the company's latest financial statements.

"Let's look these over." They begin to discuss the company's condition. The boss reviews all of the cost-saving steps the company has employed. "It looks to us like we're going to have to make some further cuts, George, unless we can find some other way." The boss does not abdicate his power, but George has been brought into the problem-solving, decision-making process. Whatever the decision is, George will feel as if he had a fair opportunity to be heard, and the boss will feel that his decision, whatever it will be, will not be viewed as arbitrary.

When I make a final argument to the jury, I often employ a story that is now well known among trial lawyers—"The Bird Story." I no longer remember its origin. I did not create it, but it is a parable that wonderfully empowers the jury and at the same time beseeches them to do justice—the justice on my side of the case. The story goes like this:

Once there was a wise old man and a smart-aleck boy. The boy was driven by a single desire—to expose the wise old man as a fool. The smart aleck had a plan. He had captured a small and fragile bird in the forest. With the bird cupped in his hands, the boy's scheme was to approach the old man and ask him, "Old man, what do I have in my hand?" to which the wise old man would reply, "You have a bird, my son."

Then the boy would ask, "Old man, is the bird alive or is it dead?" If the old man replied that the bird was dead, the smart aleck would open his hands and allow the bird to fly off into the forest. But if the old man replied that the bird was alive, the boy would crush the bird inside his cupped hands, and crush it and crush it until, at last, the bird was dead. Then the boy would open his hands and say, "See, old man, the bird is dead!"

And so, as the story goes, the smart-aleck boy went to the old man, and he said, as planned, "Old man, what do I have in my hands?"

The old man replied, "You have a bird, my son."

"Old man," the boy then said, his voice dripping with disdain, "is the bird *alive* or is it *dead*?"

Whereupon the old man looked at the boy with his kindly old eyes and replied, "The bird is in *your* hands, my son." It is then that I turn to the jury and say, "And so, too, ladies and gentlemen, the life of my client is in yours."

This story is a wonderfully empowering story that places in the hands of the jury the fate of one's client. No longer is there any contest between the attorney and the jury. Yet the jury knows from the story that, despite their complete power, they must not kill the bird—the life of my client, which I have put in their hands.

Patronizing people: There are many ways in which those who make arguments attempt to open up the *Other* to receive their arguments. Some speakers, undaunted by the intelligence of their audience, begin their speeches in an offensive and condescending manner. How often have you heard a speaker begin by saying, "I can't tell you how delighted and privileged I am to be here tonight with this distinguished group of great Americans and their beautiful wives," or some such other bunkum, when everyone knows the speaker was hired to speak, and that he would rather be herding turtles barefooted over the coals of Hades than standing in front of all of those boring half-drunk jerks to give them, half-drunk, an equally boring speech. No amount of patronizing will succeed in opening up an audience. The opposite is true.

Again, empowering the audience is the better way. One might begin: "I'm here to tell you about my dream. You have the power to make my dream come true." Do you want to hear what the speaker's dream is over which you hold such power? "I want to tell you about a new program that will put the homeless to work, that will return them to our fold as useful, proud members of our society." Now the audience is into it. There has been no patronizing, no cosseting. The audience is not turned off. Empowered, it is ready to exercise its power.

The joke is on the jokesters: Some speakers try to warm up their audience by telling them a joke. The joke may or may not be funny. If it fails, the speaker faces a catastrophe. The audience is forced to laugh, but a forced laugh sounds like a gurgle from hell, and the speech is already a failure. If the joke is inappropriate or irrelevant, or its relevancy is stretched, one would have been better off to have left the joke in one's joke book. And when the joke is in conflict with the tone of the presentation, the whole speech suffers. It's like running into the auditorium in a clown's suit, doing some silly tricks, and then, having changed back into one's dress suit and tie, expecting the audience to take one seriously. I never tell my audience a joke to warm them up. I have come to share with them something that is important to me. I usually have come a long way, for Jackson Hole, Wyoming, is a long way from anyplace. I do not have time for jokes, although before the speech is over the audience will have often laughed.

None of the great speeches in history had warm-ups. Following Pearl Harbor, Roosevelt did not begin his famous "a date which will live in infamy" speech with a joke. Martin Luther King's "I Have a Dream" speech did not begin with a joke, although the Reverend Dr. King could make an audience laugh at will. We do not go to the boss when we want him to accept our proposal and warm him up with a joke. We do not begin our argument to husband or wife for something important in our life by telling a joke. Jokes set the tone for having fun. We want our audience to like us, to be sure. But audiences do not necessarily like joke tellers. We have not come to perform as stand-up comedians, but if we create that expectation with a beginning series of jokes, we most often fail as both comedians and speakers of substance. I have heard many a delivery when the audience, if it were afterward polled for what it remembered, would, perhaps fortunately, remember only the jokes.

The introduction as bridge: If the speaker has enjoyed a good introduction, the warm-up is often unnecessary. You can tell. The faces of the audience are eager. You, the speaker, feel warm inside, complimented, accepted. I often start right out. Never, however, do I begin a speech with that ghastly descent into irrevocable boredom one endures when the speaker begins with a history of how he got there and what he encountered as he prepared himself to address his audience, such as, "When George, your president, asked me to speak, I thought . . ." That cruel and banal trip into the place where the eternal doldrums dwell makes me want to jump up and run for the nearest exit.

The positive need for the positive: Whether one's argument takes the form of a speech, a plea for help, or an effort to convince the *Other*, the presentation should begin by creating a *positive contact* between us and the *Other*. Let me show you what I mean:

We are walking along the pike and a stranger stops us. "Hello," the stranger says, stepping in front of us. "I've just opened a fresh bottle of beer." He holds out the bottle. "Could I interest you in a swig?" You step around him and reply, "No thank you," and hurry on, leaving the stranger standing there looking lonely and rejected.

On the other hand, if you were seated in a bar with friends and an admirer across the room whom you had never met sent the waitress over to buy you a drink, you might accept. The first encounter with the stranger on the street was a negative contact, an intrusion. The latter was a positive contact, an offering, a compliment.

We must begin our argument by creating a rapport between ourselves and the *Other*, a *positive* contact. But how can we make people like us? We all want to be liked. On the other hand, I have spent a lifetime with a perfect understanding that some people out there are not my friends. When I represent an unpopular defendant in a criminal case, all of the victim's friends and family at once see me as their enemy. When I take on an unpopular cause, the opposing side views me with hostility. When I answer the iconoclastic urge, when I attack cherished beliefs, confront tradition, when I

flaunt my ideas in the face of political correctness, I create hordes
of enemies, like one who pounds on a beehive with a hammer. To
be renounced is the price one pays for one's personhood. It is the
price paid by the advocate. Rejection is the bed the iconoclast has
prepared for himself.

Still, the question remains: How do we create a positive contact
with an audience so that the audience will be open to our arguments?

Smiling: How about smiling a bunch? We see people with a per-
ennial smile plastered on their face, a habit acquired from the
premise that a nice smile usually begets a nice smile. Moreover,
nice people smile, and we like nice people, do we not? Nice smiles
make money. Television hucksters smile at us constantly. We are
sold cars and shampoo and hamburgers with nice smiles. Although
there are numerous kinds of smiles—happy smiles, sexy smiles,
knowing smiles, "I told you so" smiles, evil smiles, teasing smiles,
sad smiles, and ornery smiles—the just plain nice smile is the favorite weapon of those who want us to like them and who, in turn,
want something from us. Politicians give us nice smiles as an ac-
couterment without which, I take it, they would feel naked. The
tattooed "Mr. Nice Guy" smile is the exclusive property of politicians and hucksters, and those who are not to be trusted.

Being nice: But I argue that it is not nice to be nice. It is nice to
be respected. It is nice to be right. It is nice to be real. It is nice
to be loving and caring. It is nice to be committed and courageous.
But it is not nice just to be nice. When I am told that someone is
a "nice person," I avoid that person as one who will likely aim an
endless supply of nice smiles at me. A person who agrees with all
I say is one who engages in social onanism. When I die, one epitaph
that I pray will never be chiseled on my tombstone is: "Here lies
a nice guy." Fat chance, my friends assure me.

If you attend a stand-up cocktail party and stop to look around
the room at the people engaged in conversation, you will see that
there are nice smiles stamped on nearly all the faces. It is as if
people have put on their nice-smile masks when they entered the
room. No matter where you look, people are smiling at each other.
One thinks, "What a great and glorious time everyone must be
having! And how nice, how very *nice* everyone is!" Yet we know
that the room is not filled with nice people, but with a splendid

assortment of bastards, fakes, wife beaters, child abusers, crooks, and social thugs of one type or another, not to mention a few decent people who are bored out of their minds and can't wait to get home.

If you could watch the couples walk from the party to their cars, you would see that they have now taken off their smile masks. Some are bitching and moaning about the party. Some are mad at their spouses for not having shown them enough attention or for having shown too much attention to someone else. Some have aching arches or vexatious stomachs. We all know this, even as we smile back to those who have shot us one last disingenuous nice smile when they bid us good night and exclaim what a wonderful party it has been.

Smiling a lot, assuming the stance of the nice guy, does not lend credibility and does not open the *Other* to our arguments. A smile should not *cover* our feelings. Instead, we should smile when we *feel* like smiling. We should smile if we feel happy or friendly toward the *Other*. We should smile if we are amused. But let us not smile to open the *Other* to our arguments, for their credibility detectors will identify those of us whose smiles are not in sync with the circumstances or the person delivering the argument. Instead of winning acceptance by nice smiling, we will likely create a swamp where our argument will become bogged down in distrust and doubt.

I say, to be liked, one must be respected.
To be respected, one must be believed.
To be believed, one must be believable.
To be believable, one must be who one is.
No masks.
Naked.
No nice smiles when one does not feel like smiling.
To be accepted, one must simply tell the truth.
Just tell the plain old truth!

Telling the truth, the painful truth: So how does one gain rapport, a *positive connection* with the *Other*? *Why not tell the truth?* To an audience with whom I want to get close, I have said, "I don't know most of you and most of you don't know me. I wish we were old friends. I wish we had known each other for years. I wish I knew your kids and had shared important times in your lives. Then it would be so easy for us to talk together. But before I am through here I hope we will know each other a lot better, and we will become friends."

To a mean-looking prosecutor to whom I want to make an argument for concessions in a trial, I begin by telling him the truth: "I don't know you, except by reputation. I am told you are a fair-minded man and that you are not as fierce as you appear. I hope we can speak frankly and openly. I need to make a bargain with you, but that will be impossible if I am unable to convince you that I am also a fair person you can trust."

To gain rapport with a hostile judge—and most are (I have come to the belief that donning the black robe magically transforms what was once a good and generous heart into a black and gloomy void)—I tell the judge the truth: "Your Honor, I know your job here is to follow the law, and that sometimes that job is made very difficult by attorneys who will not tell you the truth. In our case, the truth is that the majority of the cases do not hold in my client's favor. In the past, most judges have not seen the law as I wish you to see it in this case. Although the majority of cases are not on our side, justice is, and, at the end of the day, rendering justice is what successful judging is about. Let me show you why justice is on our side."

I remember hearing the story of an old-timer who had come to Wyoming from Arkansas to homestead. He had worked hard all his life, gradually expanding his small cattle ranch by buying up neighboring homesteaders until he became one of the largest ranchers in the county. The old rancher's name was Henry.

One day Henry decided he needed another loan from the banker with whom he had done business over the years. Henry, still riding his mule, rode into the small cow town of Lander, Wyoming, where the bank was located. He wore his bib overalls and an old dirty black hat and looked the part of the hillbilly he was. He clomped through the bank in his clodhopper shoes to where the bank president was seated.

"Mr. Hayes, I come to see ya," Henry said.

"Always good to see you, Henry. Have a seat. What's on your mind?"

"Well, Mr. Hayes," Henry said as he sat down across from the banker, "I was wantin' to ask ya a question."

"Is that right, Henry? What question?"

"Well, Mr. Hayes, I was wonderin' if ya took a bath this mornin'?"

":What?" the banker asked, too astounded to be offended.

"Well, I was wonderin' if ya took a bath this mornin'," Henry repeated.

"Why would you ask such a question, Henry? Of course, I took a bath this morning!"

"Well, I was wantin' to know if ya took a bath because I want to borrow some money from ya, and I know I'm gonna have ta kiss yer ass fer it." Henry got his money.

Sometimes when the *Other* is hostile, the truth concerning that hostility is the only way to open the *Other* to the argument. Once I was asked to address a realtors' convention. I had been chosen as one of the speakers because of my well-known stand in favor of the environment and, on the other hand, the chairman's need to present a balanced program. I was, to some, one of those tree-hugging infidels who were causing the real estate business most of its troubles.

The introduction was perfunctory, and mean. It went something like this:

"Mr. Spence, as you know, once sued a corporation for having accidentally killed a couple of trees with their weed killer. The trees belonged to the corporation's neighbors, and Spence got his clients a huge settlement in court, one that was worth more than the land itself—trees or no trees. Mr. Spence has been a thorn in the side of real estate development in this state for many years, but in fairness, his side of the issue ought to be heard if for no better reason than to know what his arguments are so we can be prepared to answer them." Laughter. "I therefore give you Mr. Gerry Spence, the renowned lawyer and tree hugger."

How do you open up a door that has been slammed shut like that? I began by referring to the introduction.

"If I knew I was going to get an introduction like that, I wouldn't have shown up this evening," I began. That was truthful, all right, and the audience knew it. They laughed—but only a little. "I feel like a worm in the chicken yard," I said. They sputtered a little again. "And as for my suit on behalf of those trees—the trees that were killed were friends of mine. I had hugged each and every one of them dozens of times." They laughed, but it was more like a jeer.

"One of the trees was named Shirley. One of the trees was named Lulu Bell." They laughed again. "I remember one of the trees I especially loved. She had darling black eyes, and she wore a lovely yellow dress in the fall. Her limbs were lifted to the sky when she sang in the spring and her leaves quaked and shivered at the slightest passing breeze. She was beautiful. I could not introduce you to all the bluebirds and chickadees that nested in her arms over the years. I could not list by name the downy woodpeckers who found shelter for their babies in this wondrous tree. I do not know how many lovers picnicked under her outstretched limbs and how many children played around her, year after year. Her name was Gladys, and they killed her. They killed her, and her sister Betty Jo, and they killed all of her other sisters, and they killed the wildflowers that gathered at their feet. Then they laughed and mocked at those who loved them, who cared about them, and who came to court and asked for justice."

There was silence in the room. You could hear the chairman grinding his teeth. I waited. I heard a nervous cough or two from the back of the room. "I came here tonight not to defend myself for caring about trees, nor to defend myself for having fought for causes I believe are just, but to ask you to join me in a fight against that which is plainly wrong."

Then I began my argument against cutting up the beautiful Jackson Hole valley in ugly subdivisions for the profit of the developers. "Let me begin by telling you a story," I said. "Before the Venus de Milo became the property of the Louvre in Paris, it came into the hands of a Venetian art dealer. Already the statue had become the focus of great public interest. The pose and drapery of the figure gave the Venus great nobility and was, indeed, a masterpiece with all of the power that exudes from perfect pieces of art. People came from distant places to see the statue. And, as time went on and as the statue's popularity grew, it was attributed with the power to make all women who touched it beautiful.

"The art dealer realized he could reap huge profits by exploiting the public's demand to own a small piece of the Venus. Women from across the land came on pilgrimages to view the Venus, and yearned to own but a small chip of her, believing that they might, by such possession, become beautiful themselves. The art dealer had a plan. He would preserve the Venus in a plaster copy and thereafter break the original Venus into thousands of small pieces, for he realized that the profit to be obtained by the sale of the many parts would vastly exceed any sum he might ever realize from selling the whole unbroken piece of art.

"So he summoned workmen with sledges to appear at his shop where the Venus was displayed. 'Break her up, men,' he commanded. 'Break her into a thousand little pieces.' He raised his arm to give the beginning signal, and just as his arm was about to fall the merchant's arm was severed from his body as if by an invisible sword. And at the same time, the opposite arm from the Venus de Milo was also severed. Both arms fell to the floor, one of flesh, the other of stone, and where they fell they formed a cross, which the workmen took as a divine sign that the Venus must never be destroyed. Shortly thereafter the Venus de Milo was acquired by the Louvre, where it has remained to this day for all lovers of beauty to behold."

I stopped for a moment. The room was silent. The people's faces were as stony as the Venus herself. Then I continued, "This valley was not the creation of a mere human sculptor. This valley is a work of art created by God. To many world travelers who should know, they adjudge this valley with its towering peaks and its pristine lakes is the most beautiful valley in the world. As the Venus de Milo was once in the hands of an avaricious art dealer who wished to destroy her for his profit, so is this valley in your hands."

I left the podium. There was no applause. The room was silent. When I walked out, people did not speak to me. I thought the speech had been a horrid mistake, a miserable, shameful indulgence, until a few days later when I met a local realtor at the grocery store.

"That was some speech you gave the other night," the realtor said.

"I guess it wasn't very well received," I said.

"Well I don't know about that. I had two parcels down by the river I was intending to subdivide. I sold them yesterday but placed covenants on the land so it can't be cut up. Didn't want to cut the parcels up and have some invisible sword hack my arm off." He laughed. And I laughed.

On another occasion I was invited to speak to a national media conference. I had just tried the Miss Wyoming case, a suit I had brought for the former Miss Wyoming against *Penthouse*. The magazine had published what it claimed was a humorous article in which Miss Wyoming was held up as such an expert at fellatio that men were actually caused to levitate by her "art." The story so humiliated my client and so destroyed her ability to live a normal life that she eventually had to quit school. She could find no employment at home and at last joined the army as a chaplain's assistant. The jury awarded her a verdict in excess of $25 million.

The media are, as are we all, fervent advocates of the First Amendment. The media association had interpreted my verdict against *Penthouse* as an assault on the First Amendment, and the audience was hostile. The chairman had introduced me simply by saying, "Here, in the flesh, is a living, breathing enemy of free speech, one who, by contagious hyperbole, was able to talk a jury into foregoing our sacred rights to free speech and to thereafter award his client twenty-five million dollars in damages for her alleged hurt feelings. That's justice, right? Well, ladies and gentlemen, here is the man who knows how to butcher the First Amendment, Mr. Gerry Spence."

I stepped to the lectern and looked over a silent, hostile crowd. I felt like I had been accused of raping Little Red Riding Hood and was facing the lynch mob just before the hanging. I waited. Nothing. I waited some more. Nothing.

Then I said, "Well, fuck you, too." With that, the audience burst into great laughter. Some began to applaud, and the ice was broken. My having told the audience exactly how I felt—the truth—permitted us to breach the gap, to relate to each other, after which the audience was able to conclude that my suit against *Penthouse* had not been an assault on the First Amendment after all, but one to obtain justice for an *abuse* of the First Amendment by *Penthouse* for its profit.

In another setting I was once saved by simply telling the truth. I had been deep in the *voir dire* examination of the jury, the process in which prospective jurors are questioned by the lawyers preparatory to their selection or rejection as jurors in the case. In Wyoming that process occurs in the presence of the entire panel, about a hundred prospective jurors, who sit in the courtroom listening to the questions the lawyers ask and the answers each juror gives.

For many years I had practiced law in the small community of Riverton, Wyoming, where I had been elected the prosecuting attorney. As a consequence, I had put people's kids in jail and had taken on unpopular causes. Later I had practiced as a private attorney and had fought tenaciously for the causes of my clients and I had acquired my share of enemies in that small close-knit county.

Realizing that proposition, I wanted to make sure—as sure as I could—that I didn't seat one of my detractors on the jury. I began to ask questions that might reveal who such persons might be.

"Do any of you know me or know of me?"

Almost all of the hands went up.

"Are there any of you who know something about me that would make it hard for you to sit on this jury and fairly listen to our side of this case?"

A young man wearing an old western shirt and a pair of faded Levi's raised his hand. "I know something about you." And before I could suggest that we go to the judge's chambers to discuss the matter, he blurted it out for everyone in the room to hear. "My old man says you was his lawyer once and he says that you sold him down the river." I was stunned. I didn't know who his father was. I didn't know how to respond. The entire panel of jurors were listening and would be poisoned against me—this lawyer who had betrayed the young man's father.

After a long while, during which I attempted to regain my composure, I said, "I know I asked you to tell the truth, but I have to say that hearing your answer in front of all of these people embarrasses me. I really don't know what to say." And I didn't. I must have looked miserably nonplused.

"Oh," the young man replied. "Don't think nothin' of it, Mr. Spence. My old man says stuff like that about ever'body." Suddenly I was saved by the same juror who had done me in, saved because he saw that I had openly revealed who I was, a man who had been hurt and humiliated. In the end, the exchange served to bridge the gap between me and the rest of the jurors.

AND SO: To open the *Other* to your argument, tell the truth. Be yourself. That's enough.

10

How to Deliver the Winning Argument

RELEASING THE SOUND AND THE FURY

The instrument we call "voice": We speak with an instrument we call "the voice." If we were not so equipped, we might communicate with violins or tubas or drums. All such instruments, including the voice, are intended as mechanisms with which to make music. We forget that. If we were able to amplify the sounds of earthworms, as they burrow their way through the soil, their groaning sounds would simulate those of many people who burrow their way through the drudgery of life. The sounds of their voices always betray their sodden march in the bogs of boredom.

The voice plays the music of the soul. Listen to the sounds people make when they speak—only the sounds. Listen to the sounds made by your wife, by your children. Listen to the sounds made by the boss, by your colleagues, your husband. Listen to the sound of television announcers, to the preachers, to actors. Listen, not to the words, but to the *sounds*, and you will discover something of the person who is playing the instrument.

The voice reveals who we are and how we are more than the words we choose. We can, of course, easily confirm this truth. Begin with the words, "I am the happiest person in the world." You can read these words from this page like a computer reading words— flat, slowly, spaces between each word, each word sounding like the word before. Go ahead. Read the words that way. The words do not convince. If such words represent happiness, I can do without it.

Now deliver these same words—don't read them—as if your fondest dream has just come true. Listen.

Now say the same words as if you were held captive by terrorists.

You are tied in a chair and your tormentors are sticking bamboo slivers up your fingernails as they make you repeat the words into a tape recorder. How do the words sound now? Do you not agree? Words do not carry the meaning as much as the sounds.

I am always in awe of my brothers and sisters of the bar who can, by simply opening their mouths, transform a courtroom into a sepulcher. Their arguments are dead. They themselves are so unalive that they cannot hear the dreadful scraping sound their instruments are making. Sometimes I feel like offering them a cold bottle of formaldehyde to liven them up. Porcupines that indolently mumble a few indistinguishable grunts to each other at the apogee of their sexual climax emit a more moving music than many lawyers at the height of their argument.

One judge I know closes his eyes, as if asleep, while he listens, even to a lively argument. I am convinced he does so to confuse the lawyers. Since his eyes are closed and he occasionally grunts or coughs, lawyers assume he is awake all the time, which permits him to sleep through the agony of the droning verbosities he must endure as the words, as wonderfully crisp and exciting as soggy toilet paper, engulfing him, consuming him, smothering him. His outbursts at the lawyers are the only suggestion of life in this catacomb of ghouls. No wonder he screams, from time to time incoherently. He was once a nice man. Remember? But that was before he was elevated to the bench and subjected to such everlasting torture.

Think about the eternal languor of most company meetings. Who can listen to the reading of the auditors' reports? Think of the infuriating droning of the Sunday sermon. No wonder children would rather be whipped than go to church. Think of the lifeless, interminable palaver of the expert in court. No wonder jurors have begged to be jailed rather than to sit through a whole day of it. Think of the endless, agonizingly dull of committee meetings, union meetings, political meetings, church meetings, school meetings, and meetings about meetings. I tell you, to choke some boring blatherer to death rather than to listen to him another second might be successfully defended as justifiable homicide.

We have a duty never to attack with tedium, but to be acutely aware of the sounds we make with our instruments. I daresay more husbands and wives bolt from the misery of their matrimonial ties not because their spouse is clumsy in bed, not because the spouse has been unsuccessful in the affairs of the world, but because the spouse has, finally, proven to be just plain and irreversibly boring. And if we bore the *Other*, the likelihood is that we also bore ourselves. That is hell on earth, for no greater pain can be endured than to be eternally trapped with some wearisome person you call "you." And the first defense against boredom is to put some aliveness in the voice.

Utterly ugly up-talk: And consider the current fad of "up-talk," a style of speaking in which the voice, at the end of each clause, ascends as if the speaker is asking a question when instead the speaker is merely making a statement. "I went to the grocery store *yesterday* (*yesterday* goes up as if the speaker is asking the question, "Did I go to the grocery store yesterday?") and I bought just a small sack of *stuff* (*stuff* goes up as if he is not sure what he bought and needs your confirmation) and it cost over a hundred *dollars* (*dollars* goes up so we are being asked if that is the correct amount. How should we know?)." The function of up-talk, of course, is to manipulate the listener, to ask a question that must be answered "yes," and thereby to control the listener, a clause at a time. Similarly, the use of "you know," inserted where a comma should go, and the insertion of "right?" at the end of each sentence are speaking habits that serve no legitimate purpose. No one listening to another wishes to be forced to agree or to be transformed into a nodding puppet.

The magical stuff called "charisma": We have experienced the charismatic preacher, the charismatic orator. We feel caught up, taken in, absorbed in them. The great actor moves us to tears. The great comedian grabs us and shakes us into uncontrollable laugher. But what is it? How can one speaker actually transform an audience into an angry mob or reduce the audience to tears while another speaker, who delivers the same message, immediately lulls the audience to sleep? What is this thing called charisma? Where does it come from? And how can we get it?

Charisma is energy, energy from the *heart zone*. If the speaker has no feeling, he has nothing to transfer and hence he cannot create charisma. We shall endure, instead, only his dead sounds, or the sound of the trained television voice that is little better than dead. *Charisma occurs when the speaker's feelings are transferred in their purest form to the Other*. Charisma is not diluted feeling. It is not disguised. It is raw feeling. Charisma is the passing of our pure energy, our pure passion, to the *Other*.

Think of it in this way: Suppose you possess a feeling reservoir brimming with excitement. Can you see the excitement there in the reservoir, bubbling, steaming, splashing up against the walls of the reservoir? Suppose you want to transfer this excitement to another. How do you do it? If excitement were water you might insert a hose into the reservoir and siphon the excitement from the excitement reservoir to the empty reservoir of your listener. This is the method of the charismatic speaker. His feeling reservoir is filled with pure feelings and he is able to transfer these feelings through his siphon pipe, his voice, his presence, to his audience. And how? Oversimplified, the process is as follows:

- In his mind's eye, the speaker inserts his communication pipe into his reservoir.
- He opens the pipe. The energy, the feeling, flows upward, outward, freely.
- The energy flows over his voice box and activates his vocal chords.
- The energy is transformed into sound and rhythm that reflect the sounds and rhythms of his feelings, naturally.
- Simultaneously, the energy activates his body, naturally.
- The muscles of the face, the arms, the hands, the legs—the whole body—respond, in sync, naturally.
- This escaping energy of voice and body enters the invisible pipe of the listeners' ears and eyes and travels down into the waiting reservoirs of all who make up his audience.
- We are moved, excited, motivated, indeed, changed in response to the charisma of the speaker. We become as he.

Some listeners are more open to the speaker's energy than others. Some are greatly moved. Some are closed to the energy and deprived of much of the experience. But all are affected by the energy. We may disagree with the speaker. We may even be repelled by him, but we *feel* repulsion. We have not escaped the power of the charismatic speaker.

Since charisma is the process by which the emotional energy of the speaker is transferred from speaker to audience, it should be no harder to be charismatic than to operate the metaphorical siphon hose. If you have never siphoned anything before, you might be better able to visualize the experience of the charismatic speaker by actually siphoning something. Find a short hose. Fill your wash basin full of water. Then suck on the hose until the water comes into your mouth and, holding the pressure, lower the hose into the waiting pail. You will drain the basin, and, as you do so, think of the water that is being transferred from one receptacle to another, as the speaker transferring the emotions feels from his reservoir of feeling to his audience.

Opening the floodgate: Now, in our mind's eye, we are ready to transfer our feelings to the *Other*. Focus on your feeling. Don't forget, you must feel your feelings, feel your passion for the argument you are making. Remember, nothing in, nothing out. Feel the fervor that comes steaming up when you seek justice—justice for a raise, justice for a promotion, justice for a wrong done to you or a loved one. Feel your passion surging for a reform. Feel the love that caresses, feel the joy! Feel the feelings.

Where are these feelings? You can touch where you feel. That is the place where you insert the siphon hose—into that reservoir of feeling. And now that the hose is inserted, you simply open up the hose and let the feelings *run free*.

THE LOCK: I'm not sure I can feel all the feelings you talk about. And if I can, I don't know how to let them go.

THE KEY: One way to release feelings is to sing. Read on.

Many claim their feelings are trapped behind impenetrable walls. Their feelings cry for escape, but they cannot release them.

One way to release the feelings is to sing. Release the bird within. The lyrics of simple songs, of country and cowboy music, the music of the blues singer, are merely sounds the singer attaches to feelings, even as birds sing their joy and their sorrow. We could understand the feeling of the singer, bird or man, without knowing the language. Most blues songs contain substantially the same words and are sung to essentially the same tune with variations mostly identifiable by the sounds and rhythms of the singer.

Today many achieve adulthood without having learned to sing. Instead they have only learned to listen to other singers, to those who have captured them on television or radio. As audience, they become a part of the great listening masses collected by the networks and sold by the hundreds of thousands to advertisers. But the people, so captured, rarely sing. What a sadness this brings to my heart. Imagine how it would be if all the meadowlarks and song sparrows and warblers were gathered up in huge nets, held captive, and never permitted to burst into song? How can we exist in this world without singing—especially without the children singing? Yet I know children in the supposed best homes in America who have never been sung to by a single *living* human being—father, mother, teacher—no one. We are forgetting how to sing, and, in so doing, the singing part of our souls becomes atrophied. We wonder about the source of violence in this country. I would guess that a singing country would be a less violent country. But that is another subject.

When I hear the sounds that painfully, tunelessly, escape the mouths of lawyers, I sometimes ask a simple question. "Can you sing?" Most often they say, "No." "Can you carry a tune?" I ask. Many doubt it. Many have never tried. But most can. I strike a note. "Dummmm," I hum. "Make the same sound," I say to them.

"Dummmm," they imitate. We begin to sing. It is like teaching someone to play the guitar who has poked one or two strings on the guitar all his life but has never learned to play a tune. We must learn to sing again. We must learn the sounds of sadness, of joy. We must learn the excited rhythms, the soft, endearing tones of love, the heavy, powerful sounds of anger.

THE LOCK: Singing or not, I am still locked up.

THE KEY: Let's go back to our beginnings, then.

Releasing the warbling bird, the howling coyote: Listen to the children. Listen to the sounds of their laughter, their whimpering, the sound of discovery, of fear. Hear the children's anger, their pleasure, their surprise and pain. These children were born knowing how to feel and how to express their feelings in sounds and words. Natural sounds. Simple words. These children already possess what has been stolen from us and what we must retake.

And so perhaps might we try an exercise that is intended to reintroduce us to the ways of children? Are we so sophisticated we cannot try to be as children again? We cannot learn to feel with sophisticated minds. We cannot learn to feel by *thinking* how to feel, or *thinking* how to express our feelings. Feeling is not an intellectual exercise. We must *feel*, not think about feeling. And so let us do something we all recognize as childish. Let us take the risk of being children.

Go into the woods where you are alone. Go to a barren hilltop where no plow has disturbed the soil. Go to the beach where you are alone and where there are no tracks in the sand. Go to some small natural place where you can be alone—even if it is but a little pocket in Central Park. Go where you can look in all directions and see no people. Take this book with you. Open the book to this page. Mark this page. Turn over the corner. It's your book. Or if it came from the library, commit this one small crime. You may enjoy it. Now find a log or a rock. Or sit on the ground.

First, listen to the silence: The silence creates a small anxiety, does it not? The silence is like the pure, white canvas upon which the first stroke of the painting is yet to be made. Dare you desecrate the canvas? Dare you break the silence? What if someone is listening and hears you? Are you afraid to speak out in the silence, to break the whole engulfing silence? To be as a child again requires an act of courage.

Whisper then: When you were a child you pretended you were an adult. Now that you are an adult, pretend you are a child. You are a child, alone. You are happy, perhaps excited. But you are afraid to sing a child's song. Despite your anxiety, undertake this small act of courage. Hum a tune you know. Hum something like "Row, row, row your boat, gently down the stream." You know the rest. Hum any song that expresses your feeling as you sit there. Perhaps a song from *Oklahoma!* "Oh, what a beautiful morning. Oh, what a beautiful day. I have a beautiful feeling. Everything's going my way." Now sing the words softly. Sing the few words of a song you may know. Any song. Sing the words a little louder, a little louder still. Are you afraid to sing the words very loudly, like a child at the top of his voice? Like a lark on the first day of spring?

You must not be discouraged. It took many years for us to lose our spontaneity, our freedom to express our feelings. Such freedom is power. Children are very powerful. Perhaps you cannot regain the power of a child all at once. The mind interferes. The mind says, "I am a grown, intelligent person. What am I doing here? What am I doing singing this tune out loud here in this place, alone? Enough of this foolishness. What will people think?"

If you must shut the book, I will understand. It is difficult to be a child on command. We have had little practice at this. You may, of course, shut the book. You are free to do so. But having shut the book, do you not wish to open it again, to feel again the power of the child, to experience a new feeling, something very simple, something called "the courage *to be*," as the great theologian, Paul Tillich, calls it.

But before you go, let us try one more thing: Take off your shoes and your stockings. Now wiggle your toes.

Stand up with your bare feet on the ground: Do you feel something new? Do you understand how long you have been separated from Mother Earth? Think of all the layers that have separated you from her all of these years. Think of the stocking-layer and the shoe-layer made of several layers. There are usually the floors, perhaps many floors, sometimes hundreds of feet above the ground. On the ground there is the pavement, and below that, the roadbed. How does it feel to touch the Mother Earth once more? Can you feel her now?

As children we had a connection with her. We were aware of our Mother, as animals are aware of her and live attached to her. As children we loved to roll on the ground, to kick at the leaves, to lie in the sun and to feel the wetness of the dew on our feet. We smelled the springtime. We could smell the fall. We could touch the air, and talk to the moon and the stars, and we were filled with wonder. But we have lost this magic. We have forgotten that our power to feel came from the earth, from those certain energized proteins that burst into simple life, from those tadpoles and pollywogs and creatures of the sea, from the reptiles and scurrying little animals in the trees, from the soaring birds, from three million years of man and man-type bipeds, all of whom played out their immortality through our genes. And they all could feel. They all touched the earth. And they are all there with us.

Let us therefore commit an act of courage dedicated to the memory of our childhood. Let us reintroduce ourselves to the Mother Earth. Does it take courage to speak to the earth, to our Mother? The child can do so without hesitation. Shall we try?

Why not say, "Hello, Mother." Perhaps this simple experience makes you feel childish. Yet, in feeling childish, do you not feel the child? Perhaps you feel only the embarrassed adult? It does not matter how you feel, *if* you feel. But why should one feel embarrassed to speak to one's mother? Is the earth not our Mother? Were we not born out of the womb of the sea, and were we not nourished by the breasts of the land? At last, is not reintroducing oneself to one's Mother but reintroducing ourselves to ourselves?

Perhaps we are ashamed of the way we have treated our Mother, ignored her, poisoned her, defiled her all these years. Perhaps you feel like saying, "I'm sorry, Mother." Perhaps you feel something else. Perhaps this seems silly and the suggestion that you speak to the earth angers you. Feel it. Say it. Say it out loud. Say what you feel the way you feel it.

How does it *feel* to say these words, your words, whatever words you have chosen? In this forest, on this beach, in this meadow, in this park say out loud how you feel. Say, "I feel sad," or "I feel happy to come home," or "I am embarrassed to be standing here in my bare feet speaking like this. I hope no one is listening or watching." Say out loud how you feel.

Is this painful for you? But are we not seeking that which we have lost? And is not rebirth, like birth itself, painful? Our minds fight against it. We are afraid to feel. Feeling often has been painful. We do not wish to rediscover the child. Being a child often has been painful. Yet we wish to *be*. Do we not realize that with the loss of our child we have also lost a kind of courage? Perhaps it is the courage of innocence.

Perhaps this exercise in childlike behavior is nothing more than our work to regain the courage we have lost, the courage to feel, the courage to express our feelings, "the courage *to be*." So if it is painful to speak to the earth—for embarrassment is painful, is it not?—then does it not follow that to overcome the pain we must acquire a certain courage? And realizing this, must we not, no matter how painful, provide ourselves with such courage? Must we not, therefore, do that which we are afraid to do, do that which embarrasses us, do that which is painful? Must we not speak to our Mother Earth in order to acquire the courage we have lost? Can we live without such courage?

Therefore, must we not sing, sing aloud? Therefore, must we not do those childish things that would otherwise repel us? Must we not, as has always been the teaching of Christ, "to be as little children"?

If you wish, if you have the courage, if you can quiet the mind that jeers, if you can turn your back on the intellect that points its accusing finger and adjudges you as silly, you may retake the most important part of the self—the part that has been stolen from you for so long you have forgotten it.

> Say what you feel.
> Hear yourself say it.
> Listen!
> The courage to retake the self seeps in.
> Are you not discovering something magical?
> Is this not a time of rebirth?
> How do you feel?
> Say out loud your feeling—without words.
> Say out loud the sounds of your feeling.

The visit is over: But tell your Mother you will return. She will be waiting. She will always wait for you. That is the way of mothers. Sing her a small farewell song if you wish, if you have the courage. She will hear you. Mothers love the songs of their children.

Tomorrow: This is tomorrow. Before you go to your secret place, let us first speak more about this business of feeling. Humans, of course, are not the only animals who can feel. Have you ever watched a proud rooster as he crows to the early sun? Have you seen him strut? Have you heard a hen cluck with that terrible racket when she lays an egg, proclaiming to the world that she has just given birth to the king of the barnyard? Have you seen chickens run with fear as the neighbor's cur chases them, screaming like chickens scream? Have you heard the anger of two roosters as they fight to the death? Even the lowly chicken that we eat in a chicken burger feels all the primary feelings that we feel—pride, fear, rage, even love as a hen clucks to her chicks.

Pigs and dogs and chipmunks also feel all the feelings that we feel. Dogs feel love and anger. Dogs know loyalty. Dogs can laugh and play. So can the pigs we chop up into chops. So can the muskrat and the beaver and fox, whose hides we take as if they were not peeled from the flesh of once living, feeling creatures. Animals are filled with humor and with joy. Every animal on the face of the earth can feel. Flowers that are loved grow best. It is said flowers shrink in fear when someone stoops to pick one. I try very hard not to step on flowers when I tramp in the woods. I can hear their silent cry.

Every living thing feels because feeling is a dimension of the universe. I daresay rocks feel in the way of rocks. I daresay the stars feel in the way of stars. If we can feel stars, feel their beauty, feel their majesty, how could we so arrogantly insist that a star, one that has existed in the universe for billions of years, one that came into being at the time of the "big bang," cannot also feel? Any astrophysicist will tell us stars have lives of their own. How can we of such piddling knowledge, of such puny understanding, of such fleeting existence, how can we who live but who cannot fully explain the life of the simplest of cells—how can such as we proclaim that the universe is bereft of all feeling except our own? Can we not leave room for the possibility that the universe itself is composed of endless feeling?

Be that as it may, if we wish to become effective in our speech, if we wish to evolve beyond the monotonous hum of our computers, if we wish to be heard, if, at last, we wish to win our arguments, we must learn the *science of feeling*. Like life, the science of feeling is not an exercise in thinking. It is an experience.

It is time again to go back to your secret place: Once there, first go through yesterday's exercises. Leave nothing out. Perhaps yesterday's exercises are easier today. Perhaps by now we have gathered the courage to experience a new feeling and to express the new feeling.

How does anger sound? Do not be discouraged. Even the great actors fail here. Few can express their feeling of undiminished rage with believability. Instead, the sound is often emitted as a high screech, a sound more pathetic than moving. The true sound of rage originates from the depths of the person's being, from the bottom of the person's heart. It is expressed out of the full capacity of the lungs exploding against the diaphragm. Rage is not the pitiful sound of a choking goose, the cackle stuck in the throat.

What is the sound of anger? Hear the crash of the tree in the forest. Hear the pounding of the waves on the beach. Hear thunder. Hear the growl of the wolf.

Why not growl? The wolf is in all of us. The hunter. The warrior. Growl like the wolf. The sound is not a shallow scraping in the throat. Take a breath and force the sound from deep down into the chest. Can you feel it reverberate in the lower lobes of your lungs? Can you hear the growl, the universal growl? The growl of alpha wolves standing face to face in the moonlight. It is the growl of ancient man confronting the enemy. It is the growl of a million ancestors who abide in our genes. It is a growl out of the pit of your being, a growl from under the heart itself. The sound is a powerful sound.

Can you feel the power? The stomach tightens when the sound is made. The stomach tightens in preparation for battle. The stomach, the diaphragm, force the sound upward and out. How does the power feel? How does anger feel? Can you express the feeling without words?

Anger is not a thing. Yet it is real, as real as the earth. Do you dare believe that before the first amoebae split in two there was no anger? Anger, ah, yes, and joy, and sorrow and love have filled the universe from the beginning, for as we came out of the universe, so did our anger and our love and our joy and all of our feelings.

Now look about you. Find a tree. A rock. Perhaps you are not as afraid as before. Perhaps you do not care so much about what others think should they happen onto you, this stranger, speaking to this rock or to this tree. They will likely shy away. They will likely appear alarmed as if they have stumbled onto a madman. But you have not come here for them. Besides, most of them are underprivileged, because most have had little experience in speaking to trees and to rocks. But trees and rocks are often more understanding, more patient than our neighbors, and less likely to cause trouble when we practice expressing our anger to them.

Why were you angry? Do you remember? Try to call up your last memorable anger. Did you speak of your pain and no one heard you? Were you lonely? Did you feel abandoned, frustrated, hurt? Were you afraid? Were you betrayed, slighted? It makes no difference why. Call up the memory of the anger. Do you feel the anger now?

Perhaps now you can now express the anger with the sounds, not the words—the growl, if you please. If you please, any sound that expresses your anger. Say the sounds to the rock or the tree.

"Uhhhggg. Hay-tee! Hay-Hay-tee!" What are your sounds?

Let the sounds escape. Say the sounds with abandon. Say them out of your chest. Say the new angry words to the tree. To the rock. They will listen. Patiently. They will hear you in ways you have not been heard before.

Feel your power. The energy. Hear the sounds.

"I-ee! I-ee!"

If you wish, pound your chest. If you wish, let the arms fly. Let the feet stamp, the fists strike at the air. Let the sounds of your anger well up. Feel the sounds push up against the gut. Feel the sounds escape through the voice box out into the air, over the rock, over the tree, out into the universe, out into eternity.

Stop before you leave: Sit down beside the rock or the tree that you have talked to. Now ask yourself:

Have I learned anything?

Who taught me?

To be sure, you have learned nothing from me. If you have learned, you have learned it from *your* experience, from discovering yourself. You have learned that you can speak feelings—your feelings.

You have learned that feelings have sounds.

You have learned that words are nothing more than sounds that carry feelings, the way telephone wires carry sounds. Words are the conduits, the agreed-upon sounds of a social order, that may or may not carry the feeling of the speaker. We call these sounds language. The words by themselves are, however, not the expression of truth. *The feelings communicated in the sounds of the words are the only truth.*

If you say, "I am angry," but the word sounds like the wind whistling through the barn—a low sort of moan—the words do not convey your feeling. I have heard people who are angry sound as if they are reading a sheet from the financial pages of a banking corporation. The words do not communicate the feeling. "Ey-ee—*yah*!" out of the gut conveys the feeling. You can read the phone book and make it sound any way you wish. The sounds. The sounds!

It can be painful to free up: Freeing up is like having had one's arm in a cast for months and now the cast is taken off. It is painful to move the arm. The arm is weak. It is atrophied. So too are our stiff, hidden psyches where our feelings abound. Remove the cast. Take the risk. Be brave.

So let us continue to work at freeing up.

It is the third day: Perhaps you should bring along your phone book. We will speak of it later. When you return to your secret place bring along this book as well. Begin by repeating each step you have gone through in the two preceding days.

Now think of something that has brought you great joy. Now feel the joy. Say the one word that stands for your joy. Perhaps it is "Ah!" Perhaps it is "Oh!" Perhaps some other word. Say just the one word that expresses your feeling. Let the word go free. Think: I am transmitting this feeling of joy through one word, only one word. I am freeing up my feelings and putting them all in this one word. I can feel the word coming up. I can feel my feelings saturating the word.

Now listen to the sounds. To anger. To joy. To disappointment. To sadness. To indignation. *Listen to the sounds of feeling.*

Read the phone book: We read the phone book because the words make no difference. The power is not in the meaning of the words, but in their sounds. Read the phone book out of your angry feelings. Read it out of your joy. Read it to express sorrow. Read it to express supplication. Read it to demand justice! Read it to tell your Mother that you love her, your Mother Earth. She will know. She will understand.

Now you may wish to speak two words: Only two words, two words for anger or love or sadness. Two simple words: "I am." You can say these two words to convey anger.

"I am!" Hear in the sound of these words your ancestors beating their chests?

Do you hear the rooster crowing in the morning proclaiming "I am"?

You can say these two simple words to convey sadness, to convey happiness, to convey the existential question: "I am?"

Only when we can say these two words to express every feeling can we truly assert, "I am." Like the painter without a full palate of color, we cannot fully be without a complete spectrum of feeling. The painter may not use every color on his palate for every painting. But the colors must be available to him.

Return to your secret place often: Go through the liturgy we established the first day, and the days that followed. It is easier to practice in one's secret place. I have returned many times to favorite places of my own. I have spoken to the sky, to the wind, to the creeks and the trees. I have touched them as I spoke, touched them lightly, reverently. I have spoken to my Mother, beseeched her, learned from her, loved her, for as a true mother she will not judge you, nor shame you, nor embarrass you.

After you have practiced in your secret place, perhaps you can begin to practice in some other place where you do not touch Mother Earth. Perhaps you can practice while driving to work in the morning or on the way home at night. Here are the steps you can follow in this practicing:

First, choose a feeling: Perhaps the feeling is an unwelcome feeling you bear this morning as you drive to work. Perhaps you are on the way to a meeting where you must make a presentation. Will you fail? Will they criticize you? Locate the feeling in the gut. Is it up high around the ribs? It is lower? Where in your body does it lodge itself? Now say a sound that permits the feeling to be released.

"Ah-hhhh." Whatever word you choose. It is *your* word.

Now while you are driving, say the sound out loud. Shout it! Pull down the rearview mirror and watch your face as you shout it. Do not let loose of the feeling. The sound and the sound-word you have chosen must be soaked in each other. Now choose a common word that expresses the feeling and say the word. Perhaps the word is "Please." Perhaps the word is "Damn!" Never let the word escape your lips unless it is soaked in the feeling. The word as spoken must always be saturated in the feeling. By now, of course, you understand.

Say, "Damn!" Say whatever feelings you are feeling, without words.

As a young lawyer I drove twenty-four miles from the town of Riverton, Wyoming, where I lived, to Lander, the county seat where I tried my first cases. Often the roads were icy and the prairies white with blowing snow. As I crept along I would tilt the rearview mirror so I could see myself and I would practice making sounds and rhythms of speech. The words weren't important. In fact, I couldn't think of the words fast enough or in proper sequence to use them. But I could make music with the beat of my voice:

Ta-ta, ta-ta.
And ta-ta, ta-ta, ta-ta.
Nowhere has there been so much ta-ta.

Nowhere have we seen such ta-ta.
Nowhere have we felt the depth of the ta-ta.
Nowhere.
Nowhere at all.
I say not here. Not there. Not anywhere.
And so, ta-ta, ta-ta, ta-ta.
And, so, ladies and gentlemen, that is all I have to say.

My voice rose to a thundering crescendo and fell to a wisp of a whisper. The tempo of the sounds grew faster and faster, and then the cacophony was broken by a screaming silence. In my mind's eye I looked out over the spellbound jury. They waited breathlessly for my next words. Then they came bursting forth like a torrent from hell, and I drove on through the storm.

You must begin to speak out of the full palate of feelings that are yours. Sing the sounds in the shower. Say the sounds in the car on the way to work. Sing new songs to your children. Sit your wife down and sing to her. Sing to your husband. Be shameless. You cannot be loved as much if you are not shameless, if you are not open, open like the crowing rooster, open like a cooing dove, open like a joyous puppy. Open like the child. Open like the universe. Shout! Cry! Be! Be open!

Do you want to really be brave? Do you want to test yourself? Perhaps to grow? Go with some friends to dinner. Tell them not to panic, that you are about to perform an experiment. You might start out in this fashion: First tap your glass with your spoon for attention. People are trained to become silent whenever they hear the tap, tap, tapping on the glass with the spoon. Then get up on your chair in the restaurant and begin to address the people. You might now begin: "Ladies and gentlemen. I am trying to get over my stage fright and at the same time to learn to free up my feelings." The people will, of course, think you are quite daft, but don't worry. You will be finished before the manager can throw you out or call the police. Tell the people about the movie you saw last night, and the feelings you had about it. Tell them something your child said or did and how it made you feel. Remember to soak your words with feeling as you have done so often in your secret place. Whatever you tell them will take little more than one minute. Then thank them for their gift of listening and sit down. (Some may even clap.)

Soon you will wish to practice your new discovery, indeed, your new power, at work, at home, with your friends. Your ordinary conversations will take on new life as you convey your feelings. Where before you spoke without much awareness of the sounds of your voice, now you will become acutely attuned to the sounds, not only the sounds of feelings, but the music, the rhythm, the power of the crescendo and the whisper and of silence—the power of the music. Already you have learned about the reservoir of feeling that you possess and how you can arouse and excite the people around you because you have learned the secret of charisma, which is the secret of simply releasing your feelings.

We have learned to speak the truth out of our hearts, out of our feelings, with words that are soaked in our feelings. All other words are like empty bottles floating in the ocean. They pollute the beach. They annoy. They cover the beach and nothing grows. Nothing.

Learning from painting: When I teach young trial lawyers how to deliver their arguments to a jury I first introduce them to painting. I place a large white piece of butcher paper before them and hand them a brush and a palate containing the primary colors. My instructions to them are simple: Paint how you feel.

As a young lawyer I learned much about argument from painting. I built a log studio in the back of the house with a large glass window facing north. And there, brush in hand, and alone, I painted, and as I painted I made the sounds of the orator. As I stroked the canvas I began to compose the arguments I would be delivering in my next case. There in my studio with brush in hand I learned much about the musical composition of argument. I would attack the canvas wildly with the brush, letting the paint settle on the canvas where it would. The brush struck the canvas with the rhythm and beat of the sounds of my argument. I learned that a painting could not become a painting without contrast in shade and color and without small, delicate brush strokes carefully laid on. For these the sound of my voice became a whisper. Sometimes I spoke with very high, staccato notes, sometimes with slower, lower notes, and as the sounds varied so did the brush strokes.

I learned that, like a painting, an argument could best be made with a variety of color. Yet it could not be a jumble of every color for sale at the artist's supply store. Simple words were enough. Too many colors caused the painting to lose its power. As in language, the colors become muddy, the design blurred, the meaning lost.

Moreover, the negative spaces in the painting, as in speech, were as important as the positive. Instead of painting the figures or objects, one might paint everything but the design—which became the design. I became as aware of the negative space as of the positive. Looking at the spaces between the limbs and leaves and clouds became as interesting, as important, as the objects in the painting. In the same way, I learned that the spaces between words were as important as the words themselves. A word could be emphasized and a thought underlined by silence, by space. In a painting, the eye can take in only so much detail before the details blur and merge to become something else. So it is in argument. The rapid, close, unbroken delivery of words causes the ideas, the visuals to become blurred and to recede into common noise.

I have learned from painting, like argument, that one must have the courage to begin. Beginning is breaking the silence in your secret place. It takes courage. Before you stands a white virgin canvas on the easel, unspoiled, waiting for your first stroke. It will be helpless against you. So it is also with beginning an argument. The first stroke of the brush, the first word spoken in furtherance of the argument stains the canvas. It is frightening to stand before something as perfect as an untouched canvas. What an incomparable act of arrogance to defile its perfect emptiness! To release the first sound of one's argument—dare we? It takes courage to strike with the brush, to strike with sound in the silence of one's secret place or in the courtroom or anywhere else. Yet silence cannot exist without us. If there were no song of bird, no chirp of cricket, no crash of thunder, no bursting out of our souls, there could be no silence.

Knowing when to start and when to stop: The most important times in every painting are when to start and, indeed, when to stop. One stroke too many can destroy a painting. How many paintings I have ruined because I could not bear to stop! One word spoken after the argument is complete can destroy the argument. *We must know when to stop.* How many times I have labored over a painting because the painting was not good to begin with and I had painted on and on, hoping somehow to salvage it with more and more paint. In the same way we must know that a poor argument cannot be made better by the use of more and more words. Have you heard a poor argument made worse by more words? Have you seen the good argument, even the great argument, diminished or finally lost by one who did not know when to stop?

One learns by studying them what kind and style of paintings flood the art market. I live under the Tetons. I never tire of seeing them. They come dancing out onto the stage in different dress every day. But I have tired of paintings of the Tetons. I am tired of paintings of cowboys and Indians and mountain landscapes. I am wearied with paintings of little Indian children with a sparkling tear dripping like morning dew from an innocent eye. I want to see fresh paintings, out of the fresh souls of original, passionate painters. If the argument is to be fresh, it cannot be a replay of the old, banal, expected arguments of others. The argument must be new, out of one's own creative cauldron where one's psychic witch stirs the magic brew.

And so, paint: And as you paint, make music, both with the brush and with the voice. Leave the silent spaces. Transfer to the canvas by brush and space the cadence of the voice's music. Paint your paintings. Sing your feelings. There is a magic there. Again I think of Van Gogh. Ah, could we have but joined him with the crows in the grain field in the late yellow summer! Could we have but felt the feelings, not from his brush, but from the sounds in his mind's ear, we would have heard the throbbing music of the universe.

But not all who see a Van Gogh painting are comfortable with the feelings that created it. Van Gogh himself was confounded by such feelings. At last, the feelings were so raw, so frighteningly unconfined, that he began to reject them, and thereby to reject himself. He cut off the piteous ear. Then, in that one infamous moment when he could bear his feelings no longer, and as the Earth Mother wept, he cut off his life.

I say this loss beyond losses was not because Van Gogh could feel, not because his feelings were so naked, so painful, but because he could not accept his feelings, embrace them, cherish them, become them. To feel is to feel pain as well as joy. To feel is the most exquisite affirmation of life. The corpse does not feel. But in his search for peace, Van Gogh sought to discharge his feelings on the canvass, and when the canvasses were full, when they could no longer absorb the pain and the power, with desperate fingers he raised up the dastardly pistol.

The goal of many educators, albeit unconfessed, is to condition our young, who are perfectly alive with perfect feelings, to become separated from their feelings, to repress them, to deaden them. The scheme of too many parents and too many teachers is to teach these perfect little living creatures the attitudes of the dead and to instill in them the virtue of death, which is, of course, to be perfectly still, as if in the graveyard, perfectly silent, as if in the tomb, for the dead exhibit the most exemplary behavior. The dead never speak up or cause trouble. I say too many teachers and too many parents love the dead more than the living. But death comes soon enough. Death ought not be imposed upon our young before their time.

Once I spoke of feeling to a young lawyer named Jim, a brilliant student who had acquired a fine Harvard use of words. He had been taught to deny the *heart zone* by professors with deadened innards and lobotomized right brains. He was taught to imitate them. I had been discussing the issues we speak of here, of feeling, and the transmission of our feelings to others.

"That's all very well for TV evangelists and shysters," Jim said. Echoing the father of all dead lawyers, the late Christopher Columbus Langdell, who sanctimoniously proclaimed the law to be a lofty, ethereal discipline, the exclusive property of intellectuals and academicians, Jim protested, "But the law is a science. The law is an honorable profession, not an excuse for an emotional outpouring." Then unwittingly admitting his own loss of self he said, "Besides, I could never speak like that. I'm not *that* kind."

How strange, I thought, that we are able to argue so well against ourselves but so ineffectively *for* ourselves. That evening I was his dinner guest. He brought along his friend Dianne. They sat very close to one another and stole furtive glances like timid children.

Without warning I said, "Tell me how you feel about Dianne."

He stared at me incredulously and started to say something, but held back.

"Go ahead," I said. She smiled at the young lawyer as if to give him permission.

"Well," Jim said, "I feel like we have a lot in common."

"That's not a *feeling*," I said. "That is a *thought*."

"We communicate on a mutually cognitive intellectual plain."

"That's not a feeling either," I said. "That is something stillborn from the intellect."

"Well, we reciprocally project and bear an appreciation for the other's separate entity."

"You sound like you are describing a severed kidney at the autopsy," I said. How do you *feel* about her?"

He was silent for a long time. The silence grew uncomfortable. Finally he blurted it out: "I feel like . . . like . . . I love her." Then he looked away embarrassed. Suddenly Dianne grabbed him and kissed him and then they both began to laugh.

Recently I was talking to my friend Dick Cavett, the great wit and interviewer of television fame. I read him some of the passages I have just written, the ones about how to free up our feelings by getting into contact with Mother Earth.

He said, "Yes. What you write about reminds me of the dancing of Fred Astaire. He could be surrounded by a chorus of dancers, all of whom were dancing the same exact step as he. Yet there was this difference, this magical difference, that was so easily discernible." I say, as Cavett surely meant, that the difference between the dancing of Fred Astaire and the dancing of his surrounding chorus was that Astaire's dancing was born of his soul, his deepest feeling, while the chorus worked out of quite another more mechanical place, a head place.

I remember many years ago standing in the court of appeals before three judges, old cadaverous drones who looked as if they hadn't seen the good light of day for fifty years. They sat high up there in their black robes, black as death, and stared silently, maliciously down at us, the frightened lawyers. They stared with empty eyes over slumping jowls. I was afraid, and so I launched into my argument with abandon, my then best defense against fear.

But before long I had tuned in to my feelings. I knew them. I trusted them, and the passion sloshed over the courtroom's red carpet and up its stodgy walnut-paneled walls and some of it must have splashed on the old judges themselves. Suddenly the chief judge came alive. His voice sounded like the proclamation of the chief of the grave robbers.

"I remind you, Mr. Spence, we are *judges*, not jurors," his voice laden with deadly sarcasm. He was telling me my argument was too filled with emotion for him, that it made him feel uneasy. Judges aren't supposed to feel. Judges don't like to feel. How can you feel and take little children from their mothers? How can you feel and condemn living human beings to death? How can you feel and deprive men of their good names, their hard-earned fortunes, their deserved justice, their hope? Theirs is a cold, impersonal logic that too often misses its connection with the human beings whose lives will be inexorably altered by the law in which judges find refuge.

"You are the only jury my client has left," I replied to the chief judge. "You *are* his jury. And I hope that you will permit me to talk to you about justice, for weren't we taught that the law is the handmaiden of justice?" Then I began anew. I talked to them like men, not judges; persons, not legal automatons.

"It must be difficult to base one's decision on justice," I said to those old, hanging faces. "Justice is not always easy to discover. Sometimes it hides in the shadows of logic. Sometimes it is painful to behold. It is easier and far less risky to deal with logic. No one can criticize us if our logic is perfect. But what if, in the pursuit of logic, we abandon justice?" I talked about how it must be hard to bear the responsibility of other human beings who hurt and who suffer and die. It must be difficult to manipulate the law so that the decision comes up just. Then I said, "Logic, Your Honors, without justice, is like a man with a great mind and a piddling heart."

When the court's decision was handed down, the tone of the judges' language was softer and more direct, and although judges often occupy such high ground that justice fades from their vision, I could hear its distant cry through the stiff words and stilted phrases of a favorable opinion. I am not so fortunate so often.

Crawling inside the hides of the *Other*: Sometimes we are asked not to speak out of *our* feelings but to understand and express the feelings of others. When I represent a man who has been unjustly charged with a crime—with murder, say—the question is, how does my client feel? It is one thing to say my client is unjustly charged with murder. It is quite another to say that my client lies awake at night, helpless to throw off the terrible blanket of fear that smothers him, that turns his life into hell on earth. The accused feels trapped, helpless, tortured. He cannot escape the agony. He cannot run. He cannot hide. He cannot find any comfort, any relief. He wants to scream out his innocence, but the public sneers at him and claims his protestations are merely those of a murderer attempting to escape his well-deserved doom. His family has abandoned him. And his lawyer, how does his lawyer see him? His lawyer sees him as "a client," more an object, a problem, than a person with feelings.

How do we express out of our hearts the feelings suffered by another? There is a cold intellectual word for it. It is called *empathy*. I call it *crawling into the hide of the Other*. It is the magical process of becoming the *Other*. Can you become the child who was born as a spastic quadriplegic, who cannot speak a word, who cannot stop the slobbering, who cannot control his bowels, but whose little mind is as bright as your own, whose little soul wants to run and play and to be loved by the other children? Can you crawl into the hide of your adversary? Can you feel his fear or feel her longing? I sometimes even feel the feelings of one who is among the worst of human beings—a despicable snitch, one who has betrayed a fellow human being; worse, one who has lied about my client in exchange for small favors from the prosecutors. I once conducted a cross-examination of a snitch who took the stand to testify that my client, his cellmate, had confessed to the crime with which he was charged. My cross-examination of the snitch went this way:

"It must be very hard to be a prisoner in the state penitentiary." ("It must be," as we remember, are the magical words by which we crawl into the hide of another.)

"Yeah," he replied.

"How long are you in for?"

"Thirty years."

"You will be a very old man when you get out."

"Right."

"That must hurt you a lot. You must feel very helpless?"

He said nothing. Looked down.

"Do you sometimes cry at night?"

"You get used to it."

"Used to the pain?"

He didn't answer.

"Before you went to prison, what did you like to do?"

"I liked to fish."

"How long has it been since you've had a fishing pole in your hands?"

"Long time."

"Do you have children?"

"Yes."

"A wife?"

"Yes."

"How old were your children when you came to prison?"

"Sarah was five. Becky, seven."

"Have you held either of them since?"

"Once."

"How about your wife? Is she waiting for you?"

"I don't know." He looked down again.

"You must be very lonely."

He didn't answer.

"It must be hell for you in there. You must feel like you are dying."

He didn't answer.

"And you would do anything to get out, isn't that true?"

He still didn't answer.

"If getting out of that hell-hole required you to tell an untruth about my client—well, would you do it?" His answer will, of course, be "No." "I have no further questions," I said in a kindly way. There was no reason to go on.

The power of love, of understanding, of being able to feel the feelings of the *Other* vests us with a much greater power than the more common ability to attack.

Love is power.

Understanding is power.

Feeling is power.

But one cannot feel as the other must feel without first being exquisitely aware of one's own feelings. It all begins with us. With our feeling.

"*It must be hard* to be the foreman, to have to answer to some vice president who never has to get his hands dirty," one might begin one's argument to the boss.

"*It must be hard* to be a child of parents who love him too much, who protect him too much when he needs to grow and discover things on his own," one might begin the argument to one's child.

"*It must be frustrating* to live with a person who can't always understand you, but who wants to," one might begin one's argument with his spouse.

AND SO: The trick to the delivery of the powerful argument, which, as always, is a nontrick, is to *feel*.

We have always had the ability to feel. We were born with it.

We must become *reborn feelers*.

Feeling! If we feel, we know such feelings permeate the earth, and flood the universe. If we feel we know that the *Other* feels as well. Only when we do not feel are we alone, and empty, and dead. And when we do not feel, our arguments are lifeless and hollow as empty cans. When we do not feel the words from the voice carry nothing, communicate nothing. But when we feel we can deliver the great argument, the powerful oration, the charismatic inter-change, the winning argument at home. It all begins with feeling. Our feeling.

To feel we must take the risk, the risk of pain—our pain. We must take the risk—the risk of criticism, even of rejection. But the reward is to be alive. The payoff is to deliver the winning argu-ment, for remember, no winning argument was ever delivered by the dead or by those who imitate the dead.

The Magical Argument

ARGUING OUT OF THE *HEART ZONE*

THE LOCK: I don't believe in magic. What's the matter with logic?

THE KEY: Great arguments do not originate from the head, although the head is at work like a rudder on a sailboat. Great arguments come erupting out of a magical place, and we shall learn where, and we shall learn how to make them.

Most speech teachers teach what the speech teacher knows—the intellectual carryings-on of those who have never made memorable speeches. What I teach you here is how to get to where the great speeches abide, speeches that come bursting forth from the soul. I speak of an art. I speak of an awareness. I speak of a risk that is soaked in fear. It is something like achieving Nirvana. Yet every spellbinding orator, every unforgettable singer, every great running back and wide receiver, every true jazz musician experiences it. The performance is magic. It is not a performance of the conscious mind, although the mind is activated and alert. It is not a performance of logic, for art transcends logic. It is not calculated or thought out. Yet it is exquisitely planned. It is magical. And we shall learn how to do it.

How does the *Magical Argument* feel? Describing the magical argument is like describing an orgasm to one who has never known one, which is not to say we cannot experience it. Describing the orgasm only confirms our inability to attach words to the experience in some logical fashion. The dictionary describes an orgasm as "the climax of sexual excitement typically occurring toward the end of coitus." Such words convey little information about orgasm if we have never experienced it. I might try to improve our understanding by calling it "an all-encompassing explosion erupting within, one that seizes the body in shock waves of pain and joy and in spasms of ecstasy." That doesn't help much either. I might try a more poetic approach: "It is all purple and pink and wild and rolling in delirious daisies." But still I have not described an orgasm. So how do I describe the *Magical Argument* to you?

Let me begin by telling you a story: Early in my career I was standing before a jury making my final argument. Stiff with fear, I held tightly to the lectern. I had prepared my argument as I have beseeched you to prepare yours, written it, outlined it—I'd tried to memorize it, and now all I could do was read it. I was afraid to look up for fear I'd lose my place. I was afraid to look at the jury for fear their bored looks would be so disconcerting I would fumble and stammer and then go blank. Suddenly my papers fell from the lectern and went flying across the courtroom floor. Red with embarrassment, and sweating, I began picking them up. I could hear the snickers of the people in the audience. I caught a glimpse of my client's face frozen in horror. When I had finally retrieved my papers they were in hopeless disarray. I didn't know where I had left off, nor where to begin. I thought I would die. I prayed I would.

But God did not oblige. I had no choice. In terror I looked at the jurors and they looked back. "Sorry," I mumbled. And then it came blurting out: "I wish I could talk to you without these notes. I wish I could tell you what's in my heart, and how I really feel about this case. If you could only know. Why . . . the facts are clear. Jimmy, here, my client, is innocent. And you know why I know?" and suddenly the *Magical Argument* had begun.

An hour later I realized I had finished my argument without a note! And it was an *argument*, not a stilted reading of something I had written. Some mysterious force, some guiding, unconscious intelligence had taken over, picked the words, and formed the thought line. The same mysterious force directed the torrent of words to a climax, knew when to stop and even how to construct a perfect ending. The mysterious force chose the sounds, the music of the language, the rhythms. It selected the hand movements and the body language, as we now call it. In short, it composed the music, and choreographed the song and the dance of the entire argument.

When I finished I sat down, sweating and exhausted and over-come with joy. The people in the audience gathered around me and congratulated me. It was a great argument, they said. I was a great lawyer. The jury was out for less than half an hour before it returned a verdict for my client. I was staggered and befuddled and ecstatic.

Later, when I read a transcript of what I had said, I was even more confounded. Surely these weren't the words that had influenced the jury, these broken sentences, these false starts, this illogical syntax. The court reporter who took down my argument verbatim must not have heard me correctly. I was ashamed of the language, of the composition. Then I began to understand: what is written and what is spoken are as different as Swahili and Bach. Slowly I began to realize that it is not the words alone, not even mostly the words, that carry the meaning, but, as we have already seen, the sound, the rhythms, the body, the gestures, the eyes—indeed, the whole person.

Slowly I came to understand that reading a written speech and delivering the Magical Argument are different arts. One is the art of writing, the other of speaking. One is like painstakingly drawing a picture of a child, line after careful line, while the other is like giving birth to the child. The written speech always lacks *credibility*, not only because it is composed for silent delivery, but because it has been obviously, painfully premeditated. But the Magical Argument comes exploding forth with life, bearing the pain and the blood of its mother. Its mother cares for it, enfolds it, and finally releases it into the world where it continues to live, to grow, and to work. No matter how well the written argument is delivered, it can never move the listener, it can never transform a jury, it can never win like something born spontaneously from the soul.

The numerous imperfections I recognized in the written transcript of my Magical Argument were the very marks of authenticity the jury heard with the ear of their hearts. People who tell the truth do not choose the best words and render the cleanest, the most literary sentences. People who are telling the truth are not as concerned with making pretty phrases as they are with letting their souls run free. Concentrated on their feelings, people who are telling the truth speak from the heart, which is incapable of composing the precise linear thought of a plodding brain. And hearing stuff from the heart, the listener is called to listen from the listener's heart as well. That the speaker lays the argument out in defectively constructed sentences and fails to choose the most appropriate words is no measure of the argument's power. I must say it again: Power comes from the *heart zone*.

A young writer who was compiling a book on jury arguments for trial lawyers obtained a copy of my final argument to the jury in the Karen Silkwood case. He wrote asking for my comments on the argument. I wrote back, telling him that after I had read the final argument I was astonished by it. I had no idea why anyone would want to publish it. I wrote, "The only thing that that final argument could stand for would be that if it could win a $10.5 million verdict, then tongue-tied grade school children could do as well." And indeed they probably could, given the fact that children usually speak the truth, and that their speech is so superbly eloquent, not with the chosen, intellectual word, but with the simplicity and honesty of their natural language.

I was concerned that my argument, which had proven to be adequate when presented in person and received by the eyes and ears of the jury, would appear foolish and amateurish on the written page. I tried to defend myself: "After three months I was nearly exhausted and perhaps the jury understood that." I asked that the false starts be edited. I argued, "The ears clean them up when they are heard. When I argue, I never attempt to speak as if what I say will be literally transcribed. If one thinks the linear thoughts of a written argument, one that proceeds from left to right as it takes its place, word by word, on the page, the magic is shut off, the pure power that drags from the bottom of the soul all the elixir of the oratory dries up. I therefore ask you to do what the ears would have done for the jury—that is to make the argument a little more presentable in writing. . . .

"I do, however, believe that you suffer a very severe disability by having not heard the argument in the context in which it was given—that is, a human being standing open-faced, sweating, worried, exhausted before the jury. Had you been there, what you would have seen and heard would have changed the tenor of your comments. Then your comments would have been grounded principally in the tone in which the argument was given, that is, in the music by which the argument was delivered. It is the music of sincerity, of a man trying to be honest, not always honest, but trying *to be*!"

I went on to point out that I "do not attempt to determine what is or is not clever and crafty. Juries are wiser than that. What I try to do is to determine how to tell my story in the best way. Final arguments should be stories, not strategies. Your comments," I wrote, "deal with strategies, and I think from that standpoint, insofar as my efforts are concerned, if one must speak of strategies, then the tactic should be to try to tell the truth as simply and as graphically as you can. Every human being appreciates that."

Despite my protestations, my argument was published substantially as delivered. Any argument, when reduced to writing, is like stuffing a dead grizzly bear and standing it up in a showcase for all to behold. Although it has been mounted on its hind legs as if attacking, its motion exists only in the mind's eye. Although its mouth is open as if emitting a horrifying howl, the stuffed grizzly is heard only in the mind's ear. The bear in the glass display case is not the same bear that walked through the forest and, when confronted by the hunter, reared up on his hind legs with a ferocious roar. Publishing a speech that was delivered orally is something like that. The living speech, full of motion, rhythm, sound, and life, when mounted on the printed page is quite a different animal.

In the same way, an argument that has been written and then read is also a stuffed bear, but with mechanical legs and an artificial voice. Although the bear now moves, and is heard to bellow and roar, it is still a dead, stuffed bear. Although we might shy back from its attack and laugh, we laugh because we know it is not real. But when the bear is alive, when we see it rising up on its hind legs preparing to charge, when we hear it scream in rage and feel the ground underneath us vibrate, when we see the flash of deadly fury in its eyes, we experience something we shall, if we survive, never forget. In this same way, the live argument delivered out of the living heart and the living soul makes its mark on the soul of the *Other*.

The elements of the Magical Argument: But one asks, how do we open the headgate so that our arguments come rushing up and out fully formed, correctly balanced, bearing the energy and charisma of the great orator who moves multitudes? After having made many Magical Arguments since that desperate day when, by accident, I delivered my first, the formula remains the same. Two simple elements are necessary: the first, *preparation*, which we have already explored in Chapter 8; and the second, *mustering the courage* to give one's self over to the magical power of the self.

Freeing the frog: Now that we are prepared, how do we call up and release the Magical Argument? The task to which I am about to set myself is like being told to try very hard to go to sleep when the harder I try, the wider awake I become. I do not intend to initiate the mystical. Yet mysticism floods in whenever we attempt to reduce to intellectual thought that which we do not understand. The miracle of life is as real as turnips until we begin to ask head questions like "What is life?" and "Where does it come from?" and "Where does it go?" and "What is its meaning?" It is only when the intellect cannot answer that magic prevails. So it is with the Magical Argument.

Once we have prepared it, the Magical Argument abounds within each of us, and when freed will come bursting forth as easily and as naturally as a frog jumps. But if we catch the frog and cut it limb from limb and examine all its parts, we shall never discover the life's energy that caused the frog to jump in the first place. The question then is not "Why does the frog jump?" but "How can we make the little beast jump?"

The frog, of course, has to be nourished, a matter we have already addressed when we examined the necessity of preparation. But it must also be freed. When we stand before a crowd or sit down in the boss's office, *we become the frog* and we are, as we have seen, afraid, oh, so afraid, that we shall never jump at all, but instead we shall only emit a lowly, dastardly croak.

Letting the frog go is a metaphor for living our lives. It is frightening for most of us to let go. I remember a time in my own life when I was hanging on to unhealthy places of the past. I could not let loose. The fear of falling into an unknown abyss was too overwhelming, and I clung to the past even though I knew it was destructive to do so. One night during those dreadful times I dreamed I was hanging at the edge of a cliff by a single branch. In terror I looked down to the canyon floor thousands of feet below. As I hung there I realized I could never save myself. My hands, at last exhausted, began to slip. Finally I had to let go. But as I fell I suddenly felt free. I realized I could either relax and enjoy the fall or I could scream all the way down. In the falling I felt exhilarated beyond all expression, utterly free. At the risk of again mixing my metaphors—and why not—I am suggesting that we, the frog, jump over the cliff, that we trust the experience and enjoy the trip. Let it happen. Let go.

Jump!

Letting go: So now we are standing in front of our audience. How can we speak? How can we let go? The experience is similar to jumping the first time from the twelve-foot diving board at the local swimming pool. As you stand up there looking down, your stomach grows tight and your knees begin to quake. You want to turn nonchalantly around and go back—acting, of course, as if you have just forgotten something important. Instead, a wee voice inside urges you to jump. Letting go for the Magical Argument, releasing one's self without being tied to the notes, standing there naked, speaking out of the heart and not the head, speaking, not reading, is like that. *The Magical Argument is a leap into yourself.*

I have suggested to young lawyers that they actually experience the leap into the Magical Argument by first going to the local swimming pool and jumping from the high board. One of my students who couldn't swim actually learned not only how to dive, but, in the process, how to swim as well. Argument is like that. When he walked before a jury he envisioned himself standing on the high board about to jump. He felt his terror. As I had suggested to him, he spoke of his fear to the jury. He explained why the case was important to him, why he wanted to win, why he was afraid of losing. He was afraid for his client. But he was afraid for himself as well. Afraid because he cared. Afraid of the pain that he would suffer if he lost. He had jumped. He told me that after that the Magical Argument came bursting forth.

Another student of mine had dived competitively in college, so diving was old hat to him. "Well, go do something you are physically afraid to do," I suggested. The next time I saw him, he was aglow with this experience. He had jumped out of an airplane. He'd held back on opening the parachute until he was a few thousand feet above the ground, and the fall, he said, was glorious. He said he envisioned the same experience in his next argument to the jury. He spoke to the jury of his feelings, his fear, his love of justice. He said he could not remember the words he chose because he did not seem to be choosing them. He merely let them come as if in a free fall. And it was, he exclaimed, magical. Whether you jump from a high board or out of an airplane, or let loose before an audience, the experience is the same: facing fear, looking fear in the eye, and staring it down.

Every triumph is preceded by fear. Fear always initiates the act of breaking free. And why? What is the biological advantage of a trapped psyche? Breaking out, walking freely through the forest, leaving old trails for new ones always entails a certain quantum of risk. Might we not come face to face with the lurking enemy? Might we fail to measure up? Might we not be injured or killed? But both the forest and the enemy are within. Life entails risk. If it were otherwise, one could not bear to live it, for the risks of boredom, of being trapped within the self—the chick dying in the egg—of dying without having lived, are risks far greater than any that lurk in the forest.

That we should overcome our fear of a physical threat as a way of overcoming our fear of a nonphysical act, or vice versa, is nothing new. To overcome the fear of the actual crash of an airplane, pilots put themselves in simulators where they learn, in a nonthreatening environment, to deal effectively with the emergency. Cowboys ride simulated bucking bulls in barrooms.

Once in San Francisco, I saw a young woman with a shrunken leg dancing in the most crowded part of the airport. People had gathered to watch her. She nearly fell when she spun, but there was a grace, a dignity about her performance that gripped her audience. She and I boarded the same plane, and as we walked up the ramp I asked her about her dancing.

"I dance in public every chance I get," she said. "Sometimes I dance in the street. I need to dance. It's good for me." That is all she would say.

How to jump: Once again we stand before our audience. The *Others* wait for us to speak. Still we ask, how can we jump free? How can we speak? I say, turn inward. Feel the fear. Again, touch where it resides—yes, just above the solar plexus, that one glowing spot in painful spasm. Feel it, for there we can begin with something we know is *real*. And now can we jump?

Sometimes when I begin a speech, I look each member of the audience in the eyes. In a large group it sometimes takes a half a minute or more. The silence grows uncomfortable. The people stare back. I hear the nervous coughs. But something has happened between us. Without words, I have shared with them the same feelings I suffer. I have felt fear, and they, in turn, have felt its discomfort in the pressing silence in the room.

Finally I begin. "It is all right for us to feel uncomfortable as we launch our relationship. We do not know each other. We have no experience upon which to trust each other. Why shouldn't we feel uncomfortable? I wondered as I looked at you what you expect of me. What do you think of me? And as I look at you, you, too, must have wondered what I am thinking of you." I have jumped. "We are going to have a valuable time together." I have broken free.

Once I was speaking to a large group of lawyers in Philadelphia. I was introduced by the chairman of the meeting, but he had obviously made no effort to prepare his introduction. He got up and said, "Mr. Spence needs no introduction. I therefore give you Mr. Spence." An introduction is the bridge by which the speaker crosses over to the audience. Otherwise it is as if two strangers meet on the subway. It is hard for them to get a conversation going. The chairman's failure to introduce me to his audience also carried another message: that the speaker was not really important enough for him to have prepared an introduction. That hurt me, and it hurt me with the audience—it was as if he had said, "This guy really isn't worth introducing." And if the chairman of the meeting was not enthusiastic about the speaker, how could he expect his audience to be? At this point in the speech, I felt empty and flat. The Magical Argument would never come. I also felt angry, not afraid, for anger, the secondary emotion, always replaces primary emotions such as fear. I went with how I felt. I went with the anger. I walked to the podium and tapped into my feelings.

"Your chairman has told you that I need no introduction. I don't agree with him. I *do* need an introduction. I need the introduction in order that I can feel welcome. I need the introduction to get my juices flowing, and you need the introduction to get interested in what I am going to say. Now, considering that both you and I need a good introduction, and that I have had none at all, is there anyone in the audience who would care to come up to properly introduce me?"

A horrible silence followed. I waited. I looked over the stricken audience. No one stirred. Not a sound. Suddenly a large, muscular man got up, said nothing, and headed in long, quick strides toward the podium. I didn't know whether he was coming up to throttle me for my effrontery or what. He stepped in front of me and took over the lectern.

"Ladies and gentlemen," he began. "I would like to introduce to you a man I have admired all of my professional life. He is a man who for many years I have wanted to meet and to know better. Now he is here with us. This man . . ." He spoke of some of my better-known cases. He talked of my books he had read and how they had influenced him. When the introduction was over, the audience gave him a standing ovation. My own speech that followed was full of incredible life and excitement and energy, one of the best I ever made, and the man who introduced me later became one of my closest friends, and after that an associate in my law firm, all the result of both of us having jumped, of having taken the risk to break free.

To jump! To let loose! To break free! Perhaps you should give yourself permission to say the first thing that comes to your mind. I have said things like, "I wish I knew what you wanted from me. I wish you could see what I see up here—you all looking up at me, expecting me to say something entertaining, something insightful and magnificent. I think to myself, 'I can't say anything magnificent—I can't say anything that is even original.'"

Jumping at home: At home, breaking free is to express your feelings, but breaking free can never become a judgment of fault on the part of the *Other*. It's "I feel upset," not "You upset me." It's "I feel sort of cheated," not "You cheated me." Sometimes when I feel totally frustrated and helpless in a courtroom circumstance, perhaps when an angry judge takes after me or continuously sustains the opposing side's objections, I walk up to the bench and quietly begin to speak to His Honor. I do not say, "You are unfair," or, "You are being rude to me." I speak of my own feelings. I say, "Judge, *I* feel helpless. I don't know how to proceed. I wish I didn't feel so intimidated. I wish I didn't feel so ashamed." Magically, having faced my feelings, I no longer feel so intimidated or ashamed. At first the response of the judge may be even more caustic, but the issue is not the judge's feelings but my own, for it is I, not the judge, who must break free.

At home, if I can transcend my anger, I can win my argument. I say "transcend my anger" because anger, as we have already seen, is most often a replacement emotion, one that takes the place of fear or frustration or disappointment or a sense of loss or guilt or even loneliness. If I am angry, I need to ask why rather than express my anger. I may be angry because I feel unloved or ignored. What I should be saying at home is, "I feel lonely for you. I wish we could be closer. I need you. Oh, how I need you!" I shall speak more of this in Chapter 13.

Jumping and courage: The *ultimate courage* is the courage required of man to affirm himself, that is, to affirm his fear of being and his anxiety of nonbeing. Once we have done so, once we have given ourselves to the trip and have jumped, the Magical Argument will begin.

The overself: I have struggled with analogy and metaphor because the experience of the Magical Argument is not an intellectual one. Yet the only tool I have for its exposition is the black word printed linearly by machinery upon empty white paper. It is not easy to explain multidimensional magic on mere two-dimensional pages. Still, the Magical Argument does not abandon reason. There remains a conscious *overself* that acts as the control center, that hears the argument springing forth, that edits it and keeps it within bounds. The overself sets the margins and becomes the chaperon for the *heart zone*. Those many years ago when I delivered my first Magical Argument over my strewn papers, I was keenly aware of what I was saying although I was not consciously composing the argument. From time to time I made conscious decisions—how close to stand to the jury, which juror to speak to. The overself was vaguely aware of the passage of time and interceded to bring the argument to a close. But the argument was being fed and formed from the spring within, and orchestrated and delivered through a magical mechanism I had never before encountered and do not now fully understand today.

Struggle in the heart zone: The magic of the Magical Argument bursts forth from the same place in us in which the argument is *heard* by them, from the same place from which the decision of the *Other*, for or against our arguments, is always made. If our audience speaks and understands only English, we would be foolish to attempt a winning argument in Latin. Why then would we choose to speak to the *Other* with a different language from the language employed by the *Other* in making his decision? Why would we choose to speak to the *Other* in *head language* when the *Other's* decision is always made out of the *heart zone*?

Judges are said to make their decisions in accordance with the logic of the law. But I say that good judges like the rest of us, make their decisions from their *heart zones* first, after which they support their decisions with logic. In the same way, your boss, your neighbor, your customer will make their decisions out of their feelings even though they may support their decisions with reason and logic.

The argument the customer makes to his spouse (and to

himself) when he buys a new car is usually couched in terms of logic: "The old car was nickel-and-diming me to death. And it was unsafe for the family to drive in anymore." But the customer's decision to buy a new car is really motivated from the good *feeling* he experiences when he proudly drives his purchase home. We make decisions with our mates out of our feeling of love, or the good feeling that comes from doing the right thing. We feel right about giving or about rendering justice. Our decision to visit our old aunt may be based on the feeling of guilt that pains us when we realize we have sorely neglected her. Feelings of fear cause us to decide against dangerous or hurtful acts. All decisions are based on feeling. Although logic may be factored in, as, for instance, the logic of buying low and selling high, the decision to sell high after having bought low is based on the good feeling of having realized a profit, or the feeling of anticipating a greater profit when we decide not to sell. Decisions are always made out of the *heart zone*. As Pascal once commented, with reason, "The heart has its reasons which reason does not know."

Therein lies the great power of the Magical Argument, for it originates out of the *heart zone*, employs the language of the *heart zone*, and addresses the *Other's heart zone*. And although it sometimes argues with logic, although it sometimes urges fairness or pleads for justice, it always addresses the *feelings* of the other. And because the Magical Argument originates out of the *heart zone*, it always carries with it an energy, a rhythm, a sound, an indomitable power that is heard by the *Other's heart zone*.

AND SO: I have attempted to explain what I call the "Magical Argument." It is no more magic than the making of bread. The ingredients are all well known and understood—the flour, the milk, the oil, the sugar and salt and yeast. Yet when these common ingredients are mixed together and the bread rises, and thereafter the dough is kneaded and kneaded again, and then baked, a quite different product is retrieved from the oven. In the same way, when we have prepared our argument by mixing in the essential ingredients of fact and logic and commitment, when we have outlined it and reduced it yet again, when finally we have baked it in the heat of doubt and fear, what comes out will be quite wonderful, indeed, quite magical.

If you have never taken a step, it would be impossible for me to explain to you how to dance. I can only urge you—take the first step. Experience the courage to be! Again and again, I can only assure you that it is all right to be afraid, that facing your fear will free you, that facing your fear will permit you to jump and will set you free. I can only ask you to trust the idea of the Magical Argument. In the end I can only admonish you to trust yourself.

Do it!

Jump!

Jump!

12

The Unbeatable Power Argument

DELIVERING THE KNOCKOUT

THE LOCK: Same old lock—even though I've read these chapters, I still have doubts that I can get it all together.

THE KEY: Same key—same person—in the same hand—your hand. Let's begin by assuming the *power stance*. Listen up.

More about power. Preparing to take the *power stance:* The *power argument* is an argument so powerful in its structure, so compelling in its delivery that when we assume the *power stance* the argument cannot be defeated. The power argument need not fill the air with noise. It need not create pandemonium. It need not destroy the opponent. It can be quiet. Gentle. It can embrace love, not anger, understanding, not hate. It can employ ordinary language. The person delivering the argument need not emulate Martin Luther King Jr. or Churchill or Roosevelt. There is one compelling, overriding reason always to deliver the power argument: Losing is so painful.

Is losing a necessary part of our lives? I remember how losing felt. When I began to practice law, before I had become a prosecutor, and before I had tried any criminal cases at all, I lost civil case after civil case. Winning, when it came, was often an accident, a mystery. Winning was the prerogative of those who sat at the top of the legal totem pole where there was no permanent place reserved for me. No one offered help. I thought perhaps I was beyond helping. And, of course, when I lost, my clients also lost. I witnessed their disappointment, their pain, their unspoken accusation—I had taken their good and just cases and had lost. It was my fault. I felt like a fraud. I felt dumb and dull and desperate. The pain of losing felt as if a cold, blunt instrument had been driven through my heart. I felt as if I were bleeding slowly to death and no one could stop the bleeding. The pain of my continuous losses was so great. I nearly gave up the practice of law. That was before I had discovered the Magical Argument of which I have already written. In the years that followed, I learned the essential elements of the *power argument* as well. So shall we.

But before I had discovered and understood the ten essential elements of the power argument, I found myself wondering if there were reasons, yet unrevealed to me, that explained my continual losses. Obviously people weren't irresistibly drawn to me. Likely I was not as quick and clever as other lawyers. Maybe I lacked something I couldn't see in the mirror. One day, utterly lost and helpless to discover the reasons for my continuous defeats, I began to consider a simple question: *Is losing a necessary part of my life?* Is there some invisible scorekeeper who keeps tabs on one's losses, so that for every so many losses one earns an occasional win? Over and over the question returned: *Is losing a necessary part of my life?*

Assuming the role of the prey—giving permission to be beaten: If losing is not a necessary part of my life, then why do I lose? Who gives *permission* to my opponents to beat me? *Permission!* I remember as a child being whipped by the bully on the block every day, until one day being whipped was no longer an acceptable way of life. Once I withdrew *my permission* for the bully to beat me up I was no longer beatable. The *shift in the paradigm* from one who granted permission to be beaten to one who withheld such permission was the magic. The power did not arise out of bolstering myself with false courage. I was still afraid. I did not deny my august failings as a young lawyer. I recognized that I lacked many skills, indeed, most skills, of a competent trial lawyer. The power was in a single word: *permission.*

For there to be prey, the prey must agree to play the role of the prey. Once recognizing my power to give or withhold permission to be prey, I would never again give permission to my opponent to beat me, and I would never again give myself permission to play the role of the vanquished. It was that simple.

Something magically happened when I withdrew my permission to be beaten. How do I describe the changes that occurred? One does not see one's own expressions or observe the way one walks across the room. One cannot perceive accurately the effect one's energy imposes on others. I can only describe the phenomenon from the feedback of others. People perceived me differently. I looked different. I walked differently. The sound of my voice changed. I thought differently. My attitude, the attitude of a winner, became pervasive. I remember reassuring my client, "We will win. Do you know why? Because they have to kill me before they can get you, and they cannot kill me. They cannot kill me because I will never give them permission to kill me." The change permeated my being. An astounding metamorphosis occurred. I became a winner.

Casting the characters in life's drama—the law of the "*I-nucleus*": I am still surprised when I am told that as I walk into a room people can feel it. That is *their* perception. But also for me, the room, the territory, is mine, and I am at its nucleus. Everything in the universe begins with me—for me. Let us call this the law of the "I-nucleus." This law is also true for you.

Is this not a childish view? Are these not the blabberings of an infantile personality? For only a child sees the world in this ego-centric way. But I cherish my infantile view of the world. I fight against the adulthood demanded by the therapists. Maturity and death are cousins. I resist the cold, judgmental view of the psychic scientists who label us but do not understand us, who dissect us but do not love us, who can write a cold report in black and white about us, but cannot write a single feeling line about our joy, our love, our sorrow, or theirs.

I vow never to grow up, never to lose my childlike views, never to abandon the child who feels joy, never to give up the child's sublime spontaneity, his magical creativity, his innocence. I shall die (if ever) still clinging to the last of the child in me, for only with the awe and innocence of the child may one experience death.

Look out at the stars. View them from three hundred sixty degrees. Are you not in the center of the universe? Look at the occupants in the room. As you turn, are they not, from your perspective, also turning, with you as the axis? Admit it. Are you not at the nucleus of your universe?

If I do not see myself as the sovereign occupying the nucleus of my universe, then some other person or power occupies this position. And that *Other* occupies my center only because I have given them permission to do so. But, as we have already learned, it was *my power* that placed that person or power there. If one possesses the power to crown one self or at the center of our universe, ought we not give respect to such a person with such a power?

Let us think about this further.

More on permission: No one else, no other power, can seize my position at the center of my universe without my *permission*. Permission, then, becomes the word of power. I give permission, as do you, to whoever occupies my nucleus. I give permission to myself to occupy the center of my universe. I give permission to you or to my mentor or to God. But permission comes from me.

I have the power to give another permission to defeat me. I also have the power to grant myself permission to win. How, then, can we be defeated when permission to be defeated is vested solely in us? Is not the obvious answer that we can be defeated only by our giving permission to the *Other* to defeat us?

Truth and choice: *Truth* in the form of revelation is that which we already know, but have never heard in words before. Truth in the form of discovery is that which we already know but have never before confronted. Truth as judgment is the product of our experience. To a child with an abusive father, the truth is that men are monsters who can never be trusted. To a child with a loving father, men are the opposite.

From the standpoint of our belief system, truth is what we accept out of our history. Truth is what we accept as true. To some, God is truth. To some, Christ or Mohammed or Buddha is truth. To some, quantum physics is truth, while to others it is merely an exercise unrelated to the real world. To some DNA is the omnipotent god that dictates our lives, while to others the structure of DNA is transcended by a universal intelligence. But what is scientifically true today may be scientifically rejected tomorrow. *We choose truth.* Therefore, when I tell you that the truth for me is that I occupy the center of my universe, I have merely told you I have made a *choice.* I can choose any dynamic, any paradigm, any fact, any condition as the truth—the truth for *me.* I do not endow my parents or a priest or a minister or a guru or the Bible with the power to decide what is true for me. For me, truth begins to reveal itself only in proportion to my ability to discard all that has heretofore been presented to me as true. I am the truth, as, indeed, are you. That is why you are at the center of your universe. Let me say it again: I would rather have a mind opened by wonder than one closed by belief.

Choosing our role: Think of it this way: There are two people in a room who are about to put on a play. One will play the part of the hero, who against all odds will win the contest. One will play the part of the victim who, after the same struggle, is unfairly defeated. You are one of the players. Which part will you play? *You have the choice.*

We were not all born with sensuous bodies and magnetic personalities. We are who we are. Yet I remember a small dog in the neighborhood. It was a mutt with crooked front legs. It was not nearly as large or powerful as many of the other dogs. Yet it was *the* dog on the block. It dominated. The block belonged to this crooked-legged cur. The other dogs occupied the territory only at his sufferance. We, too, can cast ourselves in the role of the winner, the loser, the hero, the victim, the insightful, the jerk. I am not speaking of conceit. I am speaking of choice.

The arrogance of power: One must be cautious in assuming such power as I have suggested. It is a very great power, indeed. Do we not understand that by possessing such power we can easily slip over the fine line into arrogance? Unaccustomed to the heady experience of feeling our power, we can easily abandon humility. That one occupies the center of one's universe does not preclude humility. One must remember that. One occupies the center of one's own universe only because one has made the choice, not out of arrogance, but out of truth. Truth is never arrogant.

Trying and winning: I warn you, a winning stance is never achieved by *trying*. I hear some say, "I will try as hard as I can." Trying is for losers. Trying implies the possibility of losing. I will *try* to win. I will *try* not to lose. If after trying they have lost, well, they *tried*, did they not? *Losers always try.* Winners never try. Winners only win.

I remember when a young buckaroo, who had just been thrown from his horse, dusted off his pants and, embarrassed, came limping up to the old cowboy who had witnessed the kid's humiliation.

"Why didn't ya ride 'em?" the old cowboy asked.

"I tried," the kid said.

"Ya tried?" the old boy replied. "Ya see that steer over there?"

As most know, steers are castrated bulls. Their fate is to grow fat and to be butchered.

"Well, ya put that steer in a herd of young heifers and what's he gonna do? He's gonna try. That's all. Steers try. You ain't no steer, kid. Now go ride that horse." And the kid did.

Argument and war: The trial of a case in court is war. The casualties are apparent. People are sent to prison or freed as a result of the war. People die at the hands of the executioner. Others are saved as a result of the war. Children are taken from their parents. Fortunes are lost. The warriors, the lawyers, when defeated are pitied, when they win, they are respected.

The argument of a cause before a city council, or a board or any committee with power, is war. As a result of the war, the use of land will change. An airport will cover the fields and destroy the hedgerows where the meadowlarks nest. As a result of the war, the neighborhood will change. The corner house, where old Mr. Hardesty played his banjo to the children on a warm summer evening, will become a parking lot.

When decision-making bodies with power are gathered to hear our arguments, we must understand that the dynamic is one of war. And to the victor go the spoils. In such a contest, there is usually an opponent who speaks for power, most frequently the government, industry, money. Usually the odds are against us.

When I take on the United States in the defense of a client who is charged with the violation of a federal statute, the government has unlimited resources to wear me into submission. The prosecutor is not interested in justice. He is interested in a conviction. When we contest the city, ostensibly the organ of the people, we most often face the corporate oligarchy behind the city. We face money. The city is not interested in our lives. It is interested in its administration. When we come before the school board, most often we do not face those interested in the education of our children, but those who are interested in the maintenance of power. These contests are war. Any other paradigm is an illusion. It is not a mere contest, like athletes plunging down the hill on skis for the fastest time. It is not a dance in which the most graceful will be rewarded with a medal. *This is war.* Once we understand that the struggle is war, we can wage war and win.

The key to winning any war is to *control* the war. This does not mean I seek to control my opponent. I am not in charge of his decision-making processes. Although my strategies may indeed influence the decisions of my opponent, I do not dictate where or when he will attack or the method or time of his attack. I do not dictate his defense. But to win, one must always be in control—in control of one's own forces, one's own self, and, hence, of one's own war. We control the war when we are exquisitely in control of ourselves. I do not speak as one who brags or beats the chest or threatens. Bragging is a standard symptom of insecurity, and threatening is a universal display of weakness. The strong do not threaten. They need not.

Again, I am speaking of a simple mind-set. The mind-set does not make room for loss. The mind-set is one that extends permission, but only to win. The mind-set is alert, creative, aggressive. It is willing to take risks, but unwilling to act foolishly. The mind-set is willing to accept fear as a necessary step in the preparation for battle. If given a choice in which all potential consequences are equal, the choice will be to attack, for attacking establishes control. It is *our* attack, is it not? If there is no clear strategy available, the choice will likewise be to attack, for attacking will require the opponent to alter his position in relationship to the attack, which places us in control. The attack creates the opportunity for our more decisive and focused strategy. If the opponent has attacked, we may retreat, but we do not relinquish the initiative. We retreat only to take a better position for the counterattack.

Many lawyers are afraid to ask the telling question, to make the definitive statement in court, to attack, for fear the opponent will respond in some way. "What if he objects?" the lawyer asks me. "What then?" He is, of course, afraid that the judge will sustain his opponent's objections, that he may even be admonished by the judge and suffer embarrassment in front of the jury—that the jury will hold him in disfavor.

But whenever my opponent objects to my attack, he sets in motion a dynamic that will only lead to my victory. I will respond to his objections, or let them pass as I choose. I will reveal his unfairness. I will show that he is attempting to hide facts from the jury. When he objects, he takes the risk of a new attack from me. When he objects, his position is not well calculated, for he has not had time to analyze his objections carefully. His objections may be overruled. His objections may spotlight his weakness. If his objections are sustained, the judge's bias may become apparent to the jurors, who decide that the judge is unfair. Whenever someone responds to my attack with objections, that is, when they are willing to engage me, they take the risk of making serious strategic errors, of opening up their vulnerable places.

Therefore, when we refuse to take the initiative because we are afraid that our opponent will respond, that is, when we are afraid the opponent will engage us, we operate in a safety zone. But we can do no damage to the opponent in the safety zone. Operating well back from the line and delivering the margin of safety to the opponent is a common cause of loss. In the end, we lose the war because we are unwilling to win.

When does one attack? Sun Tzu, in *The Art of War,* declares, "Invincibility lies in the defense; the possibility of victory in the attack. One defends when his strength is inadequate; he attacks when it is abundant. The experts in defense conceal themselves as under the ninefold earth; those skilled in attack move as from above the ninefold heavens. Thus they are capable both of protecting themselves and of gaining a complete victory."

When in doubt, take the initiative, release the attack, institute the offensive. Such is the best strategy. And let our attack be relentless. The relentless attack creates invincibility. When a small boy and a bully meet, it is better for the small boy to strike first. He will get up and attack again. When he is knocked down again, he will get up and again he will attack. When he is knocked down, he will get up, over and over, until at last he will win. Nothing in the world is as fearsome as a bloody, battered opponent who will never surrender.

When attacking is the wrong strategy: I have spoken of the strategy of control, of the strategy of attack. I am speaking of strategies in war. Although it may seem so, we are not at war with our loved ones or with our children. We cannot be at war with our friends and employers. I have, therefore, devoted separate chapters to the art of arguing at home and at work.

There are other times when we also must forego the attack. As we shall see, we cannot attack the person wearing the white hat. We must wait until our white-hatted adversary has been revealed as the villain who misappropriated his white hat. Before we launch our attack, the decision-maker—most often the jury, the city council, the school board—must see our opponent as wearing the black hat. Were we to attack before our adversary has been revealed as the true owner of the black hat, we would be attacking the decision-maker, because the decision-maker is always aligned with the wearer of the white hat. And, of course, we never attack the decision-maker.

As a consequence, we obviously do not attack a mourning mother. But if the mourning mother, under the gentle prodding of a good cross-examination, becomes an angry, vindictive shrew, we may then attack, but gently. We do not attack an overtly nice person until the nice person's story, again through a gentle cross-examination, takes on an air of apocrypha. We do not attack a weaker opponent, a child, any person obviously frightened, any person who, for any variety of reasons, is unable to defend.

That we attack does not necessarily mean we attack the *persons* representing the other side. We may attack their case. We may attack their view of justice. We may attack the truth of their witnesses. We may attack motives. But we do not attack them, except when it appears, frequently from our cross-examination, that they have been untruthful in their testimony. Then it is often better that our attack reveal our sadness rather than our anger that they are unable to tell the truth. And the attack must always be fair. *Fairness is the tiny voice that thunders from behind every argument.*

Arguing when our side wears the black hat: One who commits a heinous crime is hard to care about. But we must make the decision-maker care about our client, about our errant son, about our daughter who has stepped over the line in some unfortunate way. The crime, the wrongdoing, whatever it is, becomes the *bare facts*. We, and the rest of the world, most often judge those who are charged with wrongdoing merely on the *bare facts*. We judge the man charged with murder on the bare fact that he killed. We do not ask why. We judge one who has been charged with a rape or with child abuse or with any scandal on the bare facts of the charge. We do not ask if the charge is true.

But there is no such thing as a set of "bare facts" that tell the whole story. Two worlds *always* exist: one is the world that is apparent, the one we see, the bare facts; the other is the world we do not see, a world that is personal, sometimes secret, the world in which the respondent lives and acts. In defending the actions of one who wears the black hat, we must discover that world, understand it and reveal it.

I once defended a Hispanic man from Rawlins, Wyoming, Joe

Esquibel, who was charged with murdering his white wife. On the "bare facts" there was no defense. He shot his wife between the eyes in the presence of two of his children, several welfare workers, and a deputy sheriff who had drawn his gun. The "bare facts" provided an open and shut case of first-degree murder. The prosecutor sought the death penalty.

If we were concerned with only the "bare facts," in most cases we would have nothing to try. But mitigating facts always lie beneath the bare facts. In every case they lie there waiting to be discovered and presented. That is why Americans cherish the presumption of innocence. Citizens cannot be convicted on "bare facts." They can be convicted only after the jury has heard the whole story.

Let me show you what I mean. The following excerpt reveals but one day in the life of my client Joe Esquibel. These are among the secret facts behind the "bare facts," as I reported them in *Of Murder and Madness*, a book that chronicled the murder as well as my defense of Esquibel.

A distant yard light shone on the face of the kid sitting in the corner of the boxcar, fat-faced little kid, big brown eyes as wide as dollars, scared, shinning in the dark, his black hair stubbing out all over, making him look like a little animal who needed to have his hair licked down smooth. Kid looked crazy. But he was mostly dirty and afraid of the dark. The light shining into the boxcar occasionally caught the naked white ascending ass of a man, and there were the noises, like animals fighting, panting noises, and the groans of animals struggling. The trainman gave the woman a dollar. Enough for a boxcar woman.

The woman, of course, was Joe's mother. The scene depicts his earliest memory. By the time the jury got the case, they knew every facet of Joe's life, his degradation, his humiliation, his wretched pain, mostly inflicted on an innocent child by an unjust, insensitive system in that small railroad town. By the time the jury passed judgment on Joe, they had no choice but to see him *from inside his hide*. They came to care about him, and, in the end, acquitted him of the murder. The defense, of course, was insanity.

When our side of the case wears the black hat, we must always *crawl inside the hide* of the person accused. There is always wretchedness there. There are always miserable, pitiable pain and confusion and sorrow. There are always the scars of injustice, the deep slashes of abuse across the soul, the evil mangling of the mind of the once innocent. It is too easy to point and accuse and to hate on the "bare facts." To do so relieves us of the responsibility of understanding. We would not punish a child for crying out, even striking out, against the power of a father who has brutally beaten the child. But we refuse to hear the child, now a man, still crying out when he flays against another power, a power against which he feels equally helpless—a power that may be equally cruel.

Always I hear the self-righteous, the arrogant, the mighty, the haughty, the privileged, the lucky decrying even the smallest of our gifts—the gift of human understanding. I hear their hateful preachments against their fellow man, their callous judgments. "They did wrong. Punish them!"

Punishment! Ah, yes, punish them! Born with less fortunate genes, some are punished. Born into poverty, they are punished. Born into an environment of filth and disease, they are punished. Born into neighborhoods of crime and hate, they are punished. Born to a twelve-year-old girl cook on crack, they are punished. Judged and then banished as unworthy to participate in the fruits of the system, they are punished. Deprived of an education, they are punished. Deprived of opportunity, they are punished. Deprived of simple human respect, they are punished. Most have done no wrong, but they are punished. And those who judge them from their lofty places now look down on them with hate, with spite, with fear. Those who judge them shake their haughty heads adorned with crowns of good fortune, and with disdain and scorn demand that they be further punished. Punish them!

We cannot permit those who must wear the black hat to be judged, not ever, on the "bare facts." We must crawl inside their hides, and from that dark and frightening place shout to the world what we see.

Revealing the liar: When our opponent presents what we believe to be a nontruth, do we call him a liar? To call another a liar is seen by most as bad manners. People do not like to hear someone called a liar. When one points a long finger at another and calls him a liar, one reveals a part of oneself that is equally ignoble. Yet, as the old saw goes, a man must sometimes call a spade a spade. In the Karen Silkwood case I dealt with the issue in this way:

I have been taught from the time I was a little boy in Sunday school that you should never call anybody a "liar" even if he is one. I do not like people to be called liars. We use all kinds of words to keep from saying the word. I have even used a fancy word for it, like "this is the worst *mendacity* I have ever heard." The word *misrepresentation* is also a word that lawyers use in place of the word *lie*. But, if I am going to demand in this case that we speak the truth, the plain old truth in ordinary English, if we are to demand that the nuclear industry tell the truth—and I ask you to make them speak the truth—then I, too, had better start speaking in ordinary English—as Dr. Gofman did. He called this "the big lie." He said this was a "license to murder." And so, following his guide, I'm going to call it, in plain old three-letter English, what it is: "The big lie." . . .

But note, the attack is on the issue, on the argument of the nuclear industry. The attack is not against the lawyer who represented the defendant in the case.

THE LOCK: I need something more concrete. Give me rules. Give me a formula. This is who I am—a formula person.

THE KEY: All right. Here are the ten elements that make up the *great power argument.*

1. *Prepare. Prepare until we have become the argument.*

Prepare until you know every scale on the hide of the fish.

Having prepared, next understand that good preparation is like writing a script for a screenplay. Proper preparation requires one to tell the story and to assign roles to the parties. Cast your side as the good guys, as the side that is unjustly accused, wrongly despised, gravely misunderstood. Cast your side as the underdog. And, when those for whom we argue cannot wear the white hat, argue their case from *inside their hides*.

2. *Open the Other to receive your argument.* You have already learned how: empower the other to receive or reject your argument.

3. *Give the argument in the form of story.* As we have seen, we are genetic storytellers and listeners to stories. Remember, fables, allegories, and parables are the traditional tools of successful argument. Every movie, every soap, every sitcom, most lyrics in popular songs, all operas and plays, most successful television commercials are in story form. So do not forget what you have learned already: jurors, the boss, the family, the *Other* are conditioned to listen to stories.

4. *Tell the truth.* With ordinary words you have learned the incredible power of credibility. Being who you are is powerful. Saying how you feel is powerful. To be open and real and afraid, if you are afraid, is powerful. The power argument begins and ends by telling the truth. Truth is power.

5. *Tell the* Other *what you want.* If you are arguing before a jury for money, ask for money. If you leave the *Other* to guess what you want, their guessing may be wrong, and guessing spoils your credibility.

Remember the power of justice. Jurors will circumvent the law to mete out justice. People will break the law to obtain justice. People will die in wars to win it. People can live without food or shelter or love. This is a species that can bear every kind and character of pain except one pain—the pain of injustice. Discover the natural justice of your argument and ask for it—demand it.

6. *Avoid sarcasm, scorn, and ridicule. Use humor cautiously.* Hold back insult. No one admires the cynic, the scoffer, the mocker, the small, and the petty. Giving respect to one's opponent elevates us. Those who insult and slight do so from low places.

Remember: Respect is reciprocal.

The employment of humor can be the most devastating of all weapons in an argument. Humor is omnipotent when it reveals the truth. But beware: attempting to be funny and failing is one of the most dangerous of all strategies.

7. *Logic is power.* If logic is on your side, ride it—ride it all the way. If logic is not on your side, if logic leads to an unjust result,

it will have no power. As Samuel Butler said, "Logic is like the sword—those who appeal to it shall perish by it."

Logic does not always lead to truth—or justice. Logic defeats spontaneity. Logic is often dull and is more comfortable with the dead, for it is often without spirit.

Do not give up creativity for logic. However, the creative mind will soon see that creativity is often served by logic.

8. *Action and winning are brothers.* The worst of head-on attacks is often better than the most sophisticated defense. Never permit your opponent to take control. Do not defend when you can attack. Counterpunching is for boxers, and counterpunchers most often lose. The great champions of the world take control. The great generals attack first, and attack again. Take the initiative. Do *something.* But with those we love, the best attack is often to attack with love, and, as we shall see, winning is often accomplished by the art of losing.

9. *Admit at the outset the weak points in your argument.* You can expose your weaknesses in a better light than your opponent, who will expose them in the darkest possible way. An honest admission, having come from you, not only endows you with credibility, it also leaves your opponent with nothing to say except what you have already admitted.

10. *Understand your power. Give yourself permission—only to win.* But remember, arrogance, insolence, and stupidity are close relatives.

Take the winning stance. Turn on the Magical Argument. Open up and let the magic out. Trust it. Take the risk. Jump.

And how do we get this all together? Let us think about it in this way: Suppose you have never seen an automobile before. One day you are shown one. You are told this is a machine that weighs more than two tons. It has the capacity to hurl itself down a road in excess of sixty miles per hour creating hundreds of thousands of foot-pounds of energy. Suppose you are told that you will be required to drive this machine down a narrow roadway at sixty miles an hour and that oncoming like machines will be speeding at you at a similar speed. You are told that if you let the steering wheel veer to the left but an inch, and hold it there for more than a second, two at the most, your vehicle will cross over the line and strike, head-on, the oncoming vehicles. In such a head-on crash the likely result will be the death of all occupants in all cars. You are advised that some who drive these automobiles at the very moment you are also driving will be blind drunk, some nearly blind, some blind and drunk, some inexperienced, some aged, quite a few will be crazy, countless will exhibit the mental capacity of a demented slug, some will be asleep, some will be awake but sleeping, some will be ill, and most can, at any moment, be guilty of such negligence that a Sherman tank would be at risk. Under such circumstances, would you not conclude that to get into a car and drive it on any highway would exhibit the approximate intellect of a multilobular water organism?

What interests me here is the *mind-set* that permits us to overcome these seemingly insurmountable odds and to safely drive our cars to work every morning and home again every night. We do not consider the apparently overwhelming probabilities that we and everyone else on the highway will wreck. When we decide in the morning to drive to work it does not occur to us that we cannot get to work safely. The possibility of impending injury or death is simply not factored in. We will get to work. We will undertake that goal and win. We do not cower in fear as we enter the automobile. We do not tense up and clutch the steering wheel as if driving to our doom. We make no other alternative available to ourselves except to drive easily, successfully to our destination.

The other alternatives to safe driving are eliminated from our assessment because we have the experience and skill. We have a long history of driving that reduces the risk so that it is seen as minimal. Yet we know the risk is real. We know the facts I have outlined above are true. Still, none of us could drive if we reacted to the potential dangers of driving and as a consequence froze at the wheel. Although we are aware of the underlying dangers, our mind-set assumes no other result but a safe trip.

Taking on the *power* mind-set: How do we accomplish such a winning, *power* state of mind? We have already trained and prepared to accomplish this feat. We have taken driving lessons to begin with. We have driven thousands of miles. We have had a close call or two, perhaps a wreck. We have learned from these experiences. However, there comes a time when we feel in control. At that moment the act of driving the car is no longer an act of pure madness.

So it is in making the power argument. We have prepared. We know our case, our argument. We know it so well that its presentation will become as automatic as driving. We have learned and understand the elements of argument in the same fashion that we have learned to steer or shift or brake our cars. We know the rules of argument and we will follow them in the same way that we obey the rules of the road. We have learned to analyze the traffic ahead and to create a strategy that will take us safely through our journey. So, too, will we begin to analyze the arguments we make before we make them.

On the road, as well as in our arguments, a cast of characters exists. We are the heroes in the highway drama—the good guys. If you don't believe me, see how we react when someone cuts in front of us too closely. In our universe, the only cars on the road that have relevance to us are those that *we* are encountering. We are at the center of our universe. We give permission to no one to run into us. We give ourselves permission only to win by achieving our destination safely. No other alternative exists. And we win. We win every day. That we drive safely many hundreds of thousand of miles is nothing short of miraculous. Yet the miracle is but the result of mind-set. So, too, with making the power argument.

The making of a power argument: Let us see if we can compose a power argument together. Suppose we find ourselves arguing before the school board for the reinstatement of our son Jimmy after he has been expelled from school for misconduct.

When ours is the black hat: The facts were these: The boy was causing a disturbance in the back of the room, talking to Sally and laughing while the teacher, Mr. Lamb, was attempting to lecture. The teacher stopped the lecture and asked Jimmy to come to the front of the class. He obeyed. When he got there he stood embarrassed, waiting for the teacher to say something. The teacher said nothing. Still Jimmy stood there. Still Mr. Lamb said nothing. Finally Mr. Lamb said, "Now, you have been wanting to talk so much, why don't you tell us what you were talking to Sally about."

The boy, his hands in his pockets and an embarrassed grin on his face, didn't answer. He didn't know what to say. He'd been talking to Sally about a date.

"Tell us," Mr. Lamb insisted. "What were you talking about?"

"Nothing," Jimmy said.

"Well," Mr. Lamb continued, "it must have been a good deal more important than today's lesson or you wouldn't have disturbed us. So tell us, what was so important that you were talking about?"

"Nothing," Jimmy said again.

"We can't accept that for an answer," Mr. Lamb said. "You have brought us to this place and you can now tell us what it was that you were talking about with Sally."

Still the boy said nothing.

"Well?" the teacher said, "Speak up. We're all waiting." Now you could hear the snickers.

No answer.

"What did you say to Sally?" Mr. Lamb shouted.

Finally Jimmy blurted out, sotto voce, "It is none of your business what I said to her."

Mr. Lamb's voice grew stronger. "When you disturb an entire class it becomes all of our business. We are entitled to know if what you said was more important than the day's lesson."

"It was more important to me," the kid said, with growing defiance.

"All right, let's hear it."

"No," the boy said. His face was crimson. "It was between me and her."

"Well, maybe we will have to bring Sally up here too. Shall I call Sally up here?" Sally is slumped down at her desk as low as she can get.

"Leave her alone," the kid said. "It wasn't her fault."

"Come up here, Sally," Mr. Lamb said. "If he won't tell us what he said, maybe you will."

"You leave her alone," Jimmy said.

"Come up here, Sally."

"I said, leave her alone."

"Sally. Get up here this minute," Mr. Lamb demanded. Sally got up.

At this point Jimmy said, "You go to hell," and walked out of the class.

Jimmy did not come back to school for a week and refused to apologize to the teacher. With no other choice, the principal expelled him. Under the school's rules he could be reinstated only if the board, for good cause, agreed to reinstate him. At last, the heat of the thing having cooled, Jimmy wanted to apologize and go back to school. He wanted to get on with his life.

The casting of the characters in this drama must be carefully considered. We cannot cast the school board's faithful teacher in the role of the villain or the board, the ultimate decision-maker, will throw its protective cloak around the teacher and reject the student's appeal. Although we traditionally want to wear the white hat, we must recognize that the school board and its teacher have already appropriated this role.

Jimmy really had no choice. But his conduct left the teacher with no ready choice either. When the boy told the teacher to go to hell and walked out of the room, the teacher's position of power in the classroom was at stake. An apology or expulsion was the only course that could follow. And when the boy refused to apologize, he stripped the school of any choice but to suspend him.

Who should we cast in the role of the villain? *Circumstance* is the villain, is it not? Circumstance would dictate this same result in every case in which a similarly competent and authoritative teacher came in conflict with a similarly proud and sensitive student. Both teacher and student are victims of *circumstance*. Since we cannot be cast in the role of the hero because the white hat has already been taken by the teacher, we cast ourselves, *along with the teacher*, as victims of *circumstance*, thereby hoping to find room for ourselves under the broad white brim of the teacher's white hat.

All power arguments should begin from a position of power. By power, as I use it here, I mean the argument must begin from a position that generates acceptance or approval. We must be right, or justice must be on our side, or we must be the fighting underdog seeking redemption, or we must be the victim who struggles, smiling through our tears. We must evoke admiration, at least respect, at least understanding, at least sympathy—the latter being the weakest of the power positions. (I often say to a jury, "Do not give my client sympathy. He does not want sympathy. He asks for your *understanding*. He asks for *justice*—not sympathy.")

Therefore, we might begin the argument for Jimmy's reinstatement as follows:

"Honorable members of the Board,

(Now in a conversational tone) "When you go home tonight, no one will tell you you have done right. No one will give you any public acknowledgment for having saved a boy. No one will reward you for your caring and your wisdom. But I thank you now. This is a model board and you have intelligent, skilled, and caring teachers. Mr. Lamb is among the best of them."

(In a few beginning words we have opened the school board to our argument. Although the words are patently complimentary, perhaps even patronizing, they set a friendly tone. Next we have aligned ourselves with power—theirs. At this point the board members' silent sighs likely express their relief that there is to be no serious confrontation. Already the argument is well on its way to being won. We won before we began the argument by analyzing who the cast of characters would be and why. Think where we would be if the argument had started in this fashion:

"Well, you all know why I am here tonight. Jimmy was railroaded out of school by one of your know-it-all, power-hungry teachers, who had him kicked out because Jimmy wouldn't get up in front of the class and spill his guts.")

Now our argument continues:

"I am Jimmy's father. I have come here tonight to ask you to give my son another chance. I pray that when we leave here tonight Jimmy will be one of your students again. *(Being up-front in what we want.)* Jimmy is a good boy. I believe that Mr. Lamb would tell you so. The question then is, how did this horrible mistake come about? How were two good people like Jimmy and Mr. Lamb drawn into such an affray? *(We are now trying to share Mr. Lamb's white hat.)* The answer is that neither Mr. Lamb nor Jimmy are the villains here. Circumstance is.

"You, of course, know the facts. We merely need to review them briefly to see how circumstance became the real villain. Jimmy was at fault. But perhaps we could understand. Jimmy wanted a date for the movie with Sally. This shouldn't have occurred in class. But they are teenagers. Have any of us forgotten?" *(The question elicits further understanding and perhaps a quiet chuckle.)*

"But Mr. Lamb was entitled to the class's undivided attention, including Jimmy's, was he not? And what greater distraction can there be than a talking, laughing teenager in the back of the room while one is trying to lecture? I thought it proper that Mr. Lamb should call Jimmy to the front of the class, if for no other reason than to embarrass him slightly as punishment, as well as to set an example for the rest of the students. Children cannot learn in an atmosphere of pandemonium." *(The argument to this point is open, frank, reasonable, and truthful. It has credibility. The argument further takes the position of Mr. Lamb, thus depriving the board of that position. The board will continue to listen with approbation if we get to the point very soon now.)*

"But circumstance did intervene. Jimmy, because of the circumstance of his tête-á-tête with Sally, could not, without humiliation, tell Mr. Lamb what they were talking about, and he could not betray the confidences that existed between him and Sally. On the other hand, Mr. Lamb, the teacher, was entitled to be respected and to be obeyed. He had, under the circumstance, no choice but to insist that his command be obeyed. Jimmy could not obey him. Circumstance was the villain. I believe that you could put a hundred good teachers in Mr. Lamb's shoes facing a hundred proud, but misbehaving, boys under these circumstances, and the result would be the same in all hundred cases. No teacher could back down. No boy worth his salt would betray his friend."

(The principal thrust of the argument has now been made. "Circumstance was at fault." There are no winners or losers. It was just one of those unfortunate things that sometimes happens. How much better this argument than another possible scenario:

"But wasn't Jimmy talking? Wasn't he causing a disturbance?" one of the board members asks.

"Yes, he was, but he wasn't causing much of a disturbance. Only a power-hungry dictator like Lamb would kick a kid out of school for whispering to his girlfriend."

Under this circumstance the argument between the board members and Jimmy's father is just beginning and will grow more heated when the board member responds, "You throw a student out when a student tells a teacher to 'go to hell' and walks out of the classroom. I'll guarantee you that!" But when we admit fault simply and openly at the beginning, the argument is over.)

Now the argument comes to its close:

"What I want for Jimmy is an opportunity for him to tell Mr. Lamb how very sorry he is. He didn't go back to school for a week because he was too embarrassed over his misbehavior to face Mr.

Lamb, whom he respects very much. He was wrong, and he knows it. He has learned his lesson. He will be a model student, one you can be very proud of. And so I say, on behalf of Jimmy, let him come face to face with the man he respects so much. Let Jimmy make this right. Let Jimmy learn and grow from this. Give Jimmy another chance. You won't be sorry."

This close openly empowers the board. It beseeches power. It is not arrogant. It permits the board to do what the speaker has asked for, and in doing so, the board can feel good about what it has done. We all want to feel good about what we do. The argument addresses the feelings of the board in a simple but direct way. The argument will win.

Compare this close to another possible close the board might have heard.

"This whole thing has been unfair to Jimmy. If you were in his shoes, you would have told Mr. Lamb to go to hell too. And why should he come back to school? To be further embarrassed in front of the whole class? I think Mr. Lamb owes Jimmy an apology. The principal owes Jimmy an apology and this board, if it does not reinstate Jimmy, will owe him his education for the rest of his life. Mark my word!"

Where the teacher wears the black hat: But suppose the facts in the case were slightly different. Suppose when Jimmy said, "You go to hell," Mr. Lamb, in a fit of rage, attacked Jimmy, struck him in the face and bloodied his nose slightly. The issue here will probably be the teacher's job, not Jimmy's reinstatement into school.

Suppose we argue *for the teacher* under these unfortunate circumstances. Again let us cast the characters in this drama. Where does the power lie? With this set of facts the power position is now shifted. The teacher wears the black hat and Jimmy, although at fault himself, can wear the white hat. The power to decide, of course, still rests with the school board, but the emotional power, the power of empathy, is with Jimmy. He was attacked and injured. Mr. Lamb broke a cardinal rule that abhors the abuse of children and the use of violence.

The person who violates a firmly established social rule loses his power unless we can cause those with the power of decision to empathize with him and to care about him. But first, we have to care about Mr. Lamb ourselves. Unless we care we will be unable to cause anyone else to care.

Let us crawl into the hide of Mr. Lamb. Let us ask ourselves these questions: How is it to be a teacher and to daily suffer students who confront you? How it is to be challenged in front of an entire class? Isn't there a danger there? If the challenge is not immediately and firmly put down, the teacher can lose control of the class, can he not? How is it to have witnessed students physically attack and injure a teacher? There is a danger there too.

If we investigate, if we ask questions from Mr. Lamb's side of the case, we will discover that, as in many schools, a war was in progress—students against the school. It was an unfortunate war, but, like all wars, it created casualties.

Our questions will reveal that Mr. Lamb's reaction was too strong for the circumstance, but his reaction can be understood. He was challenged. He was confronted by open hostility. He was shown the ultimate disrespect. The teacher was wrong, but he was human.

Further questions might reveal that Mr. Lamb's brother or friend was beaten to death on the streets by a gang, and that gangs daily threaten the discipline and safety of the school. Mr. Lamb may have been exhausted from trying circumstances at home. Perhaps he was in serious financial difficulty. Perhaps his wife had threatened to leave him. Perhaps his child had been sick and the doctor bills were mounting and the creditors were screaming. Nothing screams louder and is more deaf than a creditor. If we look, we can almost always find some mitigating circumstance in a person's life that helps explain the person's conduct.

Mr. Lamb had been a respected teacher in the school district because he was tough. He was known for his fairness, but he gave no quarter to any student who threatened hostility or violence. In the end, this policy had proven the most successful in keeping the peace. Mr. Lamb, who had been strict but fair in the classroom, had been a model for the other teachers. His policy had been encouraged by the board.

Now that we have gone beyond the *bare facts*, now that we have viewed the case from inside the hide of Mr. Lamb, we will be better able to defend him. Perhaps we can even make Mr. Lamb a hero of sorts without making Jimmy the villain. Perhaps we can put Mr. Lamb on the side of power—the school board—and again make "circumstance" the villain. Remember, "circumstance" cannot argue back. "Circumstance" is unrepresented before the board.

Suppose we began Mr. Lamb's defense by concentrating on that part of the case that seems the strongest—Mr. Lamb's policy, which was not only lauded by the board but emulated throughout the school system. Several teachers in the past had swatted students. One had shaken a student in front of the class, and once a teacher actually punched a student who had called her an "ass-hole." These incidents were well known to the school board and the teachers alike, and tacit approval had been given. With this additional information we begin to think of a story that will illustrate this argument. There are many. Here is one.

"As I think of Mr. Lamb, I think of a story about a man who went to war. He had been commissioned a lieutenant. After many months of combat and under heavy enemy fire, he struck one of the soldiers in his command who had cursed him in response to his commands. Later the lieutenant found himself in front of a court-martial. His defense was, 'This was war. The soldier cursed me. I had to keep the ranks disciplined or, in the onslaught, we would all perish.' In war or peace we must possess our soldiers' respect, and if we cannot gain their respect except by striking them, perhaps we ought not lead. *(This passing remark disarms the opponent who would make the very observation we have made, but having made it first, there is little for the opponent to say.)*

"But this was a good lieutenant, a brave soldier. The lieutenant overreacted. *(Again, the admission that disarms.)* But the lieutenant had redeeming qualities. He was loyal, obedient, caring, and loved by good soldiers. *(Note: That he was "loved by good soldiers" implies what we cannot say in direct argument—that those who do not like our teacher are not "good soldiers." There is no ready response to this subliminal argument because we have not made the argument directly.)* The lieutenant was a model for the rest of his division, for although he was strict and stern, he was fair, and if he were severely punished for his conduct under the stress of war, it would greatly demoralize the rest of the division.

"A wise and caring court-martial understood that their lieutenant was not perfect. He was under extreme stress. He was entitled to be understood. To the same extent that the army expected him to treat his troops as human beings, so did the court-martial treat the lieutenant. They acknowledged that he did wrong. But the court-martial recognized his value to the army. They understood that the very characteristic that made him a good leader was also the characteristic that had gotten him into trouble. The board weighed his positive attributes against the one occasion of his overreaction under stress and dismissed the case with an appropriate reprimand to the lieutenant.

"We are not an army, of course, and we are not at war. *(Again this remark disarms. "We are not at war" permits the board to disagree.*

It is better for them to argue, even to themselves, that they are at war rather than for me to raise war as an excuse.) But we have before us a very human teacher, one who is the model for many of our better teachers in this district, one who has been held in high esteem by this board on several memorable occasions and who has many redeeming qualities. He is loyal to you. And as would be expected of him, he grieves over the trouble he has caused, the pain to Jimmy, and the distress he is putting you through. He will learn from this and be a better teacher." *(This acknowledgment of concern for Jimmy and loyalty to the board tends to eliminate the contest between Mr. Lamb and Jimmy as to who was right and puts Mr. Lamb on the side of the board.)*

The argument can now speed to its conclusion, in which the board will be asked to embrace its good and loyal teacher, to decry the circumstance, to permit both parties to learn from it, and to level, in the end, only an appropriate reprimand against Mr. Lamb. If the boy is to be reprimanded, that idea should be initiated by the board without any suggestion from Mr. Lamb's side of the case.

Both arguments, Jimmy's in the first example, and now Mr. Lamb's, arose out of crawling into their hides, for once *inside the hide* of the respondent we begin to care, and as we begin to care we also acquire the power to cause others to care. The power of empathy is nearly invincible.

AND SO: We have learned the ten elements of the great power argument. We have learned to take the power stance. We have learned that, when in doubt, attack. Yet, having learned to attack, we have also learned when we must not. We have learned to crawl inside the hide not only of our respondent, but of the *Other* as well. We have learned that love is power. And that caring is contagious.

With all of this knowledge, how to prepare, how to deliver, how to feel, how to be, we are ready to make the power argument that will win—every time.

PART III

Arguments in Love and War

13

Arguing in the Love Relationship

LOVE AND WAR

THE LOCK: If you don't stand up for your rights and for what you want, if you don't put your foot down, and put it down hard, they'll run you over like a Mack truck on a bunny rabbit. You have to fight to survive.

THE KEY: The magical irony of the argument in the love relationship is that to win, one must learn to lose.

Writing about how to win an argument at home is, some say, writing fiction. Arguing at home is a consummate skill—more, an exquisite art form. If you have mastered the art, your accomplishment exceeds that of those who have made grand fortunes or achieved everlasting fame. I know many a tycoon who has been a pitiful failure at the art of argument at home. I know many a star who cannot win the simplest argument at home. It is as if the thresholds to their homes emit some mysterious negative force that transforms powerful people into wooden mutes or babbling madmen.

I know lawyers as eloquent as Clarence Darrow who, as they step through the front door of their homes, mysteriously grow sullen and silent. I know women who maintain a steady, intelligent, well-balanced stance all day at work, but when they get home suddenly disintegrate into a schizoid stupor or explode into a psychotic rage. It is as if home is not a sanctuary but a war zone. It is as if the occupants of the house suffer from irreversible shell shock, that they are victims, as it were, of post-traumatic stress disorder.

Fail at home in the elusive art of argument and the love relationship will dry up like a poisoned poppy in the garden.

No one teaches us the techniques of successful relationships. No university offers courses on how to be, how to live, how to love, how to engage in successful relationships. There is no course entitled "Beginning Marriage, 101." Yet the love relationship at its apogee is that magical melding of the energies of two that fulfills the divine promise of the human potential. And at its low point, it is slavery, entrapment, hell. But both the best and the worst of love relationships begin with the *self*.

Creating the love relationship by *withholding the self*. How can we create a successful love relationship? We are told we must give *ourselves* to the other. But I say, never give the self away. The *self*, ah, that unique, unmatched, inimitable, immortal, supreme self! The *self*, yours, mine, the self that is different from all other selves in the history of the universe—that is the precious entity above all preciousness that we bring into the relationship. But do not give the self away.

Try to visualize this superlative self. Can you see it? Let it be something you can hold in your hand—a cup, perhaps, and within this one-of-a-kind cup is contained your spirit, the marvelous stuff of your personality—your kind of love, your brand of creativity, your unique experiences, your special wisdom, yes, your way to withdraw, to be angry, your insecurities, your fears, all of this is contained within your cup. Can you see the cup?

Suppose now that you enter the love relationship. You bring the cup of *self* into the relationship. But so does the *Other*. His or herself is as unique and incomparable as your own. To be sure, the *Other* could have choked the room with gold, but had the *Other* not brought in the *self* as well, the room would be empty. The *Other* would have brought nothing into the relationship, nothing at all.

But must the self, the entire cup and all its contents, become the price of admission into the relationship? Do we not understand that if the *Other* must give the self, then there can be no relationship? Do we not understand that when the *Other* has given the self, we are now joined with an empty person, a person without self, a person who has given the self away?

Whenever I can be heard, I declare that I cannot give the self to the *Other* as the price of admission into any relationship. I cannot give the self to my colleagues, my employer, my friends, or my clients as the price of acceptance. I will gladly take from my cup and give my love, my loyalty, my energy, my creativity, my devotion. But I cannot give the cup, for without the self no longer can we call up free will; no longer can we experience the magic of spontaneity; no longer can we enjoy the mystery, the eternal preciousness of self, for the self has been given away. It is gone.

The confusion arises when we fail to distinguish the giving of one's self from the giving of one's love, one's loyalty, one's creativity, or one's labor. The work slave, having given the self, has nothing to give that cannot be duplicated by a machine. The love slave, having given the self, has nothing to give that cannot also be duplicated by another love slave. Nothing remains. The cup is gone. The *Other* holds the cup in the *Other's* hand, and soon the cup will be empty. One begins to understand: the gift of one's self to the *Other* is a gift that is consumable and nonreplenishable.

The love relationship is something like a simple business partnership. The partners, being partners, do not own each other. They respect each other. They contribute their work, their caring, their loyalty, their creativity to the cause of the partnership. But they do not become one. If the will of one consumes the other, the partnership is destroyed so that what remains is only the dominant person and his menial, a master and a slave. The *Other* has become a thing that has been taken and in the process the partnership has been destroyed, for by definition a partnership must contain at least two independent functioning members.

How to lose by winning: Understanding that the nature of the love relationship, we also understand that all attempts to exert power over the *Other* are assaults on the relationship that put the relationship at risk, for when the self is diminished, so is the relationship diminished. To the extent that one wins this battle, to the extent that the *Other* submits, to that extent one has, paradoxically, lost.

The dynamic of the losing polemic might be plotted as follows:

"I want my way. You must give in. My will is the will of the relationship. My wish is the wish of the partnership."

"Very well. I will give in. I no longer have a will. Your will is my will."

"I am glad you see it my way."

"Yes, My Lord. I am at your command."

"If I am in command, I command that you speak to me."

"What is it you wish me to say, My Lord?"

"Say something!"

"Whatever you say, My Lord."

"Speak up!"

"Yes, My Lord."

"Why do you forsake me like this?"

"Whatever you wish, My Lord."

"My God, say something, do something! Stop this insufferable fawning. Be somebody! You make me feel alone. Don't you know how alone I am?"

"You have me, My Lord."

"I cannot feel you."

"I am you, My Lord."

Mastering the art of losing: Arguing in the love relationship, that is, obtaining what we *want* from our relationship, requires strategies. And strategies require the establishment of priorities. What is it we want *first* from our relationship?

First, we want to love and to be loved, do we not? We want to be happy; we want to be secure. We want to grow, to discover. The love relationship is the garden in which we plant, cultivate, and harvest the most precious of crops, ourselves, and in which the *Other* is provided the same rich soil from which to grow and to bloom. If this is what we want, only a fool would diminish its prodigious possibilities by attempting to control the relationship, for control and love, indeed, control and a successful relationship, are antithetical.

So she wants to go to the concert to hear the orchestra play Bartok, and he hates symphonies and, above all, he hates Bartok. But one with even the brains of a demented mongoose understands that by putting one's complaints in hibernation through two hours of Bartok, one will bring joy to the *Other,* and *that* is a pretty cheap price for joy, is it not? Where can you buy it cheaper? The foregoing notwithstanding, is it not better to have gone to the concert in the first place than to bring on a donnybrook over it, to suffuse the marriage with rancor and petulance that requires one to later buy oneself back into domestic felicity with pleas for forgiveness?

If the art of argument in the love relationship is the art of obtaining from the relationship what one *wants,* then an immutable psychic law comes into operation, a law as elementary and incontrovertible as "what goes up must come down." Simply put, one cannot obtain what one wants from a love relationship unless the

Other also obtains what the *Other* wants. When these opposing wants collide, the true art of argument must appear on the scene like Batman descending on his magical cape to preserve the domestic tranquillity and to invigorate it.

Having spent all but nine days of my adult life in marriage, over more than forty years in all, I can attest to the truth of the foregoing; and I have, accordingly, sought mightily to become an expert at the art of losing, to which I might add that the most satisfying losses I have experienced are those I have joyfully plotted. It seems to me one may say it quite simply as follows: *To excel in the art of domestic argument, one must master the art of losing.*

Control, the lurking alligator: We have already learned that control in battle, in war, is essential to winning. But control in the love relationship is a beast. It reminds me of a massive alligator lying just beneath the surface of the water with only its beady eyes showing. The eyes peer and peer, looking for prey to suddenly slash out at, to kill and to devour. Eventually the ubiquitous compulsion to control everything, anything whatever—except, of course, the compulsion itself—will invade even the most trivial issues. The alligator awaits. And when an issue is dropped into the pond, the alligator will strike.

Why must we always seek to control? We were thrown into this world with nothing but our naked rumps and our raw little feelings. Almost immediately we were taught to cover both. "Control yourself." "Don't you dare be angry." "Don't you dare cry." "Be quiet!" "Speak when you are spoken to." "Only cowards feel fear." As we have already observed, we were forced from the earliest age to repress our feelings. Have you ever seen a plant growing under a carelessly dropped board where, thereafter, no sun could reach it? Its life and growth were indeed repressed. Its pitiful little sprouts became pale and twisted like spaghetti. When we lift the board, we dare not leave the tender little twisted thing exposed, for it no longer possesses the strength to endure the sun.

So, also, repression sits upon the psyche. Underneath the feelings are contorted and twisted and desperate for release. We are afraid. Our creativity is smashed. We are starved for sunlight, for expression. Our personhood is diminished. Yet we smile the perpetual fatuous smiles. We fit fictive masks over our faces to hide secret throbbing places. We pretend. We must pretend. We dare not be who we are. We must not expose the tender plant, the twisted tender little thing. *We are lost under the board,* for we have never seen ourselves. We do not know who we are. We are desperate. And our need to control becomes pathological! Control! Ah, that neurotic, panicked, grasping need! Aggression and the symbiotic need to control are man's neurotic struggle against death. It is frightened man who fights death and in the process gives up his life.

Control as weapon: In the love relationship, the exercise of power as control is not an appropriate weapon. Love, in the love relationship, is the appropriate weapon—the only weapon. My entreaty is that the control-weapon, hanging in easy reach of both parties like the pearl-handled revolvers of the western gunfighter, be checked at the door. Leave the weapons outside. Take yourself unarmed into the relationship. You are still free to be who you are. You have but left the control-weapon outside, the weapon intended to do the *Other* in, that fearsome weapon of war, so that the *Other* is also free to be unintimidated in a relationship of love.

Can you see the parties otherwise? Can you see them going to bed at night, each with their six-guns strapped around their waists?

"Good night, darling. I love you," he says, lightly touching his weapon to see that it remains loose in the holster.

"Good night," she says. "Pleasant dreams." And as she rolls over she rests her thumb on the hammer.

Controlling by giving up control: People have a right to disagree; at times, a duty. People have a right to their ideas. Their differences identify them, glorify them. The issues in most marriages—where do we go on our vacation, how do we spend our money, and all the other issues—are not the issues at all. There is usually only that one ubiquitous, insidious issue: Who is going to *control*? When one examines it closely, control is at the marrow in nearly every argument in the love relationship.

As a younger man, my need to control was more urgent than it is today. It arose out of fear. When I do not trust the *Other*, when I am fearful that the *Other* will do me harm, when I am afraid to let go, when, at the bottom, I am insecure in myself, the need to control becomes crucial. As I became more consumed in my professional life, I found that I had neither the time nor the energy nor, alas, the ability to control everyone and everything.

I could entertain you with many piteous stories of my struggles to learn the simple truth I preach—that control and a successful marriage are antithetical. *But the day I finally realized I did not need to control Imaging, that, indeed, I ought not control her, that, in fact, I could not control her, and that if I could I would destroy the marriage, was the day our marriage began.*

If one can control the *Other*, one maintains a relationship only with one's self, a sort of masturbatory state that takes the place of the marriage. The *Other* becomes one's puppet, and puppeteers maintain relationships with only themselves. What a strange dynamic! When one is in control of the marriage, alas, there is no marriage.

I experienced no sudden epiphany concerning this. My understanding came slowly, seeped through that nearly impermeable barrier called the mind, and was lost and forgotten many times and learned all over again. My discovery was soaked in rage and drowned in tears, until one day I finally got it, mostly got it. But even today I sometimes fail. And the failures are more painful. Sometimes, to my mortification, I discover that after all these years, after all the painful learning, after all the solemn resolutions, after this steadfast devotion to forever defeat the need to control, I still occassionally succumb to the beast of the marriage, the control beast that will never, no, never, quite die.

Nagging as control: I used to marvel, I still do, that Imaging never nags. "How is it that you never nag at me?" I asked once. There was a lovely abundance to nag about. I mean the whole, ever-renewing list of insouciance—the flung clothes, the toilet seat, the cap to the toothpaste, the snoring, the incessant snoring that would rip the roof off the chicken house. She replied as if she were surprised. "How can anyone tell a full-grown man what to do?" What right, she was asking, do I have to *control* the life of another person? Early on she had learned that nagging is a neurotic attempt to control in its most unattractive form. Nagging is a right exclusively reserved for neurotic mothers and insecure fathers over helpless children.

The inability to wield control is often misinterpreted as inability or weakness. Giving up control is often confused with giving up. Failure to control is often misunderstood as failure. But control in marriage has nothing to do with ability or success or even manliness. Strangely, it is the opposite. Everything in the love relationship mysteriously works in opposites.

27,740 dinners: Let us imagine a relationship in which both parties have acquired black belts in verbal combat and both are earnest proponents of control. She says she is tired and wants to go to Jorge's for dinner. He says he is also tired and wants to stay at home. Obviously, one of the parties must lose, the truth of which introduces a basic proposition: Dinner tonight will be one of approximately 27,740 dinners an average person eats in a lifetime. If this were their last supper together, I predict there would be no fussing, no conflict, no control issue. It would all be as smooth as sweet cream. All would be smiles and love and tears and tenderness.

One could do worse than to consider every possible confrontation as if it were the last—the last drive home, the last opportunity to buy your loved one a dress, the last time you could take her to one of those god-awful concerts with stiffs in monkey suits screeching incoherent scores of Bartok while your pants sweat and your legs itch against the seat.

Considering then that there are approximately 27,740 lifetime dinners, only a magnificent idiot would jeopardize the marriage in order to exert control over where they will eat. But suppose the argument between these two black belts, like a boulder dumped into the cesspool, sinks to its lowest level of discontent:

HE: You always want to go out. Do you think we're made of money? I mean, I could buy enough groceries to feed us a week for what it will cost to go to Jorge's.

SHE: [*Tired, bedraggled, angry*] All you think about is money. You never think about me. All you love is the goddamned dollar. You didn't marry a dollar bill. You married a woman.

HE: I wish all it cost to eat at Jorge's was a goddamned dollar bill.

SHE: Well, I work all day the same as you. I make money the same as you. I am not your money machine. I don't work all day for the privilege of coming home and cooking your dinner.

HE: If I went along with everything you wanted to spend money on, we would have been broke a long time ago. You would have to work three jobs to pay for the things you want to buy. Why can't you just pull back a little? That's all I ask. Just pull back a little. Maybe we could get ahead.

SHE: Don't you blame me for spending all the money in this family, you asshole. [*With name-calling the argument descends to a lower level.*] I suppose I bought the new golf clubs. I suppose I went with the boys to Baja fishing. I suppose . . .

HE: Just a goddamned minute. Now we're getting to it. You have always hated it whenever I did anything that I wanted to do for myself. You hate it that I play golf and have a good time once in a while. You never got over that I went to Baja fishing instead of taking you to the fucking Virgin Islands on that cruise. And you're going to get even, aren't you? You're going to spend every penny both of us make until you get even. That's crazy! You are just plain crazy! [*He joins her at the new lower level.*]

SHE: Why you insufferable slob. Don't you call me crazy! You must have your head buried up your butt to your shoulder blades. You think *I'm* crazy? How about the time you told my mother she was a witch out of hell, and all she wanted you to do was take us to Jorge's for dinner. If that isn't crazy! You are the biggest penny-pinching, money-grabbing, dipshit who ever blew a fart over Georgia. [*Now comes the killing thrust.*] I hope you bleed to death from your hemorrhoids!

HE: You two-bit loudmouthed bitch, I've taken the last insult I'm going to take from you. [*He stomps out the door. He's been defeated.*]

SHE: Don't you ever come back! [*She's been defeated too. She screams the words, following him out. He slams the door in her face. She opens it again and hollers.*] I changed my mind. You can come back to pick up your clothes. The Salvation Army wouldn't take them.

[*He throws a stick of firewood the dog had dragged out on the lawn. And misses.*]

SHE: I'm going to call the police.

HE: Better not! They'll haul you in for being the ugliest bitch in the history of the world. [*He gets in what he thinks is the last word, and screeches off into the night.*]

[*By now the neighbors are looking out their windows. The dog is beginning to howl. The grass on the lawn has turned brown under the inferno. The sky is glowing purple.*]

Battlefields are for blood and war, for the wounded and dying, for stretchers and body bags. Home was not conceived as a battle-field. One does not win at home by having hurled the longest and vilest string of insults known to man. Sadly, more homes are de-stroyed by wrong arguments than by bombs, and more people are homeless in their homes than homeless on the streets.

The winner in the domestic argument is never the winner. How does a man who loves his weary wife come home and demand that she cook him something? As someone once quipped, "Home is a fifty-fifty proposition: the husband tells the wife what to do and the wife tells the husband where to go." The winning argument in the love relationship is most often the argument that was never made.

If the love relationship is, indeed, based on love, is it not clear that controlling is not loving?

Love, the winning issue: The husband in the example above be-lieved his wife was injudicious in her expenditures and would break them financially. He thought she was punishing him for having spent money on himself. Fearing and distrusting her, he needed to control her. The issue was not where to eat, but his fear and dis-trust. The wife, on the other hand, believed her husband was an insensitive, selfish hypocrite who had no respect for her. How could he spend the money he spent on himself and not be willing to take her out on an evening after she'd had an especially hard day at the office? Feeling unloved, unappreciated, and used, she needed to control him. Neither argument was based on what each wanted *for* the *Other*. Both arguments, soaked in the brine of past distrust and resentments, demanded control.

The issue in the melee above was not where the two should eat but how they might eat the heart out of the other. The goal was to smear the other across the emotional landscape in a dreadful verbal bloodbath. If love had been the issue, they would have been willing to eat with each other at a picnic held in the driveway.

Discover what the argument you are about to launch is really about. Is it about buying a new car or punishing for past extrava-gances? Is it about starting a new business or jealousy and inse-curity? *Love* in the loving relationship should always be the underlying issue. Most battles in the love relationship are not about the professed subject of the argument. The professed subject is most often the pretense for war. Without pretenses, wars would never be fought.

Is not the desire to provide the *Other's* wants a natural consequence of loving the *Other?* In a love relationship, does not providing the *Other* with his or her wants fulfill our own, and hence, by definition, we have won? When one loves the *Other*, what need is there to control? When one relinquishes the impulse to control, one has mastered the most important step in the fine art of losing, which, paradoxically, becomes the exquisite art of winning. Let us say it again: *To master the art of domestic argument, master the art of losing. To win, learn how to lose.*

Weeping as weapon: In the center of the hurricane comes the eye—the weeping. There are only two kinds of weeping: weeping that is meant to be heard and weeping that is not. Weeping that is not meant to be heard is a legitimate release of anguish or pain. Weeping that is meant to be heard may be yet another weapon used in the argument. Such weeping says, "Now you made me cry. Now I will make you feel guilty and suffer for what you have done to me. Look what you have done to me! I am crying. If you don't do what I want I may never stop. I may cry until the earth is flung from its orbit into the void, or at least until tomorrow morning." It is painful for most to witness crying. Perhaps we suffer a sort of primal fear that awakens the child, the memory of the first frightening sob of the mother.

The losing argument that wins: In the example above, two people began the evening wanting the same thing. They wanted a nice dinner and, ostensibly, to be with each other. But the only way this argument could have been won by either was for one of the parties to have mastered the elusive but divine *art of losing.*

The argument could as easily have gone in this fashion:

"Honey, I'm falling on my face. Could we go to Jorge's tonight?"

The husband might well look at his wife and, seeing the obvious signs of exhaustion, simply say, "Sure, honey. You must have had a hard one today." At this point his argument is already lost—*and won.*

His argument might, however, continue:

"But I'm kinda worried."

"Why?" The wife looks at her husband and listens.

"We're getting a little short this week." If the wife has the same skills as her husband and is equally committed to the relationship, she will trust that he is in fact worried. "I was wondering," he continues, "if I could take you to Taco Bell tonight (*innocent laughter*) and take you to Jorge's next week?" And when he sees that she is going to buy the compromise he adds, "And after we have a nice dinner at Jorge's we'll come home, and . . ." and he gives her that look.

"Right," she says with a look of her own she has resurrected from Lord knows where. And off they go to Taco Bell, and it's doubtful that they wait until next week to fulfill the concupiscent promise.

Modern psychologists are taken with the paradigm of the "win-win" solution. In marriage, the solutions are more a "lose-lose" solution out of which both parties win, for in the love configuration losing provides the gift, the gift that always returns.

Life on the crest of the moment: We live our lives on the crest of the moment. We usually do not have a chance to ruminate over our decisions before they are made. When she said she wanted to go to Jorge's for dinner, he could not say, "I'll take it under advisement and let you know next week." Right then it's either yes or no. It's a decision a minute. It's life on the crest of each wave as it is about to break on the shore. We usually do not have time to analyze all the unpredictable forces that will make up the outcome. Consequently, our immediate decisions, often out of impulse, often out of unconscious depths, may have long-lasting repercussions.

Assumptions on faith that win: Since we have no time in which to consider all the psychological data that might otherwise go into our decisions, since, indeed, we make our decisions on the spot, we must make certain assumptions, assumptions that are made on faith and that are usually safely made in any sound relationship. Assumptions that:

- the *Other* is trustworthy.
- the *Other* is telling us the truth—for them.
- the *Other* has no hidden agenda.
- the *Other* is not trying to do us in.

Having made such assumptions, we can make decisions that will serve the marriage on the crest of the wave. If you cannot make these assumptions in your love relationship, this discourse is inapplicable, and I can offer little or no insights except to suggest that you review the marriage, look into yourself, probably with the aid of counseling, and having done so, make those decisions that preempt the ones we deal with here.

"Getting with" as winning: I agree that marriages are not all giving, and that a book purporting to convey useful information about argument ought to say more about argument in marriage than the worn-out ideas of giving, of giving in, of giving up, perhaps, even, of giving out. But as we have seen, the strategy of every argument is tailored to reflect who the participants are and what the goal of the argument is. We do not argue to a judge or a jury in the same way we argue to our spouse. The difference in the argument, in part, is defined by the difference in the decision to be rendered. Let me explain:

In the case of a judge or a jury, the decision will be a *judgment of guilt or innocence* of the party for whom one argues. But in love relationships we should never empower each other to pass such judgments. We do not empower the *Other* to judge us as a "two-bit loudmouthed bitch" or "an insufferable slob." We do not empower the *Other* to adjudge us guilty. Instead, arguments in the love relationship are the vehicles by which the participants *get with* each other rather than by which they enter judgments *against* each other.

One day after Imaging and I were freshly married we set upon the task of picking the wallpaper for the living room. We could not agree. My taste and hers were at odds, like one who prefers apple cider and the other vinegar. That was, of course, when (according to Imaging) my taste was yet in its infancy—a matter I do not argue. As that may be, we had struggled, expressed our dislikes vehemently and loudly, and our likes passionately and with immutable finality.

"I like this one," she said.

"That one looks like a frozen section of a diseased liver."

"How can you say that? That is a classical pattern that goes back to the Venetians."

"The Venetians were inbred. They were also blind. They named blinds after the Venetians, remember? I like this one."

"I wouldn't hang that in hell if I were the devil."

And the arguments went on and grew more heated. Suddenly Imaging slammed the sample book shut. "There are two hundred samples in this book," she declared. "There are hundreds of books more where this one came from. I say that there are plenty of samples in the wallpaper books and that we should spend our energy finding the sample that suits us both instead of bickering over the ones we don't like."

And that's the way we settled it. Eventually we found one we both liked. The wallpaper book became our symbol of settling the myriad issues that arose from time to time in our marriage. "Well," she would say when we couldn't agree on the choice of a piece of furniture or the place to go on a vacation, "there're plenty of samples in the wallpaper book." And there were and there are.

But how about "Honey, I want to go with the boys on a fishing trip to Montana"? There aren't many samples in that wallpaper book, are there? There is either agreement that he go fishing or not. Already you can hear the usual power strategies that begin such arguments, strategies that, of course, won't work:

"I earn the goddamned money and I'll spend it any way I please." Or, "How come you're such a millstone? Jim's wife is happy that he gets to go. She says he deserves it."

Try *getting with*. Try *empowering* the *Other*:

"Honey, I'd like to go on a fishing trip with the boys. What do you think? They're going to leave Thursday and be gone a week. Great fishing on the Madison."

"I thought *we* were going to take a trip."

"How about in the fall during the leaves? I always wanted to take a trip with you to New England during the leaves."

"Good idea. I'll go see my mother while you're gone."

Dream on, some will say. This never happens except in fiction— poor fiction. But I say that such a dialogue, idealistic as it may sound, is born of a marriage peopled with mature members.

On the other hand, what if, after his suggestion that they take a trip together to New England in the fall, she says, "You always make promises that you never keep. This fall there'll be some excuse. There always is."

The *Other's* need to control is usually in proportion to our diminished credibility. But still I say, relinquish control. Empower the *Other*. Two are required for any struggle and when one with-draws, the struggle must end.

Perhaps, accordingly, he says, "You're right. Sometimes I don't keep my promises."

Perhaps she says, "Yes, and so that's one promise you don't need to make to me." Now what?

Again, I say, give control away. "Okay, honey," pleasantly.

"Okay what?" not so pleasantly.

"Okay, I shouldn't be making promises I don't keep. It must get pretty frustrating for you." The "It must get pretty frustrating for you" says, as we remember, "I understand you," or "I know how you feel." She's won again.

Permitting the *Other* to win eliminates the issue of control. The minute he rises up and says, "You're as full of crap as a Christmas goose, I always keep my promises," the argument is lost, and the marriage is on its way to some place south of purgatory. The minute he rises up, shakes his head like an arrogant little Shetland pony and asks the question of all fools that begins, "When did I ever . . . ?" an entire bibliography, probably in alphabetical order, of failed prom-ises with an index of exact times and places will descend upon him like an avalanche from hell.

But after he acknowledges her frustration about his broken prom-ises, suppose she says nothing more. Those are the dangerous junc-tures. The silence. The horrid, dreaded, impenetrable silences. She has won. The husband has admitted he failed to keep his promises, and she is willing to leave it at that. Now what?

Again, *get with*, and give up control. The next day, when things seem better, bring the matter up once more. "Honey, what do you think about my fishing trip with the boys? That was something we didn't settle yesterday." When she says, "I don't want to talk about it now, either," the reply might be, "Okay. But could you let me know when you want to talk about it? I have to let them know by tomorrow morning." Suppose she never brings the matter up again. She is exercising control, a sort of passive-aggressive control, if we must label it.

What if the time for decision arrives and she has refused to say another word concerning the issue? The conversation could go this way: "I'd like to talk about my trip. What do you think?"

She says, "I think you owe me a trip first." Now he must decide. Is she right? She could be, you know. Maybe he does owe her a trip. Maybe he's been with the boys a dozen times and, to her, his guileful promise is the last straw. When he arrives at such a juncture, it's time for him to *listen*. Perhaps he has given her reason to distrust him when he's been with the boys. Perhaps, because of her own life experiences, she is frightened to be alone. Perhaps she is simply so insecure she cannot let loose.

If he says, "Well, I'm going whether you like it or not, you are not going to control my life," he simply exacerbates whatever her desperate need to control is. Whatever the cause, he needs to know what it is and deal with it.

The last argument reflects a marriage between people who are not very mature, not very trusting. The parties are insecure, and the marriage is not an especially happy place to be. Perhaps the parties are trapped. No one likes traps. Remember: All creatures, including people, try to escape their traps. I can hear Imaging saying again, "What right do I have to tell a full-grown man whether he can go fishing or not? I'm not his mother." There being no traps, no permission being required, no games being played, no manipulations occurring, what is left is called freedom—freedom within the love relationship.

But freedom and responsibility are Siamese twins: Freedom also requires that we exercise our choices responsibly, for our decisions always affect the rights and happiness of the *Other* in the marriage. I am telling you nothing new. Marriages work like old Jack and Jim, my grandpa's mules, who, harnessed together, felt the jerk and the tug of the other when they were not pulling as a team. I've seen old Jack fall to his knees when he was pulling in one direction and Jim gave a powerful lurch in the other.

What if, in giving up control, we surrender our freedom, we lose our autonomy, we are manipulated, put down, used, consumed? What if the *Other* is not responsible?

I do not argue that we give up control of *ourselves*. I speak only of giving up control of the *Other*. I do not argue that we habitually surrender, simper, and appease. I argue that we ought not and must not impose our control over the *Other*.

When I empower the *Other*, I am not relinquishing control over me. *I* have made the decision to empower the other, have I not? It was I who decided.

But what do we do when we discover our needs are irreconcilably in conflict with the *Other's*? Sometimes it is not enough to say,

"There are plenty of samples in the wallpaper book." Sometimes issues are so at odds that the parties are unable to resolve their differences. But here love relationships have the advantage. For in a love relationship one can speak out of love; one can speak out of understanding; one can speak knowing that control is not the issue; one can speak knowing that one will be heard by the *Other*—heard and loved. And in a love relationship one can hear the *Other*. One can know that the issue is real and meaningful to the *Other*. And because one loves the *Other*, one will seek to understand the *Other* and to find a resolution, without attempting to control the *Other*. In no other relationship are the parties to an argument so powerfully gifted, so richly advantaged.

What if, in every argument we make from this day forward, the *Other*, the judge, the juror, the boss, the city councilperson, the traffic cop, all loved us and heard us and cared for us and understood us and desired that we obtain for ourselves what we want out of our lives? We understand now. The love relationship provides the sheltered bed within which to grow the seeds of resolution with an advantage no other relationship can enjoy.

THE LOCK: What about anger? If you don't control their anger, they'll eat you up with it.

THE KEY: Hear anger, not as anger, but as pain. *Follow the pain.*

What do we do with our anger in the love relationship? A marriage without anger is a marriage between corpses. You can see it— two cadavers bowing, nodding in agreement, gesticulating, a perpetual smile frozen in rigor mortis on their skulls. Although there may be little else to recommend the relationship, they are never angry at one another. I have known marriages like that. But in all *living* relationships between healthy adults, anger is an emotion as real as love. A person without anger is a person without feeling.

But when anger is hurled at us it hurts us. And if it is hurtful to me, why shouldn't I attempt to prevent the *Other* from turning it loose against me? If it were the symbolic pistol mentioned earlier, I would insist that anger, like control, be checked at the door.

Do you remember what we have already learned about anger? Anger, we recall, comes from hurt, from the pain of fear, from the pain of disappointment, from the pain of guilt or jealousy or rejection or frustration, or betrayal or loneliness or from the injury of attack. Anger is a response to pain. Knowing this, when the *Other* responds in anger, one must terminate the argument. *The argument must terminate because the Other is in pain.* It is that simple.

But how do we terminate the argument? Try this: Let a little space occur between you and the other. Let a small slice of silence intrude. Let the storm recede a little. Then pick up this book and, if you have the courage (it will seem as if you need a lot, but it takes only a little), read aloud the following to the *Other* whom you perceive to be angry:

> "I was told that anger stands for pain, that when a person is angry the person has been hurt. I want to know about your pain. I want to know about it before it injures us more.
>
> (You may get a surprised look. You may also get a sarcastic response, like, "For Christ's sakes, has it come to this? What kind of crap are you reading now?" There really *is* a lot of pain, right? Press on.)
>
> "I am told that anger comes from loneliness or fear or frustration or guilt or jealousy or from some other kind of pain—that anger covers hurt. I do not want you to hurt. I do not want you to have pain. I need to know *why* you are hurting. I want you to tell me so I can do something about it. I want to do something about it because I love you. Will you please tell me?"

Perhaps the *Other* will tell you—angrily. Perhaps the *Other* can only speak with more anger. But, remember, he is not repressing his anger—that much we can attest to. The anger will not come exploding out tenfold at some later time.

I say the *Other's* anger is a gift. With someone less valuable, the *Other's* anger would be withheld. We are less likely to express our anger openly to a neighbor or a passing acquaintance than to the one who is the closest to us. That one close to us expresses anger confirms the closeness. Let me say it again: *Anger is a gift.* Otherwise we could never discover the pain. We could never remain close.

The Other's anger is our teacher. It teaches us to listen, to understand. It teaches us to be compassionate. When we discover the pain of fear, the pain of having been assaulted, the pain of betrayal, the pain of guilt, we will be able to address the cause of pain, and once we have done so, magically, the anger will begin to fade.

Listen for the sounds of anger, for the words, and when you hear them, do not be put off by them. Hear them as signs of hurt. Find the hurt. *Follow the hurt.* That is the key.

Editing and winning: During our lifetimes we commit certain irrevocable acts, acts that impose irreparable injury, acts that become our or another's Rubicon. Injury to the psyche is no different from injury to the physical body. We can slap someone on the back, and the sting of it is lost in seconds. Or we can slap a loved one in the face and the injury will be long and painful in healing and will leave scars forever. When we lie to another, the injury is irreparable. When we maim another verbally, the injury is irrevocable and the destruction of trust irreversible. The act may be forgiven, and the injury may heal, but the injury can never be repaired nor its scars erased.

Take, for example, the wife whom we met earlier. You will recall her accusations against her husband when she attacked him with the slicing words, "you insufferable slob." He may, in fact, fully qualify, but her having heaved such names at him is a frontal assault. The husband, too, was no amateur at verbal abuse. We remember that he called his wife "a two-bit bitch." It was simply an unmitigated brawl.

Unless this was a marriage fashioned in hell, we can assume that neither party is accustomed to such attacks, for no marriage can long endure such slash-and-burn barrages. Thereafter, neither will fully trust the other. Although it is not beyond the possibility of human magnanimity to forgive, this experience will not be forgotten. Twenty years later the insults will still smart when called to memory. The old saw that "sticks and stones can break my bones but words will never harm me" does not, in fact, hold true.

As Ralph Waldo Emerson reminded us, "the ancestor to every action is a thought." That thought proceeds action provides us with the opportunity to edit our language, our action, even in the heat of passion. We edit action continuously. We edit action when, in anger, we do not kill or maim but withdraw. We edit action when we do not get up in church and holler at the preacher, "You are a two-headed pettifogger." We edit action when we refrain from telling a friend his haircut looks silly. We constantly edit both verbal and physical action.

Although excesses may be forgiven, they cannot be excused. Let me explain: I have argued in court before the worst judges ever to don a robe, judges who suffer from halitosis of the heart. Yet, in forty years I have never once cursed a judge. I have never once been held in contempt. I have never lost it. Why? Is it because I exhibit such extraordinary self-control? I think not. The reason I have never slipped over the edge is because I know better. I know that if I slip over the edge I will pay the price, and the price will not be worth it. I never felt the urge to take up residence in the county jail.

In the same way, I have never walked up to a man 20 percent larger than I and forty years younger and suggested to him that his mother could trace her ancestry to the canine species. I know better. It's not that I have progressed further along the evolutionary track than the average man. I have no better control over my emotions than the average man. I simply edit out the language that will get me into irrevocable trouble, even when I am outraged, even when I am operating in that zone called the "heat of passion."

Why then can I not edit my language in the same fashion on behalf of the one I love? I say I can. I say we don't because we know that in response to our excesses the *Other* will usually not send us to the county jail for contempt or to the hospital with our faces bashed in.

I hate to recount the many times I've lost arguments at home because Imaging had the simple good sense to withdraw and to listen. She watched me and saw the rage without drawing it into herself. I have heard her refer to me as her "fourteen-month-old triplets" who want it *all* and who want it all *now*, who scream and throw tantrums one minute and are gurgling with joy the next. I have seen her pull back with amazing sangfroid and observe me in the manner of one watching a passing tornado from a shelter. I have grown to feel sorry for tornadoes. When the storm has gone, what remains is the wreckage flung all over the landscape, and the sorrow. No one loves the tornado. No one remembers it as we remember a sweet breeze in the evening. When the tornado has blown itself out, it must look back with regret and defeat.

That we should edit the angry attack, that we should suppress the bully (having been bullied, most of us have a predilection for bullying), that we should give up our attempts to control the *Other*, including our attempts to control the *Other's* anger, does not mean that we must give up who we are. We are, indeed, persons with rich and tender feelings who can also be hurt, who can feel pain and who can also be angry.

What do we do with *our* anger? Must we repress it? Must we sit on it like an old hen sitting on eggs that will hatch and thereafter grow into a dozen more chickens? I say it is all right to be angry. Being angry reveals our ability to feel and proves we are alive. As we understand anger in the *Other*, so let us understand anger in ourselves. The key is to find the pain in ourselves and follow it. *Follow the pain.*

Perhaps there is a simple way to handle our anger. Let us try this:

—First *mark this page* and leave the book nearby

—So you detect anger—yours? Go pick up this book, turn to this page—you marked it, remember? Now begin reading anew.

—*START READING HERE:*
   You are not ready to deal with your anger yet.
   Do nothing yet.
   Say nothing.
   As of now, you have not examined your anger. Until you have examined it, you can no more deal with your undiagnosed anger than you can treat an undiagnosed disease.

In order to examine it, you must *disengage from your anger.* By this I mean, if you are angry at the *Other*, visualize the anger as a rope extending between yourself and the *Other*. *Cut the rope.* Now the rope, the anger, is attached only to yourself and dangles in front of you.

Follow the anger to its source. If you are angry, you have been hurt. Follow the rope to the source of the hurt. *Follow the hurt. Always follow the hurt.* That is the rule. Were you hurt by a slur, a betrayal, a remark that stung which revealed a lack of respect? Were you attacked? What hurt you? *Follow the hurt.*

—*Identify the hurt with words to yourself.* Say to yourself, "I was hurt when what he said made me feel dumb." Or, "I was hurt when she didn't understand me and accused me of something I did not do."

Speak of your *hurt, not your anger.* Anger begets anger. Dumping more anger on the *Other* is, indeed, a poor way to treat your hurt. But when you speak of your hurt, without anger, an unangry response will usually be returned in kind.

Now say to the *Other, without anger,* quietly: "I know you didn't want to hurt me, but when you said (whatever it was), I felt hurt." Or say, "When you did (whatever it was), I felt hurt."

Practice this. It is not easy to do. If, however, whenever you recognize that you are angry you will get into the habit of *stopping,* and following the above exercise, you will eventually become skilled at dealing with your anger in a constructive, loving way that will enrich the relationship rather than wound or destroy it.

The winning response when one is hurt is to acknowledge it and communicate it: It is the winning response because it is honest and tends to stop the progression of injury begetting injury. Exposing one's "tenders," becoming vulnerable to the *Other,* is, strangely, the best argument, the most effective way to obtain from the relationship what one wants. Remember what we want. What we want is love, is it not? What we want is understanding and acceptance and respect and closeness. That is winning, is it not?

Becoming the child: As I was writing this chapter a friend of mine came to visit me in my library. I stopped writing to talk. As we were talking, a four-year-old Sherpa child, who with her mother are our house guests from Nepal, came wandering into the room carrying a basket of small toys. The child had never seen the woman with whom I was talking and could not speak English. She had been raised in the primitive, high backcountry of the Himalayas where there are no cars, no highways, no electricity, no television, no supermarkets. She walked up to the woman as if she had known her all her life. Without speaking a word, she took a small doll from her basket and handed it to the woman. Then she sat down at the woman's feet and played with her toys, sometimes sharing them with my friend while we talked.

I remarked, "This is the innocence and trust I wish to have in the love relationship. Where did we lose this innocence? Where did we lose this trust? How is it that children are so wise and we, their parents, so otherwise?"

AND SO: You want to win your arguments at home? Learn to lose them.

AND SO: You want to experience joy in your love relationship, you want to feel loved and respected? You want the *Other* to grow as well, and for the marriage to become the garden for your mutual growth? Give up control.

AND SO: You want to defeat anger, both in yourself and in the *Other*? Discover the hurt. *Follow the hurt.*

14

Arguing with Kids

ALSO LOVE AND WAR

THE LOCK: I want my kids to grow up as good citizens. I want them to be successful people. One accomplishes this by proper parental control, discipline, and hard work on the part of both the parent and the child. Yet, when I argue, my child does not listen. When I argue, my child often does the opposite of what I want.

THE KEY: The "magic mirror" phenomenon of the parent-child relationship decrees that if you want a loving child, give love. If you want a child who respects, respect the child. If you want a child who lashes out for freedom, control the child. If you want a child who hates, impose your power on the child. What you give, you receive—as we shall see.

Why argue with your child? Why would one wish to argue with a child? Indeed, children are most often right. I have learned to rely on both the wisdom and the example of children. They more often know what they need and what is good for them than we, their parents. They know what they want to eat, what they want to wear, and when they need to rest. They know when they are being wrongfully repressed. They know right from wrong and they have a nearly perfect sense of justice. If I could live with the knowledge I have acquired as an adult and apply it with the innocence of a child, I would be a more successful human being.

My experience teaches me that parents do not know much about being human beings, although parents loudly and ceaselessly profess such knowledge. That parents are essentially ignorant and so often wrong may be the reason most parents want so desperately to argue with their children. These parents, who operate from a position of power yet are confronted with a child who is not powerful but right, face a mighty adversary indeed.

In truth, parents can be among the most stupid of all creatures on the face of the earth. If this were not so, we parents would not be populating the world with so many children in the first place, and thereafter supplying each generation with offspring filled with so much hate. If parents knew very much about themselves, they would not be abusing children, smothering their normal instincts, and crippling them with fear and prejudice.

I ask: Why should we argue with children? I have learned more from my children than from any guru. My only regret is that I did not listen more and argue less. Had I listened more, I could have learned much about love, about creativity, about wonder. I could have perceived the magnificence of innocence, the beauty of humility, and the immense power of honesty. Had I been more sensitive to my children, I would have learned more about feeling and less about the deluding methods of reason and logic. Had I been wiser, as I wish you to be, I would have seen my children as teachers, rather than pupils upon whom I too often foisted my seriously flawed wisdom.

My expertise: I parented and educated six children. That should qualify me as an expert, and, as a lawyer-parent, I should know how to argue with them. But, alas, the older I got the less I knew. My first wife and I had our first child, our son Kip, when we were both twenty. I was confounded. "How," I asked, "could I, who am a boy myself, suddenly become a father?" I asked that question out loud to a mere child, my wife. Her answer seemed to envision some magical transformation that, at the precise moment the child was born, would cause me, the father, to also shed my childhood. It was as simple as that.

I had learned somewhere that what parents most fear was rearing a spoiled child. If one spoiled one's child, one was likely rearing a future resident of a penitentiary somewhere, maybe the gas chamber. One night when Kip was about six weeks old, he would not stop crying. I was attempting to study for final exams, and exhausted. He had been quite happy when he had been given his bottle (those were the days when it was not stylish for mothers to nurse their children even though they had plenty of milk), and now that it was time for him to sleep, he refused. I walked him back and forth across our little living room. I patted him on the back like a good parent. I jiggled him until his little head must have been ready to bob off his poor neck. I cooed, I coaxed, I begged. Nothing worked.

It never occurred to me that he might have gas in his stomach. No one told me that babies sometimes cry just to be crying. No one really knows a damn thing about what goes on inside their little heads, what images, what feelings. He had on double diapers for bedtime. I unpinned one side, pulled them down and felt. He was dry and warm. Suddenly it became clear to me: There was nothing wrong with this child. He was merely spoiled. I recoiled at the thought. I was not going to be a father to a spoiled child. Not me! I gave the baby a spat on the bottom and put him to bed, shut the door, and convinced his mother he should be left to cry it out. Oh, how he punished us for over an hour before he exhausted himself and finally fell asleep.

I would give a good right arm to be able to take back all of that, along with other equally ignorant acts of parenting I have, from time to time, committed in generous proportions. Looking back, I wonder that my children have grown up as successfully as they have. I think it a tribute to their mothers and to their own innate resilience as survivors.

As I reflect back these many years later, my own parents had a much deeper appreciation for children than I. When I was four years old my sister, "Little Peggy" we called her, who was about three, suddenly one morning got sick and by nightfall was dead, the victim of cerebral meningitis. The death of Little Peggy left me an only child for ten years. I can recall the fear my parents had—never a spoken fear, but one I seemed to know about—that something would happen to me. I was cared for, loved, and revered. I was the center of their world. A living child was precious beyond all understanding. I was not coddled, not exactly. But I was rarely punished, rarely scolded, and often praised. I was taught to be "a little man," but I was permitted to be a child. I was given piano lessons, singing lessons, drawing lessons. I wrote poetry. I learned from my parents about nature, about the birds and the stars. I spent endless hours with my father in the out-of-doors hunting and fishing. The center of my life was the family, and the center of theirs the Methodist Church. We lived in a small Wyoming town free of crime, an isolated little haven free of racial strife. Everyone in that far north Wyoming town of Sheridan was white, and most, in those depression days, were poor. It was a friendly place where the social event of the month was a covered dish supper in the church basement, and the most exciting thing in a boy's life was to miss school for a week when the family went elk hunting with Dad, and camped out in the mountains in the old tent. How could such a child with such parents not bloom and grow? As I look back on it now, as a boy-parent I competed with my own children. We were a family of children.

Watching Imaging: It was only when I realized many years later that I was in some ways a miserable failure as a parent that I began learning how to become a better one. I watched my wife Imaging. Her view of her two boys was different from my approach to child rearing. She saw her children as individuals who were fully entitled to her respect—even as infants. She listened to them. She trusted them. She gave them freedom. She never nagged them—never once did I hear her tell them to pick up their room or do their homework or mow the lawn. As a matter of fact, she wouldn't let them mow the lawn, which resulted in their demanding the right to do so. As the important issues of their lives arose, she made room for them to make their own decisions. I found the dynamic fascinating. The more she trusted her children, the more trustworthy they became.

The key to the parent-child relationship is respect. It is not enough merely to love a child. We commit the most heinous wrongs in the name of love. Most child abuse is perpetrated under the guise of love: "I punish you in this fiendish fashion only because I love you." "This hurts me worse than it does you." I saw Imaging treating her children as friends. I remember one of my neighbors proclaiming, "I'll tell you how you raise kids. You put 'em in a stainless steel box with a few holes in it. Once in a while you stick the hose in and wash it out. When they get to be fourteen years old you plug the holes." He laughed. Yet the joke revealed how we saw children in those days—as fearsome little subhumans over whom one had to somehow assert continuous and complete control lest one fail as a parent. Children were those troublesome little blobs of living, breathing clay to be molded into good citizens. Discipline and training were the key to successful parenthood. The distinction between training a dog and bringing up a child had not been thoroughly examined.

The parent-child mirror: In the days of my early parenthood, I had not learned that a relationship is always a mirror—that children cannot respect us if we do not respect them—that if we use power against our children our children will use power, sometimes in perverted forms, in return. I had not yet learned that if we treat our children as friends they will treat us in kind. We do not use power on friends. We do not manipulate or punish friends. We trust friends, love friends, and help friends. We accept friends for who they are. We do not try to change friends. We do not try to mold friends into our own image. We do not punish friends for possessing the same instincts, the same raw desires, the same frailties we possess. Would that we treated our children as friends. Instead we demand that our children, as children, conform to standards we as adults have never been able to meet.

A sad story about a boy who was not bad: I remember the story of a boy named Wilbur as told to me by a friend of mine named, shall we say, Jake Johnson. Here is how Jake related Wilbur's story to me.

One Saturday when Wilbur was about eight years of age, his mother discovered him down at the creek with a girl whom we shall call Bessy Lou. They were reportedly playing behind a grease-wood bush, a coarse, green plant that grows waist-high on a man and thrives in the alkaline bogs in Wyoming. Jake said that when Wilbur's mother came upon them, Wilbur and Bessy Lou had their pants down and when Wilbur's mother, with no kind words of inquiry, asked what the children were doing, Bessy Lou blurted out that they were playing doctor, whereupon Wilbur's mother whacked poor Wilbur's stiff little medical instrument with a stick. Then she set upon her child, shaking poor Wilbur like a bear shakes apples out of a tree, all the while admonishing him, on the pain of death and eternal damnation, never to do such a horrible thing again.

Jake said that after Bessy Lou told all of her friends about what had happened, the kids began to tease poor Wilbur unmercifully. He began to hang back from the rest of the kids. None of the girls, of course, would have anything to do with him. Worse, everybody started calling him "Doctor," and later just plain "Doc." The boys either teased Doc or shunned him altogether, the most cruel boy of all being the school bully, Harold Hutsinger.

"Hey, Doc," Harold would holler to Wilbur. "We got a couple a sick hogs down home. Think ya could come over t'night an' doctor 'em with that little thing ya doctored Bessy Lou with?" Harold would laugh real loud, and everyone was afraid not to laugh too. Even Bessy Lou laughed, and then poor Doc would run down to the creek to be by himself.

Jake told me that no one seemed surprised that Doc became an undertaker years later, but they were horrified when, after he had worked in that capacity for several years, the local authorities charged him with having had a liaison with a female corpse. Doc's case became the talk of the town. People, especially those who remembered him as a shy, sweet little boy, could not understand how this dear child could have turned into such a despicable monster. Jake, who was Wilbur's friend, said he, too, could never get his head around it. He knew Doc to be a kind and gentle man, and the fact that he was Jake's friend only exacerbated his confusion and conflict over the whole affair.

Jake said Doc didn't have much of a trial. The local joke was that they had him "dead to rights." Jake said Wilbur's lawyer called a psychologist who blamed Wilbur's deviate conduct on his fear of women. The psychologist testified that Wilbur's conduct was beyond his control, that he could not discern right from wrong, and that therefore poor Wilbur was insane. To prove how crazy he really was, Wilbur's lawyer called him to the stand in his own defense. He had grown into a nice-looking young man, and his lawyer had him dressed in his three-piece black undertaker's suit. His hair was short and slicked down so that, all in all, he must have looked like an IBM sales rep.

"Why did you do this terrible thing, Wilbur?" the lawyer asked his client right out. Wilbur didn't answer. Jake said Wilbur just looked down at his hands and after a while began to weep.

"Tell the jury, Wilbur."

Jake said Wilbur finally began to mumble something through his sobs.

"Speak up, Wilbur!"

Someone in attendance at the trial thought they heard Wilbur mumble between sobs something about loneliness, and some claimed they heard him say something about love. No one, including Jake, could attest for a fact what Wilbur said. That's about all the lawyer was able to get out of Wilbur. Jake said Wilbur's lawyer took less than a minute to sum up to the jury. He argued that anybody who did what Wilbur had done had to be insane and let it go at that. In their hearts, most of the townsfolk agreed. The jury, however, was not going to let Wilbur escape through the insanity loophole and within minutes returned a verdict of guilty. The judge, as shocked and repulsed as the rest of the citizens, that same day sentenced poor Wilbur to fifteen years, which is longer than he probably would have gotten had he murdered the woman.

Jake visited Wilbur in jail before they transferred him to the state pen. Wilbur looked sick and helpless in his green cotton jailhouse clothes and his paper prison slippers. Jake didn't know what to say to him. They just stood there looking at each other through the bars for what seemed like many minutes. Finally Wilbur said, "You shouldn't have come here, Jake. Ya shouldn't have nothin' to do with the likes a me."

"You're my friend, Wilbur," Jake said. "Everybody makes mistakes." Jake confessed he didn't know why he said it, but then he said, "We all have our *stuff*."

"Do you have stuff, too, Jake?" Wilbur asked in disbelief. He sounded like a small boy.

"Sure," Jake said.

Jake said Wilbur was silent for a long time. Then he asked, "Is yer stuff like my stuff?"

"No, Wilbur," Jake said in a hurry.

"Is yer stuff as bad as mine?"

"Stuff is stuff," Jake said, trying not to be judgmental.

"No, stuff isn't stuff. There is stuff and there is stuff. An' my stuff is the worst stuff there is."

"No, Wilbur," Jake said, and he said he started to reach out and touch Wilbur's arm, but he thought better of it because people don't touch people in jail.

"It's awful in here," Wilbur said. "I hope they kill me. All I think of is home." Then Wilbur choked up, but he held it back because a real man wasn't supposed to cry, especially in jail.

"You'll make friends," Jake tried to reassure him.

"No. They won't have nothin' ta do with somebody that done the stuff I done."

Then Jake said, "But, Wilbur, there are murderers in there, and rapists in there, and people who beat up old ladies and who've done terrible things to little kids. You didn't hurt *anybody*."

Suddenly Wilbur asked, "What did you do, Jake?"

"Well, Wilbur," Jake said, "a man can't talk about his own stuff." Jake told me he knew he shouldn't have said that, because then all the hope drained from Wilbur's face, and his eyes looked like they were painted on with flat, blue Kem-Tone.

Then a guard as big as a beer-wagon horse came in and hollered at Jake, "Hey, you a friend of this stiff-fucker?" Jake said he acknowledged that he was. "Well, your visitin' hours is over." And Jake said that was the last he ever saw of poor Wilbur.

After Jake told me about Wilbur, I thought about how his case might have been argued differently to the jury.

"Ladies and gentlemen: Wilbur, here, is a very nice person," I might have begun. "He'd never commit rape, and he'd never commit robbery. He'd never hurt another living being; why, he's never even kicked a mean dog. This would be a better world if there were more people like Wilbur. Think of it! There'd be no poor old ladies all beaten up and little children with their heads smashed in. The FBI would be out of business, and the politicians wouldn't have to compete with each other to see who could be the toughest on crime, because there wouldn't be any. That's the kind of world we'd have if everybody was like my client Wilbur.

"Please!" I might have continued, "Wilbur has been punished enough. Not once since he was a small boy has he known a single day without humiliation. Wilbur is no criminal. He never was one. Criminals injure the living. Wilbur is only a poor lonely man afraid to be with living people. I wish you could forgive him. I wish you could understand how hurt he is, how lonely, how sick." But I knew that the jury probably wouldn't understand him and forgive him even though, when he committed that unspeakably repulsive crime, he was only obeying the admonitions of his mother those many years before.

Why have I told this story? It was such a small thing, such a small, perhaps even natural act, this curiosity between Wilbur and Bessy Lou. We can never see the scars that have been cut into little psyches. We can only see the result of the scars many years later when we hate the offender, despise the deviant, and strike out once more at the criminal. We cannot see the wounded child within. I have told the story because the story hurts me.

Our barnyard qualifications for parenthood: I think it bizarre that we should be permitted to take on the most important of all human functions, parenthood, without any training whatsoever, especially when the consequences of our own innocent acts against our children can so deform them. As parents, our opportunity to destroy lives and to maim souls is nearly unlimited. No one would think of permitting a doctor to operate without sufficient education and training. We are required to demonstrate our skill in driving an automobile before we get behind the wheel and subject innocent people to our incompetence. In this so-called civilized society we erect every protection around our members, but we let any ignorant fop who can copulate raise children. The sole qualification for parenthood in this society is merely that we demonstrate our carnal proficiency at the level of a barnyard breeding boar—this and this alone qualifies us for parenthood in America. We demand considerably more of the man we call to repair the lawnmower.

The church does not teach us: Thinking back, I ought not be so hard on myself. Where can a boy of twenty acquire the skills of good parenting? Where can anyone learn it, as a matter of fact? When I lament the fact that no one teaches us how to be successful parents—which, as we shall see, includes the skill of arguing with our children—I am reassured that the church instructs us in this skill. But the church is the first to depart from its own essential teaching—namely that love is the most powerful of all nourishment to be administered by the parent to the developing child. The church is greatly skilled at instilling fear and guilt, the worst of psychic poisons. The church has the remarkable ability to close little minds and stifle the natural ability of children to question. The church, like the parent of all parents, is relentless in its attempt to own and control the child.

The church never taught me much about how to be a parent. Good parenting opens minds. Good parenting encourages children to ask questions and provides the child with a guilt-free environment in which to bud and bloom. I grew up believing that God was the Big Voyeur up in the Sky, that God was watching at all times, that He (not She) had the ability to read my evil little mind—that, therefore, it followed that He must not approve of me—how could He, considering the evil thoughts that invaded my lecherous and conniving brain? And since God must surely disapprove of me, how then could I really be acceptable to anyone else, or to me?

To this day I find myself reserving serious doubts as to my worth.

I sometimes still fight through the fog of self-doubt that often settles in. I am always suspicious of my successes. I too readily admit that I am not smart enough, brave enough, or sincere enough. I do not measure up, and that is because God has been watching and knows the truth about me.

Preaching: I do not discount the need for children to acquire moral values, but preaching never taught me anything. Preaching is a form of power. Preaching is an overt attempt by the preacher to control. I could fill the Library of Congress with the useless sermons I have heard and given. Their preaching and mine were mostly rendered for the benefit of the preacher. We preached to our children about *our* weaknesses. We preached to them about *our* fears. We preached to them about *our* demons and *our* guilt. We preached out of *our* desperate need for *our* own salvation. We preached and preached and preached. And about all that I, or my own children learned from such preaching was that it utterly destroyed any possibility for a meaningful, trusting, loving relationship, for such preaching to a captive audience is an assault.

At home, preaching becomes even worse. It becomes carping and nagging. It is heard as anger and rule-making. It creates a mirrored hatred for the preacher, for one cannot love and assault his children with sermons without engendering equal resentment and revolt in return.

On the other hand, I admit that preaching does teach us a good deal about hypocrisy and deceit. The preaching father who delivers his sermon against the evils of drink to his children, but who is himself addicted to the race track, teaches his child about hypocrisy. The preaching father who preaches about honesty but cheats on his income taxes or on his wife impresses indelibly on his child's mind quite another value. I say we could accept liars and cheats and thieves and lechers better if they did not preach to us. We learn wrong values when the Sunday school teacher preaches to small minds that Jesus said, "Bring the little children to me," and the children on the streets in front of the church are hungry and ill clothed.

Teaching by example: Moral values are taught by example. They are taught by a mother such as mine, who during the depression years always shared the little we had with less fortunate neighbors. Moral values are taught by a father like mine, who fought for the workers in the Bolivian tin mines, who laid it all down for them, including his job and his personal safety, to help them gain the most humble crumbs of human dignity. Moral values are taught by parents who think it better to be good than to look good, who believe it better to be useful than to belong to the right clubs. All the preaching in the world does not establish right values in children. If the parents possess an impoverished store of personal values, they have little to pass on to their children. The old sanctimonious saw, "Do what I say, not what I do," has become the one predictable operative rule of law in most unsuccessful homes.

How to stop crime: Do you want to know how to stop crime? Stop the preaching and provide every child with one good parent who, by his or her own life, exhibits the values the parent wishes to instill in the child. We have become, instead, a culture that provides too many of our children with unemployed, uneducated, desperate, and addicted parents. We have become a repressive, defensive, hateful society that despises the poor, that celebrates money as its ultimate moral value, and that provides, almost inescapably, the most bloody of violence as entertainment.

As sociologists have proven, tribes that exceed about two hundred members do not function well, and in its natural environment, say in the primal forests, the tribe, after it grew to approximately two hundred members, split off into two tribes. The phenomenon was something like bees in a hive. When too many bees abound in the bee tree, they swarm around a new queen and fly off to another hole in another tree. And what does this have to do with crime? And what does this finally have to do with arguing with our children at home?

Our society in no way resembles the tribal society, to which we are as genetically suited as prairie dogs are to their towns and ants are to their hills. The principal feature of the tribal society, compared to modern society, was that the tribal society was palpably alive. Its members created a cohesive, living, integrated structure. Each member's conduct affected the other, and each member was an integral and essential part of the tribal structure.

On the other hand, each member's identity as a human being was also related to the tribe. The worst punishment that could be rendered by the tribe against an errant member was banishment. The tribe had no jails. It had no gas chambers. It did not inflict the death penalty. It merely banished the wrongdoer, a punishment worse than death, because the individual's identity as a person was inextricably attached to the tribe. The tribe gave protection, comfort, respect, caring, and security to the individual, and so, too, did the individual provide and contribute to the tribe in accordance with his or her ability. Crime in the tribal society was not necessary.

On the other hand, in our society the tribe as home is lost. Tribe as small and cohesive communities is lost. Large segments of our population have been banished from partaking in the system. They have been banished unjustly. They have committed no crimes against the system. They are banished because they are poor, or because they are uneducated, or because they were born in the wrong place, or because they are black or brown or yellow. Punish a child who is innocent of wrong and you will create the neurosis from which nearly all crime emanates. Punish large segments of society by banishment and you create the same social neurosis.

Our society has destroyed the living tribe and replaced it with a leviathan conglomerate, not of two hundred, but of two hundred and fifty million souls. It rules through rule-bound, nonbreathing, soulless bureaucracies. The bureaucracies do not know the people. The bureaucracies do not know anything. They do not think, or feel or care or love. They do not know pain. They cannot empathize. They are as inhuman and dead as any iron machine. But unlike a machine, they cannot be directed. Rarely can they be controlled. They move by their own force like glaciers, as slowly as glaciers. They destroy everything in their path. They chew up the landscape and the people alike. If we were to devise an ultimate evil, we would doubtless choose the bureaucracy. The biblical devil must at least know good in order to embrace evil, and the biblical devil serves a good and useful purpose by establishing the antithesis against which good may be understood. But the bureaucracy transcends all evil, for it is capable of understanding neither good nor evil, nor—which is the most evil of all—does it care about either good or evil, for it is incapable of caring.

This structure, this bureaucracy, in both corporate and governmental form, rules America. This bureaucracy is the new dead supertribe. And out of the dead supertribe is born the *end-evil*, shall we call it, the final alienation and denial of all of us, the tribal members. Out of this end-evil comes the repression of large segments of our people who sense the uncaring of the dead supertribe and interpret such uncaring as hatred (although the bureaucracy can neither love nor hate). Out of this end-evil, the people in every segment of our society are deprived of their tribal homes. We are left helpless against the mindless decrees of the dead supertribe. We cannot fight the governmental and corporate oligarchy that exploits us for money, sucks us dry of our resources and our creativity, that destroys our forests and putrefies our prairies and defecates toxic wastes into our rivers for dead money. We are helpless to be heard, for the ears of the dead supertribe hear only the crinkle of money. We live in the myth of freedom, but we are not free of the violence imposed upon us. We live in the myth of love, but we do not feel loved. We live in the myth of peace, but all around us the dead supertribe consumes our resources to wage war against our brothers and sisters both here and abroad.

In this society of the dead supertribe, those who are homeless are not just the few who tramp the streets at night with their vacant eyes and ragged garments. *We are all homeless.* We have no living tribe with which to associate. The TV evangelist exploits the lonely and the desperate by assuring them that if they will only give him their money they will be accepted into his tribe and there they will be loved. We are exploited further by talk show hosts who permit a few to be heard ever so briefly in order to create the illusion that we are taking part and that we count. In the meantime, the talk show host sells us gadgets and junk. We try to identify with a tribe by becoming fans of the Giants or the Jets or the Red Socks, but at last these are not tribes at all. They are corporate businesses, and as we embrace our teams, our pseudotribes, again we are sold more gadgets and more junk.

And those innocents who are punished the most by being banished the most are always the weakest, the poorest, the most in need. Theirs are the children who are impoverished and forgotten. We read where nineteen children live in two small dirty rooms and eat out of a dog dish, and we wonder why they commit crimes, and our argument in return is not to stop this punishment, not to cease our own crimes, but to build more and larger penitentiaries to house children when they are grown. It is little wonder that these children respond in kind. It is little wonder that they strike out, not only at the system, but at each other, for, at last, an insane society reflects in the inescapable magic mirror the insanity it has imposed on its members.

And what does this have to do with arguing with our children? Whether our children are members of the most alienated segments of society or the least, they are all homeless, for the living tribe has been eliminated in nearly every community. Schools are no longer tribal organizations for children, but first-step penitentiaries where kids are treated not with love and respect but as criminals. To some extent, churches attempt to fill the role of the tribe, but most are more concerned with their memberships' ability to provide the dead stuff called money. There are small rural communities that still function chiefly as tribal entities, and much is to be learned by their example.

To argue with children who are born into this dead supertribe and who are alienated from a caring, living tribe demands an understanding of *who* these children are and *where* they are entrapped. To argue with these children, these victims of the dead supertribe, especially after they have achieved the "age of reason" (as the courts like to say)—somewhere about the time of puberty, which in truth is the *age of no reason*—requires the use of certain tools of argument not generally employed in these times. The main tool, of course, is love. If I could teach parents only one thing concerning the art of arguing with children, it would be to love them better.

I believe that much of today's crime is also a function of space. We cannot pack a dozen young rats in a concrete shoebox without their attacking and killing each other. We cannot pack millions of our young into the concrete boxes of our cities without expecting them to lash out in pain and anger and violence. If I were asked to solve today's crime, and given the resources to solve it, I would take our children out of the concrete boxes. I would give them space. I would introduce them to open fields where they could roam at will. I would give them mountains and streams and wild-flowers and vast prairies. The gift of space, more than any other medicine, would do more to prevent crime than any potion I know. Instead of freeing our children from their concrete boxes, we smash them into smaller concrete boxes called prisons, and upon their release expect that they will have learned how not to be insane.

Love requires us to free our children: Love requires us to free our children and to trust them. One day when my own children were quite young, I captured some young ravens. They were too immature to fly very far. I brought them home to my children, who were also too young to fly. Immediately they fell in love with the ravens. But my children were wise enough to know that they could not truly love their captives without freeing them, and within a few days they demanded that I take the ravens back to their nest, where their squawking parents experienced the joyous miracle of reunion.

In the same way we cannot keep our children captive and love them. We must give them freedom. We must face the fear—our fear—of their being freed. The mother bird knows it must take the risk that her freed offspring will fail. The young bird will perhaps fail to fly. It will perhaps be devoured by a prowling cat. It may be eaten by an eagle. It may starve. But the mother must take the risk. And the baby bird, when it is ready to leave the nest, is not afraid.

How often I have seen myself soaring and squawking and agonizing over the fate of my children. How often I have felt the helplessness of the raven parents after their babies had flown the nest. How often I have tried to hold on to them, to keep them there, not realizing that my refusal to let them go was in response to *my* need, not theirs, in response to *my* fear, not theirs. But love not only protects, it releases. Love not only shelters, it provides freedom.

Mother Nature is marvelously wise. She understands the need of children to develop their own wings, to be prepared to fly before they leave the nest. It is we, not Mother Nature, who interfere. We do not permit the child to be. We do not give respect to the child so that the child can grow strong and confident and capable of surviving in this frightful world. Instead we punish, and repress, and preach, and fill the child to overflowing with fear. Whenever the child attempts to bloom in ways that are different from our own, we react, sometimes stupidly, sometimes even violently.

We demand conformity, which is to demand an end to creativity, which is, at last, to demand that the child join the dead. To ask that our children submit to the destruction of themselves in the name of our love is a monstrous insanity.

What do we want from our children? I have not lost sight of the fact that this chapter promises to instruct on how to *argue* with our children. In fulfilling this promise, I return to the definition of arguing. Arguing is the process by which we achieve what we *want* from the engagement. What is it that we want from the arguments we have with our children? Do we want merely to win, that is, to force the child to succumb? Do we want them to mind us, to bow to our power, to do as we say, when we say it? Do we want our reasoning to be so beautiful and unimpeachable that the child withers in its presence? Do we want the child to mimic our ideas, our beliefs, our tastes, our goals? Do we want the child to be a miniature of us, a mere poor copy? Do we want the child to respond like a servant, a slave, so that our desire is their duty? Do we want the child to do—ah, yes—not as we do, but as we say? What do we really want from our children? Before we can determine what argument to make we must determine *what we want*.

I should think that as loving, caring parents, we would be able to agree on what we want. I should think we could agree that we simply want our children to be successful. *But what is success?* Must our children achieve fame, or wealth, or status? Do we see success as occurring when our child fulfills the dreams we did not fulfill for ourselves? Is our child successful only when the child fulfills our life, as distinguished from the child's life? Would we be satisfied if our child was a happy and well-adjusted ditch digger? Would we agree that success is that state achieved by one's child in which the child happily pursues and fulfills his or her passion, whatever it is? Would we not agree that success is not measured in money or power or position or prestige, but in our child's becoming a fully evolved person? In the real world we want our children to be well adjusted and capable of coping. We want them to be successful as *human beings*. We want them to excel in the art of being persons— to live with joy, to grow, and to become who they are—to fulfill themselves.

To freely bloom—that is my definition of success.

The question then is, How does arguing with our children advance our goal that our children freely bloom?

We are, of course, concerned that our children not run afoul of the law. That is a universal concern of parents everywhere. That is the universal concern of society. I am saddened as I watch the oldsters facing, fearing, shuddering at the spectacle of the monsters they have created out of the fabric of their own hatred and rejection. It is like a sadistic man who locks his dog in a cage after which he pokes sticks through the bars—pokes, and prods, and causes the helpless dog to howl in pain. Not satisfied with his torture, the owner then starves the dog, and throws a dark cloth over the poor dog's cage so that no light shines through. One day the dog is freed. The owner now holds out his hand, claiming that the master should be loved and respected for having provided food and shelter for the dog. But the ungrateful dog bites him, and in punishment the dog is put into an even smaller cage where he is whipped and beaten even further. Little wonder that the dog would, when again released, now attack. Can we remember when the dog was a puppy and would lick our faces?

I think we ought not be as concerned with our children violating the law as with ourselves violating our children. We want our children to be law-abiding, to be sure. But assaulting our children with fear—with fear of rejection, fear of punishment, fear of reprisals, fear of criticism, and fear of banishment—is an assault upon the child that will be returned in kind. On the other hand, we cannot bribe our children to be good. "If you are a good boy you can go to the show." Later, "If you are good you can have a new car." Goodness becomes associated not with goodness but with material reward, and that is not goodness. Children ought not learn about bribery at such an early age.

The terrible danger of power: Power. Oh, power! How dreadful it is! How dangerous! What can we do with it? We can dominate with it. We can control with it. We can make children cry with it. We can make them hate. We can make them conform. We can make them despise us and hate themselves. We can make them do as we please. We can cut them with it and beat them with it. We can eviscerate their little souls with it. We can restructure them with it—restructure them into the emotionally disabled. Ah, what wonderful things power can do!

But power cannot make the child create. Power cannot cause the child to bloom, and therefore, by definition, it cannot cause the child to become successful. And one other wee thing it cannot do: power cannot make our children love us.

I have carefully observed power in the hands of people all my life. I have used it myself. It is practically good for nothing except to be used against equally ignorant power, and even there love is usually more powerful.

Have you ever thought of the power differentiation between the parent and the child? Think of it this way: Suppose you have no money. Suppose you have no friends who have power. Suppose you have no place to live except where this power-person tells you to live. Suppose you cannot eat until you are told, sleep except when you are told. Suppose you must ask for the clothes you wear and obtain permission to go wherever you go. Suppose that if you anger the power-person, he has the right to swear at you, to humiliate you, to degrade you, even to beat you. Suppose you are not even permitted to worship as you please, but, instead, the power-person tells you who you will worship and how you will worship. Suppose you have no way to escape this place of horror? Entrapped there, you can only take what is given to you. This is the disparity of power that exists between parent and child. That differentiation in power tells us that there is really no room for argument in the child-parent relationship, for where the power differentiation is this great, even the mildest persuasion can become oppression. And the ardent presentation of reason and logic by the parent, even if it is correct, even just, when there is a power differential so great as this, can sometimes become a destructive assault.

If power has constantly been used on the child, the consequences will be deadly later on. When the child is old enough to argue back, what we will behold is war, one that parents cannot understand, for have they not always sought that which they considered to be in the best interest of the child? Have they not given and sacrificed and counseled and worried themselves sick? But to the child, this has been oppression—and now that the child is old enough to possess his own power, the time for hostility, fueled with the energy of years of powerlessness and anger, has arrived. It will come bursting free with all the hatred and resentment that has been stored like rat poison in the cellar.

In this war, argument by either side is to no avail: The parent cannot achieve from the polemic what he wants. And, from the standpoint of the child, the child cannot obtain what he wants either, which is freedom and respect and love. Nothing can be said by either side at this juncture that will gain for either side what either wants. The problem is, of course, that there are sides. The problem is that there is argument. *The cure is for the parent to get on the side of the child, to argue for the child, and to end, forever, the war.* Otherwise the parents' argument is but the further presentation of power, and the child's argument is not argument, but rebellion against power. Power against power, that is the definition of war.

Editing our language with our children: As we have seen, most people edit their language as is necessary for their well-being. I have, however, said regrettable things to my children. But my children, being dependent upon me, and being inhibited by the Fifth Commandment, could not separate me from my head, nor cause my abusive tongue to be cut from my villainous throat. Yet, we can control our language if we must, heat of passion or not, and we *must*, always with children.

Children are helpless to protect themselves from hurtful language. And children never forget. The words may have evaporated into the ether, but in the deepest caverns of memory the verbal abuse still echoes against the fragile walls of the childish psyche.

We mount a false defense: "We parents fall over the edge sometimes, but the kids, God bless their forgiving little hearts, understand. They'll get over it." Bullies do fall over the edge sometimes. They fall over the edge because they choose to do so—because they are bullies and because they can. The same parent who abuses his child does not abuse his boss or the cop on the beat. And kids do *not* understand. A counselor might understand. The priest might. As a matter of fact, we all understand what makes the bully bull. But the kids can never understand why they were abused by someone who proclaims in the next breath to love them. Such abuse leads surely, inevitably, to the numerous varieties of neurosis that so enthrall and enrich the mental health professions.

The war on puberty, perhaps the most destructive war in which any child will ever engage, is also one from which many a child will never recover. So you want to know how to win the argument, any argument, when the child is sixteen or seventeen and he or she is no longer the total victim of the power differentiation? Well, it is too late. If you win the battle, the argument, you may only drive the child out of the home or encourage major, destructive revolts. The argument with children is won many years before adolescence sets in. It is won with unconditional love, with respect, and with trust. It is won by having been the child's advocate, the child's friend from the beginning, without having expected anything in return. It is not a conditional love given with the expectation of future compliance or submission. It is an unconditional love that is experienced by the child whether the child responds as the parent may desire or not. It is a love that takes the risk of loving without expectation of anything in return.

Between parent and child, love begets love, and power begets monsters.

Our need to argue: Sometimes we should ask, "Why do I need to argue with this child? What am I feeling? Am I feeling fear for the child or fear for me? Do I want the child to do as I wish for my sake or for the child's?'' The child may not have the same burning desire to be a football hero or a cheerleader as the parent. The child may have no ambition to be a banker in his father's footsteps, or to become a doctor or a lawyer like the father. He may wish to play the piano or become a mountain climber. He may wish to be a bum. Whatever he wishes for himself, he must work out his wishes, not his parent's wishes. Whatever his moral imperatives are, they are his, not his parents'. We cannot transplant the parent's soul onto the child any more than we can graft tomatoes onto corn stalks.

We parents say we want our children to be successful for the sake of our children. But I say that most often we want our children to behave for *our* sake. It is painful for us when they misbehave. We feel our own agony when they are held up to disgrace or are rejected or jailed. We wish to avoid *our* pain when we witness our children's failure. I say we wish our children to be successful because we need to be successful parents ourselves.

I think of the argument made by a friend of mine to his son. He was concerned that his son was going to take a menial job to support his first love, surfing, that he would accordingly fail to go to college and thus not prepare himself for a successful life as an adult. I found the father's argument nearly perfect.

"I've been worrying about something," he began.

"Yeah?"

"It's about your decision to go to college."

"Yeah, well, I'm tired of people trying to tell me what to do," the son replied. He was honest.

"I'm with you on that," my friend said. "The decision has to be yours as far as I'm concerned. Like you say, you're the one responsible for your life." Now the argument was being focused on the issue—*responsibility*. My friend told me that at this point he was afraid his son might get up and walk out, as kids that age can do. But my friend forged on. He took the risk. He said, "I told my son that I admired how he'd been willing to make his own decisions. A lot of kids his age refuse to take responsibility for themselves, and I told him that." The father had taken the son's side of the issue. And the boy stayed and listened to his father. "I told my son that as a matter of fact he'd done a lot of things that made me proud, but what I wanted to talk about wasn't about *him*, it was about *me*. I asked him if that was okay with him."

I stopped the father's story for a moment to ask, "What did your boy say when you asked him if it was okay with him to talk about yourself?"

"He said, 'Why not?' "

That was an important juncture in the argument, the granting of permission by the son to the father to say what was on his mind. When we are given permission by the *Other*, in this case the son, to make our arguments, the *Other's* corresponding duty to listen also attaches.

The father went on. He said to his son, "You see I've spent my whole life doing one thing—trying to become a successful parent. That's been my life's goal. That's what I want more than anything. To tell you the truth, I'm not as worried about you as I am about me."

"What are you worried about?" the son asked.

"Whether you're a successful surfer or not is something you can control. You can practice until you become a champion. Whether you're a successful adult is also something you can control. You can prepare yourself for a successful life or not. But you're in charge. So whether I can finally realize my success as a parent is in your hands, not mine. It's hard for me to give up control. It's hard for me. But I still want to be a success."

Then my friend said his boy looked at him with a lot of love in his eyes and he said, "You haven't got anything to worry about, Dad. I'll be okay." And that's where my friend said the argument ended. The most important decision he made, as is the case in every argument, was to know when to stop.

My friend's argument contained none of the fatal defects of most parent-child arguments—no blaming, no hostility, no anger, no whining, no maudlin tears, no plastering of guilt. There'd been no screaming match, no power struggle. The argument contained no demand. It didn't pull rank. There was a simple naked presentation of the father's truth. The father wanted to succeed as a parent, and he felt helpless when he realized that his success or failure was out of his hands. But he told his son what he wanted. The argument carried with it the *ring of truth*—that the father was concerned for *himself*, for his *own* success. The argument had credibility.

Whether or not the boy eventually goes to college is not the test of the argument's success. Maybe he will; maybe he won't. But the son's realization that his life is not an unrelated series of events based on his passing whim and his need for immediate gratification, but a two-way street, that he shares responsibility for his parent's success as well as his own, is the power of the argument, that and the fact that it was honest.

The rights of parents: But parents have rights as well. Those rights grow as the child's ability to take on responsibility grows. A four-year-old may not understand that his mother has a right to a moment's peace or the right to speak a full sentence without being interrupted with a whine or a demand. But children who have been respected as persons and trusted from their earliest days have already learned about respect. By the time they enter adolescence they have developed a need—their own need—to respect and be concerned for their parents.

Parents do, indeed, have rights. Parents do no service to the child by permitting the child to trample the parents' rights. We can easily distinguish between a parent who asserts his or her right with a child who has violated the parent's rights from the parent who attempts to impose his will on the rights of the child. The father who raises hell because the son borrowed his shotgun to go duck hunting, but left the gun out in the rain all night where it rusted and the varnish on the stock blistered, is justified in his vociferous complaint. The same father, however, has no right to demand against his son's will that his son go to church or paint the backyard fence or attend Yale. The mother has a right not to have a seventeen-year-old son track up her newly waxed floor with his muddy feet, but she has no right to nag him about cleaning his own room. Both parties to a relationship have rights—parents *and* child.

Punishment: I recall a time when, at about age fifteen, after returning from duck hunting, I committed the one unforgivable sin a hunter can commit. I failed to unload my shotgun before I put it in the car. I was trained to do so. I always had. Never before had I failed.

On this day I came bursting into the kitchen with my shotgun in hand to tell my father about the day's hunt. He was at the kitchen sink cleaning a mess of trout he had just caught. As I was describing to my father a shot I had made, I followed the imaginary duck with the shotgun, took the appropriate lead on the imaginary bird, and pulled the trigger. The shot ripped a gaping hole in the wall a few inches above my father's head. I was horror-stricken.

My father turned slowly, looked at me with sadness in his eyes, and then went back to silently cleaning his fish. He never mentioned the incident to me, not then, not since. To this moment, as I write, I am not sure what I learned from that frightening incident. The shock of it is still as vivid today as it was the day it happened. I learned, of course, that one must always unload one's gun. I learned that some very simple rules must be obeyed because life and death depend upon their being followed. But what did I learn from my father's silence at a time when most adults would have exploded? Perhaps I learned that children know the difference between right and wrong, that they do not need to be punished for wrongs they did not intend to commit, and that the wrong itself contains its own punishment.

My father was a very wise man. He understood children. I recall having had what I then considered a showdown with my father about a matter that sorely troubled me. By that time I was forty years old, but he was still my father and I was still his little boy. "Dad," I said, "I've had it with you."

He looked surprised.

"I have few friends," I complained. "People think I'm a smart-ass and self-centered, that I am egotistical and crass. I have no manners. You should have kicked it out of me when I was a kid."

He listened intently while I complained and derided. When I finished he said, "Well, Gerry, it's easy to kick it out of a pup. But once you've kicked it out of him you can never put it back again." Where did my father's wisdom come from? My memory of his father, my grandfather, is of an old, white-haired man with sparkly kind eyes who had a crinkly smile and a pat on the head for me when I was a little boy and who talked to me as if I were a man, just like him. He told me stories too sophisticated for my age with lessons I did not comprehend. Sometimes the stories were funny and when he laughed I laughed, too. He thought I understood his stories and that I was very bright. I think some wisdom is genetic, but mostly we are the products of our parents' parents. The biblical saw, "The sins of the father are visited upon the child," is no more true than "The virtues of the father are his gifts to the child."

Children, money, and work: In a monetary society where money and material things seem to permeate us, money can be a problem between parent and child. I have never believed that parents should buy their children fancy cars and pay for a trip to the southern coast of France for spring break. Parents should provide the necessities for their children, but in a money society, part of their preparation for life is to learn how to play the money game well enough to survive.

I was recently flying home from a lecture tour when I encountered two young, pimply-faced adolescents occupying first-class seats on the same airplane. What message do parents give children who are pampered in the first-class cabin while the majority of mankind sits crowded into tourist class? Money separates people. It separated these boys from all of the others on the airplane. Money divides us into classes—those with it and those without it. Money therefore deprives us of our right to relate to each other through the width and breadth of our humanity. Instead, we inevitably gravitate to those whose bank accounts are like our own. I have found that most bankers are dull and most moneyed people, boring. Financial statements and money are dead. Working with and for the dead tends to be reflected in the personalities of money people. I should sooner relate to a mortician, than to a professional money man. And I should like my children to relate to the living—to workers, to creators, to thinkers, to strugglers, to the confused, to the errant. Let them relate to people.

I want my children to work. Working teaches them more than they can ever learn in school. They learn not only the job, but how people live, how they suffer and struggle. They learn that money has little to do with the quality of the people who either have it or do not have it. They learn simple truths about money: They learn that the quality of the person bears often an inverse relationship to the amount of money the person possesses. They learn how hard it is for people on this earth to survive. They learn that people can grow weary and still must work. They learn compassion. They learn the satisfaction of completing a job. They learn how it is to be a subordinate, to take orders, and yet to question. Work teaches children more about themselves than any activity I know, other than play.

For myself, I was never forced to work. I was simply never given anything but a minimal allowance. I needed more money than my parents provided and found work an adventure. In the summer I drove teams of horses putting up hay on Wyoming ranches. I slept in the hay loft and hung out at the country dances on a Saturday night and, as a boy, got smashed along with the cowboys. I herded sheep and at sixteen went to sea as a merchant seaman where I worked as a messman and an ordinary seaman. I sailed to many ports and engaged in the usual vices of the young of those days.

When I wanted to graduate from high school early and go to sea, my father and mother never protested. They made no effort to control or discourage me. I remember my father drove me to the edge of town and let me out on the highway where I could hitch-hike a ride. He wished me well and kissed me good-bye and told me he'd sure appreciate a letter if I ever got around to writing one. And that was it. I remember turning back to see the family's old '37 Ford with its flapping fenders go rattling down the street. I watched it until it disappeared. There I was, alone on the highway with only my bag and my thumb. For a moment I wanted to turn around and run home. For a moment I wondered if my father really loved me. Maybe he wanted to get rid of me. Why would he leave me like this on the highway even though I had demanded this freedom for months? I would have thought he would have fought against the poor judgment of my adolescence, which secretly I acknowledged to myself.

Yet to my parents my argument had gone like this:

"I want to get the hell out. I'm sick of this town," I said one day.

"Where do you want to go?" my father asked.

"I want to go to Alaska and pan for gold."

"Is there any gold up there?" he asked. "I thought the gold rushes were over."

"Well, they sure as hell didn't get it all. There ought to be some left if you're half smart."

"Could be," my father said. "You ought to talk to Ted Johnson. He panned gold at the head of the Amazon. He could probably tell you a lot." There was no argument. My father didn't criticize me for my crazy idea or scorn or lecture. My mother said nothing. She only looked sad and helpless.

I got out the old Montgomery Ward catalog and made a list of things I would need: heavy coat, boots, socks, woolen underwear, and mittens. I figured how much money it would take to outfit myself. I talked to Ted Johnson. He said, no, the price of gold had gone down. A guy could do better trapping. So I told my father I was going to Alaska to trap. As an old trapper himself, my father was able to give me advice—the kinds of traps I would need, how to set them without leaving human scent, and how to set beaver traps so the beaver would drown itself rather than gnaw off its leg, as beavers will do when trapped on high ground. Never once did my father tell me the whole idea was ridiculous, that I was just a silly dreamer.

A few days later a friend of mine said he was going to sea and invited me to join him. He was already in school in San Diego. He told me about the ocean and the palm trees and the balmy air and the women of California. Suddenly I abandoned the idea of becoming a trapper and instead decided then and there to become a sailor and see the world. Besides, I didn't have to outfit myself with a lot of expensive clothes and traps. I was a pup. In some ways I was a very unruly, difficult, energy-packed, wild and petulant pup. But my father never kicked it out of me, for which I shall be grateful all of the rest of my days, because I have since discovered that what my father left in me was the essence of who I am.

Short of risking the child's life or well-being, children should be left free to make their own mistakes and to grow from them without argument from their parents. The parent who is always afraid for the child and argues against everything the child wishes to do has no credibility with him, for the child is not afraid. The child has been prepared by Mother Nature to take risks and to absorb failures. The toddler is not afraid to take its steps and to take the chance of falling. The old man is mortally fearful of falling. Mother Nature has prepared one to fall, the other not to fall. It is out of risk that the child learns and grows.

I used to tell my children: "A female trout lays thousands of eggs, and thousands of minnows are born from them. Most of them, however, are eaten. Only a few grow up to be a big fish." I doubt they ever heard it. I was merely reciting a story that illustrated my own fear for my children—that they would all be eaten.

At the end of the day I have usually learned and grown more from the pain of my mistakes than from the pleasure of my winning. It is easy to puff and swell and sail from the joy of victory. But I never learned much from winning, although I have always liked it a lot. What I have liked more, however, is to avoid, by winning, the terrible pain of failure, of defeat, of loss and rejection.

Some winning arguments with kids: How do you argue with a four-year-old who will not eat her cereal? Ask her what she wants to eat. If she wants a tamale, give her a tamale. If she wants candy, simply tell her you don't have any (be sure that's true), and give her another choice. If your goal is to make her hate cereal all her life, make her eat it. How do you argue with a three-year-old who does not want to go to bed? Read the child a story until the child is sleepy. For God's sake, *don't leave them in front of the television set where the arguments of corporate America will prepare them to become mindless consumers and empty-headed voyeurs.* If your goal is to make the school-age child hate learning all of his or her life, force the child to study. If you want her to hate you, force her to obey you. Force and hate are twins.

How do you argue with the sixteen-year-old who wants to spend the weekend at a friend's house when you know the friend's parents will be gone? We are afraid, are we not? Will she be hurt in an automobile? Will he be exposed to alcohol and drugs? Will she get pregnant? Today, even worse, will they contract AIDS? But note: It is *our* fear. Not theirs.

Although their lives are in jeopardy, they are not afraid. That is the curse, but also the blessing. If the child's fear were in proportion to the danger, the child could never experience the marvelous transformation from child to adult. Because youth is unafraid, we send them to war. No adult with a five-cent brain and two cents' worth of experience would go.

The puerile mind, bombarded with that most virulent of all chemicals, testosterone, has little chance to function in any normal fashion. If we were to test the average adolescent's behavior against the standard charts for the various categories of psychosis, I daresay most teenagers would fulfill the principal requirements for the most serious and bizarre forms of madness. In my opinion, teenagers are splendidly insane. They are a danger to themselves and to others. They mostly do not appreciate who they are or where they are. They suffer from delusions of grandeur, of invincibility. Their judgment is seriously flawed, their insight impaired. They have difficulty conforming their conduct to a manner acceptable to society. Some may not, in fact, appreciate the difference between right and wrong. Most crime is committed by adolescents. Most automobile accidents involve adolescents. Most of the lifelong habits that kill—smoking, drugs, and the use of alcohol—are established during adolescence. Adolescence is danger time for any child, and a time of fear, frustration, and hell for most parents.

By the time the child becomes a teenager, the best arguments we can muster will avail us little. If the child has been maintained in a domestic prison, the child will likely go wild, and nothing we can do and no argument we can concoct will prevent it. The human animal demands freedom. It cannot, without permanent and serious damage, be caged. Even the child who has been treated with respect as a person and who has grown up in an intelligent and loving household wants freedom. Such a child can experience it in a cooperative program between parent and child in which the risks are greatly reduced. If our children did not seek their freedom, we would have tragically dependent offspring with miniature psyches who, like frightened, featherless birds, could never venture beyond the family nest.

AND SO: Parents must rear their children toward that one day when the child begins to seek his or her freedom, when the insect, whether an ugly moth or a beautiful butterfly, seeks to abandon the cocoon. During the years between infancy and adolescence, the winning argument will have already been made. The winning argument will have been love; the losing argument, discipline. The winning argument will have been respect; the losing argument, manipulation. The winning argument will have been honesty; the losing argument, hypocrisy. The winning argument will have been freedom; the losing argument, control. If the child has been afforded winning arguments during the child's lifetime, there is little against which the adolescent can revolt. The child will spring forth into the world with joy, not hate; with respect and love, not fury and violence. To give to the world a child who is capable of joyously blooming is the gift of the successful parent.

15

Arguing at the Workplace

ENGAGING THE CORPORATE CYCLOPS, SURVIVING THE GOVERNMENTAL LEVIATHAN

THE LOCK: Arguing at work can be like hollering at the time clock— or, worse, pulling the tail of a tiger.

THE KEY: Like any game, one cannot play the corporate game successfully without understanding the game.

I f arguing is getting what we want from the *Other*, then what do we want from the boss? Do you say money? Do you say security? Do you say benefits? I say we want but one thing from the boss: *respect*.

If the boss respects us, he will pay us a fair wage, provide us ample security, and furnish us with safe and comfortable working conditions. He will listen to what we have to say, implement our ideas, and encourage our creativity. *Respect*. That is all we want— that the boss will not view us as disposable commodities, as a bag of rags to use to wipe the grease off the engines, and, when we are used up, discard us; that at the workplace we will not become the breathing dead; that at the workplace, despite what we think, what we do, or how hard we work, we do not become nameless, faceless units of labor; that the boss will not refer to us as "bodies" and see us as bodies. I have heard them refer to good, caring, hardworking people thus: "Give me five more bodies out here this morning. The shit's got to fly."

Before we can argue at the workplace, we must understand something of our relationship with our employer. If we do not understand the nature of the entities for whom we labor, we cannot engage in meaningful argument at work. One would not wrestle with a Cyclops without knowing something about the monster. When we work for a corporation, for us to argue without an adequate understanding of the nature of the corporate beast would be useless, perhaps injurious.

What is a corporation? A corporation is not a human being. It is not a group of human beings. Remember that. It is a *fictional structure*. A form—a nonliving, nonbreathing, nonhuman form—an invisible form. It is an entity as a church is an entity or as Citicorp is an entity. You cannot see the entity. You can see the church cathedral, but you cannot see the church. You can see the TransAmerica pyramid, but you cannot see the TransAmerica Corporation. Corporations exist only as print on paper. We can see what corporations produce, what they build and destroy, but we cannot see the corporation. No one in the history of the world has ever seen a corporation any more than anyone in the world has ever seen a thought. A corporation is but an idea. Little wonder we are so often unsuccessful in arguing at the workplace.

So tell me, how do we argue with nothing? If I were to suggest that you argue with three square inches of nothing, you would think me strange. Can you see yourself approaching with great deference and trepidation the said nothing, your courage steeped to address the said nothing? Can you see yourself arguing your heart out to the said nothing, and, when you are not heard, trudging off with a sense that you, not the corporation, are nothing?

Although corporations are not alive, they possess a life of their own, that is to say they have a beginning and presumably an end. Many seem immortal, like the Catholic Church, US Steel, and Exxon. Their founders die. The sons of the founders die. The grandchildren dawdle by. But the corporations live right on. Corporations are often absorbed by other corporations. Like some weird invisible extraterrestrial lifeless glob, they swell, split apart, change themselves into other globs, gobble globs, digest and excrete globs, and become bigger invisible globs of globulous nothing.

To understand how people are used by the corporation, let me shift metaphors. Think of a ship. The people who work for the corporation come on board the ship, jump ship, change ships, *but they are not the ship*. That must be obvious, yet most arguments made in the workplace overlook that proposition. We know that human beings serve corporations, nourish them with their lives, manage them, and are, at last, consumed and junked by them (we call the latter condition "retirement"), but the corporation, like the ship, is a mere construct and can never be understood as anything else. People are not ships. People are not corporations.

Who controls the corporation? To understand how to argue at work, it is also necessary to understand who is in control of the corporation. Many, even the corporate officers themselves, argue that human beings control corporations. This is largely a myth.

It is true that corporations are theoretically governed by a board of directors and that the ordinary affairs of the corporation are carried on by its officers and employees. But the corporation proceeds mostly by its own inertia. Shifting to yet another metaphor, one may stir algae with a stick, skim it from the surface of the pond, fuss and mess with it, but the green glob reforms itself, and, quite independent of external controls, flourishes spontaneously in response to its environment. Accordingly, if the river is being polluted by a corporate factory, and if it is the job of the corporate directors to stop the pollution, it is likely that the pollution will continue, approximately forever. Let me show you why.

Before the pollution can be stopped, the directors must, of course, learn of the pollution. This may never happen, for there is an indigenous corporate phenomenon concerning bad news. Bad news weighs a lot, and as a consequence bad news does not tend to filter upward. But should the board eventually learn about the pollution, the board can become either concerned or insouciant, the latter being most likely, for as a rule board members do not go out looking for problems to solve unless some other entity is pinching their collective nose—perhaps some gone-wild government agency that somehow has not been otherwise contained. It is less costly and hence more profitable to elect sympathetic congressmen or to influence revolving-door regulators than to stop the pollution. As a result, the board may never be required to consider the matter of the river's pollution at all.

Assume, however, that the river is so polluted it actually bursts into flames, as did the Cuyahoga River in Cleveland, and that public sentiment also flares to the point that the directors must place this irksome issue on the agenda. Once on the agenda, it is likely the matter will be tabled until the new board is elected and takes office. If a study is finally ordered, the order may or may not be transmitted to the engineers in a timely fashion, for such orders routinely become lost in the corporate paper maelstrom. I would rather face snow and storm and dark of night than trudge through the corporate papers generated in a single day in the large American corporation.

But if the order for this pollution study does not get lost, it will not likely receive priority treatment either, because there are production glitches directly connected to profit that command the immediate attention of the engineers. Or it may be that no study can begin at all until the chief engineer gets back from his foreign tour, in which case the study will take a backseat to the catastrophes that have accumulated during the Chief's absence.

However, if a study is ever begun and thereafter completed (the study may take years), the results may or may not percolate up to the president for approval. Remember, bad news is heavy. But if the president receives the study, the president, being a thoughtful person, will likely want a number of items explained so that he may make an intelligent and informed presentation to the board. This inquiry by the president will be expressed in memos which themselves may or may not get lost and may or may not be attended to by the engineers if ever received, for the engineering staff views this pollution problem as minor compared to the survival of the corporation, as an emergency room physician would view a patient who is suffering a heart attack but is complaining of a sunburn.

However, in time, the chief engineer may order the department to launch a new study. When the new study is eventually returned, if it ever is, and if the results of the same are conveyed to the board of directors, the new board, which is composed of the grandchildren of the board that ordered the study in the first place, understandably does not know what this pollution problem "back then" was all about. The chief engineer has retired and all the other engineers who took part in the original study are moldering or, at best, tottering, and, to be perfectly responsible, the new board can do but one thing—order a new study to bring them up to date.

So it goes also in the multitudinous other facets of corporate business. The corporation, although it is lifeless, chiefly runs itself. Charles A. Reich of Yale Law School says, "The corporation is an immensely powerful machine, ordered, legalistic, rational, yet utterly out of human control, wholly and perfectly indifferent to any human value." Like a ship at sea, it will float by itself and sail by itself helter skelter whether there is anyone at the helm or not. One salient trait of corporate executives is their skill in marketing the fantasy that they have the ship on course—some course. Sometimes the course is the wrong course and sometimes the officer in charge is completely lost—but the goal is to keep the ship afloat under circumstances that cause a casual observer to conclude that someone is, indeed, at the helm and that the ship is, indeed, going somewhere. If those in charge of the corporation can create such an illusion, they will become greatly sought after by other corporations, admired by all, and deemed highly successful.

Who is *responsible* for corporate conduct? The rudderless ship: Returning to the metaphor of the ship, the ship is not responsible for itself. Ships do not think. Ships do not have souls or consciences. Ships do not bear responsibility. Well, then, how about the crew? To say that the crew on the corporate ship *is* the ship is obviously wrong. They only work for the ship. They are only the crew. The captain, too, is not the ship, but a mere ship's servant. Moreover, the ship continues its life even after the captain dies of old age or is murdered in a mutiny. Well, what about the owners of the ship? The owners of the ship do not steer the ship any more than the stockholders, on a daily basis, run the corporation. Most ship owners have never seen the ship they own. Most are alienated from that which their money has purchased. At last, money, dead money, owns the ship. But money is not responsible. I have closely examined numerous dollar bills over the years, and I have yet to witness thereon the first sign of a soul.

Little wonder then that the ownership of the ship, money, which is not alive, and the ship itself, which is not alive, can undertake acts for which there is no responsibility to the living. The ship cannot be held to any criminal responsibility. We cannot put a ship in jail or lock it in the public stocks—especially when the ship, like the corporation, is invisible. Nor can we put a criminal corporation in jail or render the death penalty against it even though its mass killings may make the morbid skills of a Jeffrey Dahmer look like a tap-dance at a Girl Scout jamboree.

Corporations are mostly immune to meaningful punishment. That is why the corporate structure is in such demand for conducting business. For what better could businessmen ask than to have the protection of this mostly immune, invisible, nonresponsible entity out in front of them, this mere fiction that can be loosed to commit every variety of wrong for profit, while the persons who own the corporation are usually insulated from responsibility themselves? In the law this phenomenon is called, surprisingly, "limited liability." If the corporation is guilty of negligence that causes injury to masses of innocent people, the corporation, not the owners of the corporation, not the directors or officers or employees, is legally responsible. If the corporation is guilty of criminal conduct, usually the corporation and not its officers or shareholders is answerable, and usually the corporation will not be held responsible either, for it will summon its platoons of great lawyers, hurl them into battle against the governing agency, and carry on, as usual. Let me show you how the corporation argues.

The infamous Ford Pinto case comes easily to mind as a paradigm of corporate conduct in which the human beings who manage the corporation would never themselves engage. Ford Motor Company employees knew that even in low-speed rear-end collisions the gas tank on the Pinto could burst, causing gasoline to be spewed over the area, thus subjecting the automobile's occupants to horrible injuries and death by a resulting fire. Nevertheless the automobile was vigorously marketed. One corrective measure for the dangerous design cost but $11 per vehicle. However, in the soulless corporate milieu, human life was transformed into a commodity, the loss or injury of which was something not measured in human agony or bereavement, but in dollars.

The National Highway Traffic Safety Administration had already made certain calculations that were considered by Ford. The damages for the death of a person in those days averaged $173,3000, to which were added average medical costs of $1,125, property damages of $1,500, insurance administration of $4,700, legal and court costs of $3,000, employer losses of $1,000, victim pain and suffering of $10,000, the funeral bill of $900, and $5,200 for "other costs." The per-fatality damages averaged $200,725.

A Ford Motor Company memo showed that if the Pinto was sold without the $11 safety feature, an estimated 2,100 cars would burn every year, resulting in burn injuries to 180 people, and 180 more would be scorched so severely they would die. Now note: The corporate author of the memo was already determining how many people the corporate product was *going to kill*—how many needless deaths—or to put it otherwise, how many human lives would be sacrificed in the future for *profit*.

The Ford memo then argued that—taking the government's figure of approximately $200,000 per death, and estimating that those who survived would have medical bills amounting to $67,000, and adding the loss of the vehicle at $700 (presumably the depreciated value of an older Pinto less salvage value), and further given the marketing of 11 million cars and 1.5 million light trucks every year—a balance sheet using the above figures would show the total cost to the company of the dead and injured human beings (but only after they were forced in court to pay) at $49.5 million. On the other hand, adding $11 to the cost of each vehicle to provide a safer car or truck would amount to a total additional cost of $137.5 million. By putting its cars and trucks on the market without the $11 cost of safety, Ford, according to these figures, saved $88 million.

Between 1971, when the Pinto was introduced, and 1977, an estimated five hundred men, women, and children burned to death in Pinto crashes.

In the Pinto case, who was responsible for the deaths and the perhaps worse-than-death injuries by burning? Are they who negligently designed the car and silently submitted the design for manufacture responsible? Are they who tested the automobile and knew of its defects but failed or refused to speak out responsible? Are they who knowingly engaged in the manufacture of a defective automobile responsible? Are they who, with such culpable knowledge, in the name of profit, marketed this inherently dangerous vehicle to an innocent public responsible?

The division of legal responsibility in the American corporation bestows on the corporate minions the means by which to participate in the most heinous crimes that each, as responsible and moral individuals, would themselves have rejected in much the same way that those in the military avoid individual accountability. Ford Motor Company was later acquitted on all criminal charges brought against it.

But troublesome questions do not vanish. If One Eye George of the Chicago Mafia makes a profit out of torching the homes of the Mafia's enemies, knowing that many will die and many others will be seriously burned, we would charge him with what lawyers call "felony murders" and, if possible, ask for the death penalty. But then One Eye George does not belong to the right clubs and is not seen in the right society. He does not have the right power in Congress or control large segments of the media with his millions of advertising dollars, and, most important, his acts were not committed for the profit of an American corporation whose stock is traded in the New York Stock Exchange.

Now let us say that one Henry P. Hunt, the chief executive officer of a great automobile corporation, makes similar decisions to those made in the Ford Pinto case. Admittedly, Mr. Hunt would not engage in the crimes of One Eye George. If seated on a jury in One Eye's case, Mr. Hunt would likely vote for conviction and the death penalty. But in the corporate boardroom a certain evil pathogen persists. When good citizens come together in the corporate enclosure, their morality immune system sometimes seems to collapse and the bottom line takes over. Those who die from the wrongful acts of the corporation are just as dead as if they had been murdered by One Eye George. Moreover, the corporate profit that is gleaned from the deaths of the innocent is indistinguishable from the profit One Eye George enjoyed from his crimes.

Understanding the corporate environment: To formulate our arguments at the workplace, we must understand the environment in which we labor. The rape of the environment is one of corporate America's worst crimes. We hear little of this through the corporate media. We hear, instead, of the lost and the banished who rob the 7-Eleven or the alcoholic who knocks over the liquor store. One of the most staggering statistics I have encountered is from the Bureau of National Affairs: Every year the dollar cost of *corporate crime* to Americans is over *ten times* greater than the combined larcenies, robberies, burglaries, and auto thefts committed by individuals. One in five of America's five hundred largest corporations has been convicted of at least one major crime or has paid civil penalties for serious misbehavior. Amitai Etzioni, professor of sociology at George Washington University, concluded that, in the ten years of his study, approximately two-thirds of America's largest corporations have been involved in some form of illegal behavior. Seen from every angle, the problem is not that corporate officers are without morality. The problem is that the corporate structure itself allows the corporation to operate without regard to moral values. One does not blame crocodiles for eating babies. It is their nature to eat whatever moves and bleeds—worms, catfish, or babies.

When Judge Miles Lord spoke from the bench after approving a $4.6 million verdict against A. H. Robins, manufacturer of the Dalkon Shield, this, in part, is what he said to the firm's officers:

Gentlemen: . . . Today as you sit here attempting once more to extricate yourselves from the legal consequences of your acts, none of you has faced up to the fact that more than 9,000 women claim they gave up part of their womanhood so that your company might prosper. . . . I dread to think what would have been the consequences if your victims had been men rather than women. . . .

If one poor young man were, without authority or consent, to inflict such damage upon one woman, he would be jailed for a good portion of the rest of his life. Yet your company, without warning to women, invaded their bodies by the millions and caused them injuries by the thousands. . . .

Begging for corporate conscience, Judge Lord said to these corporate officers,

Please, in the name of humanity, lift your eyes above the bottom line. You, the men in charge, must surely have hearts and souls and consciences.

The men in charge no doubt had hearts and souls. They even had a conscience. But the plea of Judge Lord fell upon the nonexistent ears of the corporation, for corporations, as we have already discovered, have neither ears nor hearts nor souls nor consciences.

Who are we? Before we can successfully argue at the workplace, we must ask, Who are *we* in this corporate milieu? We are the crew of the invisible ship. As such, we are asked to work endlessly, to care sincerely, and to sacrifice without question for the "best interests" of the company ship. Yet, after thoughtful consideration, ought we lay it all down for a mere fiction that cannot respond to us in any human way?

We are taught loyalty and team play from our earliest days. We put on a red jersey and we fight for the red. But if we change jerseys, we fight for the blue. We are taught to love the church, to be loyal to the school, to the club, to the country. I do not preach against loyalty or patriotism or God. I simply recite the historical fact from which we derive the idea that loyalty to inanimate entities, to fictional structure, is laudable.

But how can we be loyal to a fiction? How can we be loyal when the corporation cannot appreciate or even understand our gift? The metaphor takes on the idiotic if we behold the loyal crew member—let us call him Herman—sitting on the deck of the ship expressing his undying devotion to the ship. Herman caresses its cold damp hull and lays his cheek, fevered with passion, against its rusty deck. But no matter how Herman beseeches, begs, or pleads, the ship remains cold and mute.

One can safely give one's gifts of self only to the living, to beings who can respond in kind with loyalty. The corporation, by reason of its structure, alienates us from our superiors, from our superior's superior, from our work, and, at last, from ourselves. Money, that stands in the stead of the object produced, becomes a revered object, the embodiment of an omnipotent spirit with magical powers. In our culture, money, although it is not alive, elicits unquestioned devotion. The lust for money becomes concupiscent—habitually, curiously arousing the rutty side of the species.

Where do our arguments in the corporate milieu begin? When we are loyal to a conviction, to a standard, to a moral imperative, to an ideal, we are, in fact, being loyal to ourselves. We can take our stance for an argument in the corporate workplace in this context. When we are loyal to a friend, we are loyal to one who possesses the ability to respond. Here, as well, an argument to the boss, as a friend in the corporate workplace, may begin. But if we have been reduced to a corporate-owned commodity, the cost of labor, a unit, a digit, the issue of loyalty is more difficult to mount, and an argument made to the corporate entity through any agency is like hollering at the wind. One can be loyal to people. One can sacrifice for people. But when one sacrifices merely for the corporation, one must expect in return only that which the corporation is capable of returning, which may be very little indeed.

Arguing for a raise: Almost all arguments in the corporate environment must be directed toward generating greater profit for the corporation. One does not argue for a raise on the basis of justice, for corporations do not deal in justice. One cannot win an argument for a raise by explaining that Jenny and Johnny are hungry or that Myrtle, their mother, is sick and needs a doctor. One cannot win a raise by pointing out that one has worked oneself to near exhaustion and still cannot pay the rent. One cannot win a raise by reminding the corporation that one has labored ceaselessly, loyally, for twenty years without a mumble and without a raise. Justice is as irrelevant to the corporate goal as sawdust to applesauce. In fact, justice is poison to the corporation, otherwise the employee would be paid the full value of his labor. Instead, the excess value of the employee's labor is appropriated by the corporation and converted into corporate capital. And capital is power. Hence the excess value of the employee's labor becomes an even greater power to be exerted against the employee in order that the corporation may extract an even larger share of the value of his labor. This is old dogma we all recognize in a more common aphorism, "The rich get richer and the poor get poorer"—but however we say it, it is not justice.

To argue for a raise from a corporate employer, one must always demonstrate that the higher wage will likely create more production and more profit. The arguments in support of more money—more profit—are endless:

- "I am working as hard as I can right now, but with a little more financial help I will be able to cut down my outside work and produce even more."
- "A raise will permit me to buy a new car so that with better transportation I will be able to work longer and with more dependability."
- "A raise will help me pay some of the debt that hounds me and will permit me to become even more efficient in lending my creative talents to the company."
- "A raise will help me further my education so that I can better apply my skills for company profits."
- "With a raise I will be able to eat better, sleep a little longer, and produce a lot more."

Arguments for a raise can be made on the basis of loyalty, but not to the corporation. The loyalty argument may be made only to the living, remember?—to our immediate superior. Joe, our boss, is bucking for a promotion. One's superior is always bucking for a promotion in the universal hierarchical scramble up the corporate totem pole. (If one eventually ends up at the top, there is no place to go except to jump off the pole.)

Addressing Joe's upward goal, we shall seek to assist him, to think for him, to create for him, to enliven his spirit, to help present him as a dynamic, energetic, talented, insightful leader. Having done so, we do not say, "Joe, I helped you, now you help me." Joe knows he is indebted to us. He also knows how to pay the debt, namely in the only way debts are paid in business—in money.

The more intelligent boss, being aware that much of his success is the result of our input, effort, and talent, will seek a raise for us without our having to ask for it. If not, the approach to Joe must be more subtle. Although we have engineered Joe's ascent, he does not wish us to call his attention to that fact. He wants the credit, and, of course, we will give it to him.

We begin our argument by acknowledging how we have enjoyed working with Joe, which we have, and how we hope we can continue, which we do. Then we say it simply and directly:

"Joe, how do you feel about helping me get a raise?" That puts it straight to Joe. He can now respond out of his reciprocal loyalty to you.

"You deserve one. I'll see what I can do." But Joe's argument up the corporate hierarchy on our behalf will be based not on justice, but on his assurance that our raise will tend to increase corporate profits in the future.

Arguing for a promotion: The Peter Principle—that we rise to our highest level of incompetence—is as well known to our employer as to us. If I employ a finish carpenter whose work is beautiful to behold and nearly impossible to duplicate, I am loath to convert such a man into a foreman. I may lose his extraordinary services in exchange for his becoming a mediocre leader of mediocre carpenters.

The best argument for a promotion is always the same—to demonstrate that one's move upward will advance efficiency on the job, and hence mean more production and more profit. The arguments follow:

- "I am a good teacher and I can show the others how to be as good at what they do as I."
- "I can create a whole section of skilled finish carpenters equal to myself by sharing my secrets with them."
- "The men like me, and would want to please me as the foreman by working up to my standards."
- "I will become a working foreman, thereby assuring you of my good work, but increasing my value by passing on to others what I have learned."

Whatever the argument, the rule never changes: profit, not justice, is the ubiquitous key to advancement in the corporate milieu.

Once we understand this, we can fashion whatever argument we require to titillate the corporate soul.

Sucking up: The politics of corporate existence is an alleged art that some insist must be acquired if one is to advance in the corporate community. I admit this possibility. Otherwise, how have some of the most pedestrian, prosaic, and dull types achieved the top rungs on the corporate ladder? I know some up there who have never had even a tepid idea in their life, not one. Worse, they lack the insight to recognize the good ideas of others. However, most successful people at the top are good at certain other skills. They are good manipulators. They usually have good social skills—that is, they drink with the drinkers, joke with the jokers, and play golf with the golfers.

Many a venal pettifogger has wheedled his way to the top. I often confront this type in court. I speak from my experience only, leaving room for the possibility that a trial lawyer who makes his living representing everyday people against corporate crooks is not likely to come in contact with the best examples of corporate leadership. There must be some out there with great minds and generous hearts who have reached the summit of the corporate world by good and honorable means. I have, however, rarely met the same.

I have seen the CEOs of great corporations, whose assets exceed those of many individual nations, glaring out at me from the witness stand, men whom I would not hire to run a cheap motel if it were the only motel in town. These men have nearly life-and-death power over thousands and hold sway over billions of dollars of assets. I know how most got to the top, and so do they. To be sure, some may have worked long and hard, but too many are the vain and the arrogant who have fobbed off all the way up, shaking a lot of hands and patting a lot of backs. I have seen them, their faces like old pumpkins three weeks after Halloween, unashamedly exhibiting that sickening smile cut from a lifetime of toadying. Too splendidly stupid to make a decision, they will, however, take instant credit if the corporate ship picks up a serendipitous wind and lands in some fortuitous port. But should the ship wreck, they will as quickly lodge responsibility at the door of some defenseless underling who will find himself out on the street without a recommendation.

The mindless mind of the corporation has been the role model of most CEOs I have met, and they have dutifully absorbed its worst characteristics. Rather than create new and profitable ways to utilize their loyal employees who have devoted their entire lives to the corporation, such CEOs blindly slash at the cost of labor and lay off tens of thousands without notice, usually at Christmas. Instead of cutting the fat out of the salaries of their coconspirators in management, they will cut corners in the quality of their product. They will jeopardize, even sacrifice, long-term prosperity for short-term profit. If they can show a profit today, they will do so even if their successors will suffer interminable losses as a result. They will manipulate the accounting procedures to show a profit when losses have actually been sustained. They will hide the truth and cover evidence of their wrongdoing. They will lie to analysts in order to boost the value of their stock options. They will sell to unsuspecting third-world people their stock of dangerous drugs that have been banned in this country. They will market products they know are worthless—worse, even injurious or fatal to human life—under the reasoning that all can be forgiven in the name of profit. I have heard many a corporate executive argue that he has no loyalty to his employees, to his customers, or to his country. His loyalty, all of it, is to the profit of his shareholders. In short, by the time an ordinarily decent human being with ordinarily decent instincts has labored in the corporate slaughterhouse for the years necessary to arrive at the top, he has lost, in the profit game, most of his ethical foundations. His argument is simple, banal, and predictable: "How can I say no to profit in response to someone's notion of ethics? Ethics is not the name of the game. Profit is. If you come aboard, you do so with that understanding. Ethics takes the forefront only if it is more profitable to be ethical. Don't you understand?"

"But your decision is wrong, and you know it," some brave soul protests.

"Don't preach to me. I wasn't hired to run a social institution. I was hired to run a profit-making institution." (They like to call themselves "profit-making institutions.")

"But what about ..."

"I don't worry about that either. I leave such concerns to the preachers, the do-gooders, the environmentalists, the government, and to you. I repeat myself. I run a profit-making institution, not a Boy Scout troop."

I overstate perhaps, but only because such self-indulgence brings me pleasure. Still one might make room for the possibility that my hyperbolic extravagances are more nearly the truth than a mealy-mouthed, milquetoast scholasticism on corporate politics might have been. I have no ability, no knowledge, no experience, and no will to teach you to emulate the corporate panderer, the pimp, or the sycophant. The talent of the fawning parasite eludes me, and I am grateful for that. Having failed to impart to you the subtle craft of corporate politics, you may never get to the top of the corporate ladder, but you have a chance to preserve the only asset you ever really had—yourself.

Government work: What I have said concerning corporate structure also largely applies to government structure. This is true because bureaucracies are bureaucracies whether we find them in HUD, the State Department, General Motors, or the former Soviet Union. If you work for the Labor Department, you cannot make it care. If you work for the Department of Defense, you also cannot make it care either for you or any other human being who inhabits the planet. Bureaucratic caring is reserved for numbers, for dollars in the budget, for dollars in the pork barrels, for numbers that represent potential body counts, for profits that may be realized in the government-corporate combine. All governmental entities are as incapable of responding to their human employees as any corporate entity, as any machine. A government employee can get more understanding from her GE dishwasher than from the Department of Interior where she labors. Another government employee can gain more empathy from a GM diesel engine than from the Department of the Army where he sacrifices his life and his health.

In the case of the government entity, the profit motive that otherwise blindly propels the private sector has been ostensibly replaced with a structure that is intended to promote the continuity of power. In government, one has a job that hopefully will not be taken away. In government, one has a pension that hopefully one will not be cheated of. One allegedly has a future one can foresee—based mostly on longevity, rather than on merit. The ultimate payoff in government is power. But in the end, power itself is convertible to money, because, from the power position in government, a leap over the regulatory fence into the private sector is often possible, and, once there, one may cash in handsomely on one's governmental power connections.

Despite the feeble provisions in government for merit raises and merit promotions, the same are not usually based on merit at all.

If you are an old bureaucrat who is the epitome of inefficiency and whose eyelids are propped open all day with two-by-fours, you will be paid more than if you are a young worker who has discovered a way to save the government billions of the taxpayers' dollars. We all know that. And knowing that, we understand the brilliance of preserving the energy we might otherwise expend making useless arguments to the tiny, imaginary, curled-up protrusions that constitute the non-ears of a government bureaucracy.

In government service, as is often true in corporate service, one wins by not losing. One wins by not rocking the boat, by not trying to change the system, by not demanding of the system that which it cannot deliver. One wins by being kind to one's *self*, that is by not extending one's self beyond comfort. But remember, one also wins by satisfying one's self that the job done is good and honest. One also wins by not expecting a pat on the back from the handless bureaucracy, but by patting oneself on the back for having satisfied one's self.

Remember, no matter who signs the paycheck, we always work for ourselves. No matter who hires or fires, we always please ourselves. Always we live up to our own standards. In the end, that is how we always win.

Ethics in the workplace: It is difficult to be ethical in a workplace where the employer—the government bureaucracy or the corporate employer—is essentially unresponsive to ethical concerns. That fact, more than any other, accounts for the continuous wave of crime we witness in both government and corporate service. The men and women who commit such crimes are usually not people with criminal records. They usually come to the bureaucracy from good families with above-average educational backgrounds, with high hopes, and with their morals intact. Yet along the way something happens. I think it happens so slowly the employee is unaware of the change, like growing into the next-size pants.

The principles of morality most people have cherished from childhood become irrelevant in many of these workplaces. Everything and everybody seem separated from themselves, separated from their ideals, and separated from each other. People are no longer citizens and neighbors, but economic or mechanical creatures. Like hens in the hen house whose eggs are daily stolen by the farmer, their produce becomes a unit of corporate wealth, or an item of government waste over which the worker has no dominion whatever. It was not so with native man. His labor was his. His stone tool, his. His pot, his; his basket, his. He was not separated from what he produced. He was not, as they say, alienated from his labor. His wealth, from stone and sweat, was his.

But in the modern bureaucracy, the product of the laborer, like the eggs of the hen, is appropriated from him day after day, year after year until, at last, his life has been taken from him. It is converted into that strange token we call money, most of which the worker does not get. Money becomes the god of all. It becomes the god of the employer, the worker, the consumer, the church, the politician, the school. Everyone and everything, every motive and every act are attuned to that one idea—the acquisition of dead money. Money must be obtained at any cost if one is to achieve the kingdom of heaven on earth, and perhaps the kingdom thereafter as well. Money has, indeed, become the fetish of our culture.

Money separates modern man from his neighbor. He and his neighbors are no longer peers. Each either has money or not. Each is, accordingly, respected or not, accepted or not, considered successful or not, seen as worthy or not, judged as moral (if he has it) or not (if he does not have it). Happiness, success, fulfillment, self-worth, social standing—all are dependent on money. Those few who possess large amounts of money gather on this side of the societal room and those without it congregate in large numbers on that. The two sides stare across the room at each other, criticize each other and hate each other. And what is the difference between them? Some had parents who left them money, while some made themselves poor by taking care of their parents. Some stole money, some legally, some otherwise. Some did not want money. Some had no opportunity to get it, and some never acquired the callused hands with which to wrest money from their neighbors. The issue between the people gathered on opposite sides of the room is not the law, not morality, not resourcefulness or indolence or virtue or sin. The issue between them is not crime. The issue is money. Dead money. That is all.

It is little wonder, then, that those who see themselves as deserving, but have little money, find it unjust that those who deserve money less have most of it. How can this be a just society when those who work the hardest most often acquire the least of the stuff? "Why," asks the ditch digger who sweats all day in some stinking sewer trench, "can't I earn in a week what corporate lawyers bill their clients for every dreary hour they spend sleeping through some useless deposition?" How can this be a just society when often those who possess the largest amounts of money do no work at all, except to pass moral judgment on those who have no money, nor any real opportunity to acquire it? It is strange then that crime becomes the most obvious path toward the realization of justice, that crime becomes the injudicious means by which the impecunious seek to acquire justice—namely, their fair share of the available wealth.

If parents have two children at the table and one is fed plenty while the other starves, the injustice is apparent. No one would condemn the starving child for stabbing a biscuit from the plate of the child with plenty. But when these children, now grown, now bursting with the anticipation of success, come to an unjust workplace, or are thrown out into a patently, unashamedly unjust world without work, we can expect crime, and we get it and we will always get it. Please hear me: I am not arguing for a socialist's solution. I am arguing for a *just* solution. One is not required to be a socialist parent in order to provide a just home for his children.

In the workplace, ethics are often instruments of hypocrisy that hold the employee to standards to which the employer is immune. The bank teller who unethically steals from the bank has watched the bank unethically steal billions over the years by the usurious interest it wrests from the weak and disadvantaged. Surely, the teller reasons, my crime of stealing from the rich is not as reprehensible as the bank's unrelenting theft from the poor. The stockbroker who unethically engages in insider trading has seen his firm unethically swindle the public of unimaginable fortunes by the promotion of worthless stock. Surely, the stockbroker reasons, using my insider knowledge to advance my own fortune is not as reprehensible. Corporate ethics are often the preachments of pretenders and Pharisees. How can sanctimonious, self-righteous corporations that bilk and steal and injure for money demand that the employee abide in an antiseptic, ethical void for the benefit of the corporation?

Too often corporations want honest employees not because honesty is lauded, but because it is more profitable to have honest workers than to employ thieves. Yet the thievery of the corporation is accepted as simply business and is usually protected by the law. The whistleblower is cheered on as he turns in his fellow employees, not because it is wrong for his fellow employees to steal, but because by snitching on his fellow employees, the whistleblower saves the corporation the profit that otherwise would have been lost.

And what is the function of the law in all this? Even the law is not designed to deliver justice. The law is not ethical. Instead law becomes the means by which those in power, justly or unjustly, retain power. Law preserves power—money power. Law will nearly always dignify a past evil as precedent rather than create justice by changing an unjust law.

How, then, can we succeed in our arguments? Those who succeed are those who do not enter the playing field blindfolded. I argue that successful arguments at the workplace can be made only when we have a clear, unobstructed view of the playing field. If we understand the bureaucracies in which we struggle, if we can identify who will hear our arguments and why, we can argue and win.

By now you have learned when you should argue, how to be credible, how to understand power, how to listen, and how to prepare, fashion, and deliver your arguments, and more. These tools, these techniques, these humble offerings that have meant much to me in a lifetime of arguing will serve you well in arguing in the workplace. Yet, if I have emboldened the rebel in you, I hasten to warn that rebels are rarely successful. Rebels are not understood, and people are afraid of those they do not understand: Moreover, it is one thing to be one's own person, to respond to one's own authority and to preserve one's own power. It is another to strut and swagger and make a good deal of noise about it. I am not arguing against standing on principles openly and unabashedly. I am, instead, arguing that there is usually no advantage in making a grand exhibition of it. A man who silently lives by his ethics makes a more profound argument than one who deafens us with his shouting about them.

Success in one's arguments, in one's life at the workplace, is a concept, an idea—your idea. When the head of a large corporation walks into the courtroom to testify against my client in one of my cases, he is often flanked by a whole entourage of bowing, scraping, smiling bootlickers who open doors, hand him his notes, and continually reassure him of his importance. He has acquired little true wisdom. His knowledge of himself is infinitesimal. He is, in fact, bored with himself, which may be the zenith of his insight. He is an expert in trampling those below him. He knows how to climb ladders. I do not consider him successful, except as a ladder-climber, even though he may retire with a twenty-million-dollar golden parachute. But this is only my judgment.

Instead, I consider successful the janitor who mucks out the CEO's office, repairs his chair, and washes his windows. The janitor has written a poem, and invented a device for removing rust from the office radiators without chemicals. He has helped put his children through college, and as a friend has slipped a couple of bucks he could ill afford under his neighbor's door when his neighbor was in desperate need. He pays his bills and speaks out against injustice whenever he encounters it. He has never required another to validate his importance. He is important to his family, to his friends, and to himself. He has grown from having struggled to become a person. Had he possessed the ability to make the most renowned arguments known to man, he might well have never made any at all. I consider him successful. But my judgments of his success are merely mine. You will make your own based on what winning success is about for you.

An alternative way of life in the bureaucratic jungle. Perhaps there is another way to survive in the corporate and governmental jungle. It requires a viewpoint antithetical to the reason many are in corporate or government service in the first place—security. I suggest a set of strange hypotheses: *The more one seeks security the less secure one will be.* And further: *The more security one appears to acquire, the less security one actually possesses.*

Security is not in a job. Security is not in money. Jobs, pensions, positions, all can be repossessed or eliminated by those who created them. One year we saw General Motors fire 75,000 workers at Christmastime. Thousands who had loyally devoted their lives to that corporation lost their jobs. To some, it was like losing their lives. Money, too, can be lost, its value diminished or destroyed by inflation or devaluation. Pensions can prove to be inadequate or nonexistent. Pensions that have been earned year after long year and looked to for the worker's old-age security are being eliminated daily by clever corporate lawyers. No one is more insecure than the worker who depends on the corporation or government to provide him his job or his pension. The worker is but a number. And a number is not secure. A number can be increased or reduced on the budget at will. A simple line drawn in a second can scratch through thousands of jobs.

Can you see the corporate executives working at their numbers? They must make cuts. Sometimes the cuts have nothing to do with profit. Often they have nothing to do with a better product. Sometimes the cuts are for short-term goals: to please a stock analyst, to achieve a quick promotion for the executive, or worse, simply to exercise power. Can you see the corporate decision-makers saying, "We must take a thousand jobs out of this sector by March 1"—and you are one of them?

The decision is not to cut the job of a person they know whose life will be irrevocably altered, whose family may be in jeopardy, whose children may not go to college, whose home may be repossessed, who may suffer, even die for want of proper medical care. The decision is not to eliminate the job of a man or a woman they say "hello" to every morning, whom they congratulated when little Bobby was born and whom they comforted when, eighteen years later, Bobby was killed in a motorcycle accident. The action is not against a living feeling human being whom they know. The action is against a *number*. There are a thousand other numbers like it that will be cut. Nothing personal.

Corporate and government elimination of jobs is a mass murder that is acceptable in this society if it is done in the name of profit, for profit, as we have seen, is the ultimate virtue. We have already learned that in the tribal setting, the tribe has no prisons and does not impose the death penalty. The worst of all punishment was banishment from the tribe; to the Indian, a punishment equivalent to death. But what about the corporate employee whose only tribe is the corporate workplace? What about the person whose self-worth and whose fulfillment as a person, yes, whose well-being, physically and mentally, are irretrievably connected to his corporate or government job, and that job is eliminated? What about him? What about her?

The damage such casualties inflict is unfathomable. I think of the homeless. I think of the shame and the degradation. I think of the wholesale destruction of self-respect. I think of the hatred people exhibit against the poor or the unemployed. Many are treated like lepers. The innocent are scorned and despised. I think of the pain of the family, the fear. I think of the children, once bright-eyed, yearning to grow and to succeed, who are, by the stroke of a pen, deprived of their education. I think of older workers who can no longer get a good job. I think of their banishment, and, although they are without fault, the odium that is attached to them.

No one will hear them say, "I was just a number. My number came up." No one will understand that Joe McClousky worked twenty-seven years for the company hoping for security, hoping for a pension, hoping for the good life, hoping to take his grandson fishing, hoping . . . when his number came up.

Joe McClousky did not have security. The appearance of security was another myth, another cruel and vicious lie. I say, the more one seeks security the less secure one will be. I say, the more security one appears to acquire, the less security one actually possesses. No corporation, no government, no bureaucracy, indeed, no employer can provide security. Life is the ultimate insecurity. Death is the ultimate security.

Let us, therefore, not long for security, seek it, lay our lives down for it, deliver up our freedom for it. Let us not love it too much. Let us, instead, sit on the verge of insecurity, let us look over the edge, look into the pit, let us feel the agitation in the belly. Let us, by acknowledging our insecurity, by facing it, embracing it, affirm *the courage to be.*

The ultimate security in this life is the product of courage. *The self is the source of all security.* As a worker one will be most secure if one comes to work each morning willing to be fired. What better security exists than the knowledge that one is not trapped, not dependent, not owned, and has not sucked up to the corporate plan that will, at last, reduce one to a mere number?

The ultimate security in the corporate milieu or elsewhere, anywhere, is the self. I say it again. *The self is the source of all security,* not the boss, not the corporation, not the pension plan, but the *self.* The only boss the self has is the self. It is the self that must be satisfied, not the foreman, not the superintendent, not the plant manager.

If it is necessary to fulfill the demands of your only boss, the self, I say it is all right to circumvent orders. The self will not permit you to do that which is unethical. The self will not permit you to denigrate a fellow worker. It will not permit you to do shabby work. It will not permit you to waste, either yourself or others. Perhaps you must work underground to accomplish that which satisfies the self. At the same time the self will not agree to your undertaking that which is foolish. If the self is listened to it will associate you with others who also listen to the self. Such persons are powerful allies. If the self is listened to, you will work toward good and useful goals, and the work product will be better.

Those who are the bosses will take credit, of course. But you will know who deserves the credit. The self knows and, in the end, that is all that is important.

Security is the product of dealing openly and honestly with the self. Persons who are *servants of the self* evolve into the most valued corporate employees. They are the ones who are responsible. They are the ones who can be trusted. They are the ones, finally, with power. They are the ones to whom the backslappers and yes-men, those who have sucked their way up the corporate pipe, turn when they are in trouble. For the bureaucracy, corporate or governmental, exists without virtue, life, or power, except through those who have the courage to be *servants of the self*.

AND SO: I am not against corporations. I am against mindless, life-less leviathans taking control of an often helpless, innocent public. I am against corporate power without corporate responsibility. I am not against profit. I am against the inhuman, vicious, and false doc-trines by which profit becomes virtue. My purpose is not to pro-mote unrest, but to promote a thought-garden in which justice may be planted and bloom. My purpose is not to condemn the system, but to unveil the myths that permit our system to exploit the weak, myths that will at last be its undoing. I wish us, all of us, to see clearly so that we may argue with power—our power—with au-thority—our authority—out of the place where truth abides—our truth. That is how we win, win or lose, at the workplace and every place.

16

Arguing for Justice

UNDERSTANDING THE RESPONSIBILITY OF BEING

I f I had discovered a cure for a dreaded disease, I would have a duty to share my discovery with mankind, would I not?

Each of us has an offering to make, for as we have seen, each of us is perfectly unique. This being so, can we not agree that it is our duty to discover that uniqueness and thereafter to share it? This life's process I have heretofore referred to as an "intra-personal archeological dig." At the bottom are the treasures. But they are treasures that ought not be hoarded or hidden so that these treasures die with us. That would be the worst of all crimes. For one can steal from one's neighbor his riches, but if one steals one's own perfect self from the world, the loss will be eternal.

One of the most effective means by which we share ourselves is argument. I say, therefore, one has a duty to argue. It is part of the the price we pay for the space we occupy on this earth.

Thomas Jefferson had a duty to argue. So did James Madison. Abraham Lincoln had a duty to argue. So did John Brown. Christ, Mohammed, Buddha, Paul, Joan of Arc—each had a duty to argue. Martin Luther King Jr. had a duty to argue. Mother Teresa has a duty to argue. So has Nelson Mandela. So has Ralph Nader. So do we. I have, in part, made my argument herein. Doubtless you have, in part, already made yours.

When we witness an injustice, we have a duty to argue. We know how. When we see human beings unjustly used, disrespected, ex-ploited, injured, we have a duty to argue. We know how. When we hear unjust statements, we have a duty not to permit their poison to spread unabated. We have a duty to argue at home. We have a duty to argue with those we love, with our mates and our children.

We have a duty to argue for ourselves and with ourselves. We know how. Yes, we even have a duty to argue with God. Having provided us the skill, I take it that God would be greatly disappointed should it go untested.

AND SO: Go out then, and argue, and win—every time.

Acknowledgments

Rosemary McIntosh, my assistant of many years has read nearly every word I've ever written. She is critic, editor, and confidante. I would not dare write a book without her. I could not. To her I owe much of the success I enjoy, and I accept all the blame for my literary failures, having most likely ignored her good counsel in such instances.

This book, like the last, is the child of my editor, Bob Weil. Writers are a supersensitive, frightened lot. We need more reassurance, more help, more support, and more than our share of love. Without the nurturing of my friend, Bob Weil, this book would still be a small, bothersome noise in the back of my mind.

I thank Tom McCormack, head man, for his belief that this book should be written by me and published by St. Martin's Press and for the powerful support he has given me.

I thank Mark Kohut for his faith in the book reflected by his remarkable effort on its behalf and Becky Koh, my everyday loyal friend whose tireless and selfless work has not gone unnoticed. There are others. They and I know who they are: the sales people, the marketing folks, those who labored to design the book and promote it—so many to whom I am so grateful for so much. To all of you, my thanks.

About the Author

Gerry Spence is a consummate country lawyer. Born, raised, and educated in Wyoming, he has lived in small Wyoming towns all of his life. Yet from these rural places he has conducted a national law practice, and has tried and won some of America's most famous cases—the Karen Silkwood case, the defense of Imelda Marcos, the defense of the Idaho separatist, Randy Weaver, the celebrated murder defense of Sandra Jones and many others. He has not lost a criminal case in his entire career of over forty years, and, having achieved a remarkable record of multimillion dollars verdicts, he has also not been turned away by a jury in a civil case in the past twenty-five years. A charismatic speaker, he frequently appears on television and radio, and has become known as one of the country's foremost authorities on the art of argument.

Spence believes that argument begins with the person, and that to argue successfully one must accomplish more than mere technique. He maintains that success in argument, as in life, is a derivative of personal growth, of discovering who we are, and embracing the uniqueness that is individual to each of us. Spence is also the author of six books. He is an accomplished painter, a poet, a philosopher and a photographer of note. He lives in the mountains of Jackson Hole, Wyoming, with his wife Imaging, where he conducts his law practice and carries on the many pursuits that intrigue and beguile him.

Index